Agape and the Four Loves

POSTMODERN ETHICS SERIES

Postmodernism and deconstruction are usually associated with a destruction of ethical values. The volumes in the Postmodern Ethics series demonstrate that such views are mistaken because they ignore the religious element that is at the heart of existential-postmodern philosophy. This series aims to provide a space for thinking about questions of ethics in our times. When many voices are speaking together from unlimited perspectives within the postmodern labyrinth, what sort of ethics can there be for those who believe there is a way through the dark night of technology and nihilism beyond exclusively humanistic offerings? The series invites any careful exploration of the postmodern and the ethical.

Series Editors:

Marko Zlomislić (Conestoga College)
David Goicoechea (Brock University)

Other Volumes in the Series:

Cross and Khôra: Deconstruction and Christianity in the Work of John D. Caputo edited by Neal DeRoo and Marko Zlomislić

Agape and Personhood with Kierkegaard, Mother, and Paul (A Logic of Reconciliation from the Shamans to Today) by David Goicoechea

The Poverty of Radical Orthodoxy edited by Lisa Isherwood and Marko Zlomislić

Future Volumes:

Theologies of Liberation in Palestine: Contextual, Indigenous and Postcolonial Perspectives edited by Lisa Isherwood and Nur Masalha

Fundamentalism and Gender: Scripture—Body—Community edited by Ulrike Auga, Christina von Braun, Claudia Bruns, and Jana Husmann

David Goicoechea is producing "Millennial Meditations on 2000 Years of Christian Love: A Postmodern Summa—*Agape* as Reconciliation," of which the present volume is the second of nine.

III *Agape and Ahav-Hesed with Levinas-Derrida and Matthew, at Mt. Angel-St. Thomas (A Doxology of Reconciliation from Moses and David to Today)*

IV *Agape and Bhakti with Bataille and Mark, at Loyola-St. Francis (A Mysticology of Reconciliation based on Hindu Karma from Arjuna to Augustine)*

V *Agape and Karuna with Foucault and Luke, at Brock Philosophy Department (A Therapeutology of Reconciliation based on Buddhist No-Self from Buddha to Francis)*

VI *Agape and Rahim with Deleuze, Brock Philosophy Society, and John (An Atheology of Reconciliation based on Islamic Sharia from Muhammad to Luther)*

VII *Agape and Zen with Kristeva, Wilhelmina, and Catholic School (A Semiology of Reconciliation based on Japanese No-Drama from Nishida to John XXIII)*

VIII *Agape and Jen with Cixous, Carolyn, and Pauline School (A Phenomenology of Reconciliation based on the Confucianist Family from Tu Wei-Ming to John Paul II)*

IX *Agape and Tao with Irigaray, Johanna, and the Johannine School (An Eschatology of Reconciliation based on Taoist Gendering from Moeller to Benedict XVI)*

VOLUME TWO

Agape and the Four Loves

With Nietzsche, Father, and Q
(A Physiology of Reconciliation from the Greeks to Today)

DAVID L. GOICOECHEA

POSTMODERN ETHICS SERIES

☙PICKWICK *Publications* · Eugene, Oregon

AGAPE AND THE FOUR LOVES
with Nietzsche, father, and Q (A Physiology of Reconciliation from the Greeks to Today)

Copyright © 2013 David L. Goicoechea. All rights reserved. Except for brief quotations in critical publications or reviews, no part of this book may be reproduced in any manner without prior written permission from the publisher. Write: Permissions, Wipf and Stock Publishers, 199 W. 8th Ave., Suite 3, Eugene, OR 97401.

Pickwick Publications
An Imprint of Wipf and Stock Publishers
199 W. 8th Ave., Suite 3
Eugene, OR 97401

www.wipfandstock.com

ISBN 13: 978-1-62032-153-9

Cataloging-in-Publication data:

Goicoechea, David.

Agape and the four loves : with Nietzsche, father, and Q (a physiology of reconciliation from the Greeks to today) / David L. Goicoechea.

xxii + 360 p.; 23 cm—Includes bibliographical references and index.

ISBN 13: 978-1-62032-153-9

1. Nietzsche, Friedrich Wilhelm, 1844–1900. 2. Q hypothesis (Synoptics criticism). 3. Fatherhood. 4. Reconciliation—Religious aspects. I. Title. II. Series.

B3317 G55 2013

Manufactured in the USA.

For my Father dear

with whom I still pray

my daily prayers

Mother and Daddy when they first met

My Father graduating from high-school

Contents

List of Images | viii
Acknowledgments | ix
Detailed Line of the Argument | x
Introduction | 1

Part One: **Joyful Beginnings**
Father | 20
Nietzsche | 47
Q^1 | 74
The Four Loves | 102

Part Two: **Sorrowful Proceedings**
Father | 136
Nietzsche | 163
Q^2 and Q^3 | 190
Affection-Friendship-*Eros*-*Agape* | 217

Part Three: **Glorious Finishings**
Father | 250
Nietzsche | 277
Q^3 | 304
The Four Loves | 331

Bibliography | 359

List of Images

Daddy when graduating from High School | v
Mother and daddy when they first met | vi
Lequeitio | 101
Elanchove | 101
Gramma Goicoechea | 129
Grampa Goicoechea | 129
Shamanic Beginnings when his Father died | 129
His track team | 130
His basketball team | 130
The Bounding Basque at fifteen | 131
He taught us
   to fish | 131
   and to hunt | 132
Our Log Cabin | 133
Gramma, Daddy and Me | 133
The Lequeitio homestead | 134
Bette Jo and Dad | 244
Tom, Bobby, Bette Jo, Cliff, Dad and Mom | 244
Bobby and Dad | 245
Tom and Dad | 245
Daddy Fly Fishing | 245
Our grade two class | 246
Our grade three class | 246
The report card | 247

Acknowledgments

In getting out this second volume I owe a debt of gratitude to my wife, Dr. Johanna M. Tito, who has helped me in innumerable ways. Secondly, I want to thank all those at Pickwick Publications, especially Chris Spinks and Heather Carraher, with whom it has been such a delight to work. I cannot fail to mention my gratitude to Dr. Marko Zlomislic who has helped me so much over the past 20 years.

Detailed Line of the Argument

Part One: Joyful Beginnings

I.   **Father**

I,1.   **Of affectionate beginnings with his Basque family**
I,1.1   Identification in Mother-Son Bonding
I,1.2   Daddy's Daddy and their Tuttle Ranch
I,1.3   Daddy's New Little Sister
I,1.4   Daddy's Older Sisters
I,1.5   Daddy's Last Little Sister
I,1.6   Daddy's Daddy Dies
I,1.7   Daddy's Shame in the First Grade
I,1.8   Between the Graveyard and the Sea
I,1.9   Love Stronger than Death

I,2.   **Of friendly success with his school mates**
I,2.1   Friendship with Basque Boarders
I,2.2   Friendship Seeking New World Success
I,2.3   They Ate their Peck of Salt Together
I,2.4   On Wonderfully Coached Teams
I,2.5   Friendship in the Physical, Vital, Intellectual, Spiritual
I,2.6   A Shining Star in that Constellation of Friends
I,2.7   Training up at the Sheep Camp with Uncle Pete
I,2.8   Training with Farming Friends on Silver Creek
I,2.9   All the Training Pays Off

I,3   **Of erotic exploring and finding his wife**
I,3.1   Sex, Death and Religion at High School's End
I,3.2   Starting College During the Great Depression
I,3.3   The Prohibition and Being Put in Jail
I,3.4   Riding the Rails with the Bums to Omaha

Detailed Line of the Argument

I,3.5   With Family in Nevada and Breaking Wild Horses
I,3.6   Getting His Nose Broken by the Big Black Boxer
I,3.7   Coming Back to Carey, Idaho and Dealing Poker
I,3.8   He Marries the Near Perfect Lady, Joneva Mae Coates
I,3.9   A Democrat Forever with Franklin Delano Roosevelt

Detailed Line of the Argument

II.	**Nietzsche**
II,1	**The affectionate Child finds his lost father's *agape***
II,1.1	Becoming a Pietistic Jesus Shaman
II,1.2	*The Anti-Christ* Describes Nietzsche's Life-Long Jesus
II,1.3	Jesus' Kingdom of Love Is Here and Now
II,1.4	Jesus as a Child of God Loves Everyone Equally
II,1.5	Jesus' Love Is not that of a Genius, but of an Idiot
II,1.6	The Loving Idiot Jesus Shrinks Back from 'Reality'
II,1.7	With a Loving Idiosyncratic Capacity for Suffering
II,1.8	Dostoyevsky's Sublime, Sick, and Childish Idiot.
II,1.9	The Evangel Died as He Lived and Taught
II,2	**Reconciling the Socratic Apollo with the dancing Dionysus**
II,2.1	From the Dionysus to Jesus
II,2.2	Are the 7 Traits of Dionysus Similar to those of Jesus?
II,2.3	Tragedy Is Born from the Epic and the Lyric
II,2.4	Does Nietzsche Link the "sus" of Jesus and Dionysus?
II,2.5	Socrates Is to Dionysus as Christ Is to Jesus
II,2.6	From the Affectionate Child to Star Friendship
II,2.7	From Socrates to Dionysus and from Christ to Jesus
II,2.8	Jesus – the Unknown God – Dionysus
II,2.9	The Way to Reconcile Christian Platonism with Jesus
II,3	**Reconciling Zarathustra with the eternally returning Jesus**
II,3.1	The Erotic *Agape* of Nietzsche's Zarathustra
II,3.2	An Erotic *Agape* Born out of Modernity's God
II,3.3	An Erotic *Agape* that Emanates Like the Sun
II,3.4	In a Confrontation of Friendship with the Old Saint
II,3.5	Teaching the Overman to the People of the First Town
II,3.6	Loving the Overman Who in Going Under Goes Across
II,3.7	And He Even Loves the Mediocre Last Man
II,3.8	And Saves the Tight-Rope Walker from the Devil's Hell
II,3.9	He Loves His Proud Eagle and Wise Serpent

Detailed Line of the Argument

III.	**Q¹**
III,1	**The Q¹ *agape* sayings of Jesus**
III,1.1	Burton Mack's 7 Clusters of 21 Love Sayings
III,1.2	Jesus Loves Especially the Poor, Hungry and Crying
III,1.3	Jesus Send out His Workers as Lambs Among Wolves
III,1.4	Jesus Teaches Them How to Pray and Be Confident
III,1.5	Jesus Tells the Anxious to Speak Out in Love
III,1.6	Seek Ye First the Kingdom of Love
III,1.7	The Kingdom of Love Is Like a Mustard Seed or Yeast
III,1.8	Whoever Loves Jesus Will Carry His Cross
III,1.9	An *Our Father* Summary of Jesus' Love Teaching
III,2	**The Q2 judgment sayings of the Christ**
III,2.1	Mack's First 7 Clusters of Q2 Sayings
III,2.2	The Christ of John Will Burn the Chaff
III,2.3	The Reconciling Interplay Between John and Jesus
III,2.4	Condemnation of Towns that Reject the Jesus Movement
III,2.5	Loving Praise for Those Who Accept the Movement
III,2.6	A Physiology of Exclusively Opposite Kingdoms
III,2.7	From a Kingdom of *Nomos* to a Kingdom of *Physis*
III,2.8	From a Kingdom of *Physis* to a Kingdom of *Nomos*
III,2.9	Judgment on this Generation by the Son of Man
III,3	**The second stage of Q2 judgment sayings**
III,3.1	Mack's Second Set of 7 Clusters of Q2 Sayings
III,3.2	True Enlightenment: the Lamp and the Eye
III,3.3	Pronouncements Against the Pharisees
III,3.4	On Anxiety and Speaking Out
III,3.5	The Coming Judgment
III,3.6	The Two Ways
III,3.7	Community Rules
III,3.8	The Final Judgment
III,3.9	The Epic-Apocalyptic Story

Detailed Line of the Argument

IV.	**The Four Loves**
IV,1	**Why the four natural loves need *agape***
IV,1.1	Must Affection and Wrath Give Rise to Hatred?
IV,1.2	Can *Agape* Heal Affection Becoming Hatred?
IV,1.3	Must Natural *Eros* Always Betray the Beloved?
IV,1.4	Can Plato's Sublimated *Eros* Help *Agape*?
IV,1.5	Why Is Friendship in Need of *Agape*?
IV,1.6	Can Aristotle's Friendship Contribute to *Agape*?
IV,1.7	How Do Natural and Supernatural *Agape* Differ?
IV,1.8	Can Natural *Agape* Contribute to Jesus' *Agape*?
IV,1.9	Reconciling the Four Loves In Jesus' *Agape*
IV,2	**The four loves of the pre-Christian Augustine**
IV,2.1	Can Nietzsche and Q Help Clarify Augustine?
IV,2.2	Augustine's Praise for Affection
IV,2.3	Augustine Discovers Affection's Poison
IV,2.4	Augustine's Praise for *Eros*
IV,2.5	Augustine's *Eros* Is Poisoned
IV,2.6	Augustine's Praise for Friendship
IV,2.7	Augustine Discovers Friendship's Poison
IV,2.8	Augustine's Praise for Neo-Platonic *Agape*
IV,2.9	Augustine Discovers Natural *Agape*'s Poison
IV,3	**Augustine's conversion to *Agape* heals his bipolarity**
IV,3.1	Can Augustine Help Clarify Nietzsche and Q?
IV,3.2	*Agape* Heals Augustine's Bi-Polar Affection
IV,3.3	Giving Mother and Son a Mystical *Agapeic* Affection
IV,3.4	And Gives Great Peace to All as Monica Dies
IV,3.5	*Agape* Leads to a Politics of Friendship
IV,3.6	And to a Celibacy that Still Dreams of Sex
IV,3.7	So that in Sorrow he Continues Confessing
IV,3.8	For Augustinian Sublimation Is not Platonic
IV,3.9	So Is his Conversion a Christian Sublimation?

Detailed Line of the Argument

Part Two: Sorrowful Proceedings

I. Father

I,4 **Of starting a family in war time**
I,4.1 With his First Child his Prayer-Life Grows
I,4.2 He Prays for a Good Job
I,4.3 His Prayers Are Answered
I,4.4 Bette Jo Is Born and the War Calls Him
I,4.5 Serving his Country in a Shipyard
I,4.6 Return to Carey and his Wife's Parents
I,4.7 Being a Farmer and a Boxing Coach
I,4.8 The War Ends and Bobby Brian Is Born
I,4.9 Back to Ketchum and the Good Life Once Again

I,5 **Of raising a family when shot**
I,5.1 Daddy Gets Shot But It Makes Him Stronger
I,5.2 Clifford Scott Is Born while Daddy Is still Laid up
I,5.3 Daddy Begins his New Life as a Day Laborer
I,5.4 Daddy's Fourth Son, Tommy Joe, Is Born
I,5.5 Daddy Was not Suited to Work for Others
I,5.6 We Can Live Like Kings
I,5.7 For Basques Church and Family Went Together
I,5.8 The Worst of Times Were the Best of Times
I,5.9 Lives in the Spirit

I,6 **Of Being an Alcoholic Garbage Man**
I,6.1 Daddy's Mid-Life Crisis
I,6.2 With Cigarettes, Whiskey and Gambling
I,6.3 Bette Jo Is Accepted at Portland University
I,6.4 Bobby Goes to Mt. Angel
I,6.5 Donny Dies and I Leave the Seminary
I,6.6 Gramma Goicoechea Dies
I,6.7 Daddy's Anger and his Swearing
I,6.8 A Year of Graduations
I,6.9 A New Daughter-In-Law

Detailed Line of the Argument

II.	**Nietzsche**
II,4	**Reconciling Plato with Jesus' kingdom of love**
II,4.1	From the Camel's Virtue to the Child's Sacred *Yes*
II,4.2	From Body-Despising After Worldsmen to Creativity
II,4.3	Joyfully Loving Pale Criminals
II,4.4	A Dancing God Gives his Sermons on the Mount
II,4.5	Saying *No* to Ascetics and *Yes* to Warriors
II,4.6	Plato's Republic and Luther's Nation State
II,4.7	Why Flies in Attack Jesus and Zarathustra
II,4.8	Why Plato Should Be Celibate but not Luther
II,4.9	He is Friend and Best Enemy of Plato and Luther
II,5	**Reconciling Luther with Jesus' "Resist not evil"**
II,5.1	Beyond Luther to One Humanity
II,5.2	Love not the Nearest but the Most Distant
II,5.3	The Solitary Luther and the Way of the Creator
II,5.4	Lutheran Pastor's Daughters
II,5.5	The Adder's Bite and Justice Without Noble Love
II,5.6	The Bitter Cup of Marriage can Teach True Love
II,5.7	Love Lets Anytime be the Right Time to Die
II,5.8	Bestowing Love Is the Highest Virtue
II,5.9	Bestowing Love Lets there be God's Kingdom
II,6	**Reconciling Kant with the Jesus of retarded puberty**
II,6.1	How the Enlightenment Lions Become Free
II,6.2	A *Twilight of the Idols* Summary of Zarathustra
II,6.3	The Old God Is Dead for the Enlightenment Men
II,6.4	And as Unprovable Is to Be Replaced by the Overman
II,6.5	Zarathustra Has a Spear for his Beloved Enemies
II,6.6	Kant's Critique of Pure Reasoning is Enlightening
II,6.7	His Critique of Practical Reason is Compassionate
II,6.8	His Critique of Judgment Reveals the Sublime
II,6.9	The Child Loves Everyone as a Gift

Detailed Line of the Argument

III. Q² and Q³

III,4   The Q3 sayings
III,4.1   Mack's 8 Groups of Q3 Sayings
III,4.2   Jesus Tempted by the Accuser
III,4.3   Secret Revelation to Little Children
III,4.4   Hearing and Keeping the Teaching of God
III,4.5   Qualifying the Charges Against the Pharisees
III,4.6   The Threat of Hell Fire
III,4.7   Lament Over Jerusalem
III,4.8   The Kingdom and the Law
III,4.9   Judging Israel

III,5   Three stages of *agape* in the Book of Q
III,5.1   The Unconditional Love of Q¹
III,5.2   Understands Natural Punishment
III,5.3   And Even Hates Worldly Affection
III,5.4   The Judgmental Love of Q²
III,5.5   Must Pass Judgment on this Generation
III,5.6   As Will the Holy Spirit
III,5.7   The *Agape* that Reverences God Alone in Q³
III,5.8   Is a Reverence that Fears God and Yet Knows
III,5.9   That Jesus Is Like a Mother Hen with Her Chicks

III,6   The Gospel of Thomas lacks *agape*
III,6.1   As Do All the Gnostic Gospels
III,6.2   Lack of *Agape* Kept the Gnostic Gospels out of the Canon
III,6.3   Thomas Lacks both Incarnation Love
III,6.4   And Atonement Justice Theologies
III,6.5   Are True Love and Justice Replaced by Endless Riddles?
III,6.6   Does Thomas' Hatred of Family Serve *Agape*?
III,6.7   Is Thomas More Egoistic than the Greeks and Jews?
III,6.8   They Do Reverence Father, Son and Holy Spirit
III,6.9   But There Is no Concept of Personhood for Humans

Detailed Line of the Argument

IV.	**The Four Loves**
IV,4	**The Augustinian synthesis of *agape* and John's *eros***
IV,4.1	Nygren's Luther Initiates Modernity with Pure *Agape*
IV,4.2	Defending Augustine Against Luther's Pure *Agape*
IV,4.3	And with "*Tota Scriptura*" Against "*Sola Scriptura*"
IV,4.4	And with Works of Love Against "*Sola Fidei*"
IV,4.5	Defending Johannine and Augustinian Philosophy
IV,4.6	And Johannine and Augustinian Mysticism
IV,4.7	Modern Psychological Rugged Individualism
IV,4.8	And the Modern Political Rugged Individualism
IV,4.9	By not Throwing out Augustine's Three P's
IV,5	**The Thomistic synthesis of *agape* and Paul's friendship**
IV,5.1	Nygren Also Opposes Sublimating Friendship to *Agape*
IV,5.2	For Loving the Other Half of my Soul Is also Self-Love
IV,5.3	Defending Aquinas' *Philia* Against Luther's *Agape*
IV,5.4	In that Sublimated Aristotelian Friendship can Be *Agape*
IV,5.5	And Paul Lived out this *Agapeic* Friendship
IV,5.6	By Going out to Sinners in Friendship as Did Jesus
IV,5.7	Friendly Charity Does not Detract from *Agape*
IV,5.8	But *Agape* Contributes to *Philia* as Friendship Does to Charity
IV,5.9	By not Throwing out Aquinas' Three M's
IV,6	**The Franciscan synthesis of *agape* and Luke's affection**
IV,6.1	Nygren's Loving Treatment of Franciscan Love
IV,6.2	Begins to Reveal as Sublimated Affection
IV,6.3	Francis' Sublimated Affection Goes out to All
IV,6.4	Affectionate Names Are Prayed in his Heart Forever
IV,6.5	Franciscan-Lukan *Agape* Had a Mother-Child Affection
IV,6.6	That Was Foretold by Joachim De Fiore
IV,6.7	Whose *Rationes Seminales* Inspired Bonaventure
IV,6.8	To See Affection's History so as to Aid Scotus
IV,6.9	To See the *Haecceity* that Led Ockham to Nominalism

Part Three: Glorious Finishings

I. Father

I,7 **Of *Agapeic Eros* with His Wife**
I,7.1   In their Sacramental Love Making
I,7.2   And the Sharing of Physical Exercises
I,7.3   And the Sharing of Vital Exercises
I,7.4   And the Sharing of Intellectual Exercises
I,7.5   And the Sharing of Spiritual Exercises
I,7.6   And of Being Helped by Holy Mother Church
I,7.7   And of Belonging to the Mystical Body of Jesus
I,7.8   In a Love Stronger than Death
I,7.9   With Flesh as Instrument of Salvation

I,8 *Agapeic* **friendship with his children's spouses**
I,8.1   Standing Side by Side with David's Wilhelmina
I,8.2   Standing Side by Side with Bette Jo's Bob
I,8.3   Standing Side by Side with Bobby's Genie
I,8.4   Standing Side by Side with Cliff's Bim
I,8.5   Standing Side by Side with Tom's Annette
I,8.6   More with Annette as Mom and Dad Move to Gooding
I,8.7   David's New Wife Carolyn
I,8.8   The Three Great Secret Things
I,8.9   What Is *Agapeic* Friendship in a Family?

I,9 *Agapeic* **affection with his grandchildren**
I,9.1   Being Grandfather Was Different than Being Father
I,9.2   He Took Them into his Bigger than Life Connection
I,9.3   The Legacy He Left Is as Strong as the Love he Gave
I,9.4   Memories of him Belong to the Stories of their Lives
I,9.5   And his Genes Belong to their Inheritance
I,9.6   His Story Passed on to Them his Basque Culture
I,9.7   With its Physical, Vital, Intellectual, Spiritual Values
I,9.8   And its Optimistic View of Love's Glorious Power
I,9.9   That for him Did Change All Sorrow into Joy

Detailed Line of the Argument

II.	**Nietzsche**
II,7	**Reconciling the Buddha with the evangel on the cross**
II,7.1	The Buddha too is an Enlightenment Lion
II,7.2	He too Believes in Justice, Equality and Revenge
II,7.3	But he is a Free Spirit and not a Famous Philosopher
II,7.4	Deep Down the Buddhist is a Preacher of Death
II,7.5	His Will to Power Sublimates with Celibacy
II,7.6	His Sublimation is Beautification
II,7.7	But Unlike the Child Lions do not Believe in Belief
II,7.8	Men of Pure Knowledge do not Love the Earth
II,7.9	They do not Love it as Innocent Creators
II,8	**Reconciling the romantic lioness with the here and now**
II,8.1	Besides Enlightenment Lions There Is the Romantic Lioness
II,8.2	And her *Eros* Gives Gifts to the Child
II,8.3	But Receiving can be More Blessed than Giving
II,8.4	From the Dance Song's Romantic Pessimism
II,8.5	To the Funeral Song's Dionysian Pessimism
II,8.6	On Redeeming Romantic Pessimism with Sublimation
II,8.7	A Sublimation Based on Faith, Hope and Love
II,8.8	A Sublimation Higher than Reconciliation
II,8.9	Sublimating the "It Was" into "Thus I Will It"
II,9	**On becoming Zarathustra's child with Jesus**
II,9.1	By Courageously Believing in Eternal Life
II,9.2	With a Love Beyond Wisdom that Praises Folly and
II,9.3	Goes Beyond Survival of the Fittest with a Will to Power
II,9.4	That Goes Beyond Ressentiment with an *Amor Fati*
II,9.5	Beyond Good and Evil with a *Yes* and *Amen* for All
II,9.6	And Beyond Nihilism with an Eternal Return
II,9.7	In a Loving Joy that Wills Eternity
II,9.8	And can Say *Yes* to All Sorrow as Well
II,9.9	In a Glory that Wants Deep, Deep, Deep Eternity

Detailed Line of the Argument

III.	Q³
III,7	**Matthew's Gospel of *agape* for Jewish converts**
III,7.1	Which he Explains to his Jewish Audience
III,7.2	And Introduces with his Birth and Infancy Narrative
III,7.3	The Kingdom of Justice and *Agape* Is Announced
III,7.4	The Kingdom of Justice and *Agape* Is Preached
III,7.5	The Mystery of the Kingdom of Justice and *Agape*
III,7.6	The Church Is the First Fruit of the Kingdom
III,7.7	The Approaching Advent of the Kingdom
III,7.8	And Concludes with the Passion and Resurrection
III,7.9	And Reveals One Form of Orthodox Q¹ *Agape*
III,8	**And whether Mark and John's have Q¹ *agape***
III,8.1	Does Mark Use the *Agape* of Q³ and of Paul?
III,8.2	And How Does Mark Differ from Q¹ And Q³?
III,8.3	And How Does Q *Agape* Aid Mark's Synoptic Vision?
III,8.4	Does Mark Join the *Agape* of Paul's Christ and Q's Jesus?
III,8.5	Is There Q *Agape* in John as Well as in Mark?
III,8.6	Does John Distinguish his Gospel from the Gnostics?
III,8.7	Does the Holy Spirit of Love and Truth Distinguish Them?
III,8.8	Is the Jesus of John Truly the Jesus of Q¹?
III,8.9	John's Revealed *Agape* Is Philosophical and Mystical
III,9	**Luke's history of *agape* from its Q¹ beginnings**
III,9.1	As the Holy Spirit's Well Founded Teaching for Theophilus
III,9.2	Guides Luke's Infancy Story through its 5 Joyful Mysteries
III,9.3	And Presents the Q¹ *Agape* Sayings First and in Order
III,9.4	And in Presenting the Historical *Agape* of the Historical Jesus
III,9.5	He Also Presents the Historical Holy Spirit
III,9.6	Who Guides the Historical Holy Mother Church
III,9.7	And her Historical Holy Scriptures
III,9.8	As They Present the Historical Sorrowful Mysteries
III,9.9	And the Five Historical Glorious Mysteries

Detailed Line of the Argument

IV. The Four Loves

IV,7 Luther protests the four natural loves
IV,7.1 With an *Agape* that Hates the Self
IV,7.2 Because the Law Shows that Humanity Is Sinful
IV,7.3 But We Can Be Justified by Faith Alone
IV,7.4 In the Gospel's Loving Grace Alone
IV,7.5 Which Is Revealed in Scripture Alone
IV,7.6 Urging Us to Approach our Neighbor with Works of Love
IV,7.7 But Opponents, Peasants and Jew Are Excluded
IV,7.8 And Luther Spends his Life Speculating with Reason
IV,7.9 About a Love that Condemns All but True Lutherans

IV,8 Calvin in systematizing Luther says little about *agape*
IV,8.1 For Once the Natural Loves Go *Agape* Is Diminished
IV,8.2 And Double Predestination Urges me to Seek a Sign
IV,8.3 Of my Lutheran Vocation and my Calvinist Election
IV,8.4 For as Max Weber Shows Modernity Begins
IV,8.5 With the Protestant Asceticism that Replaces the Catholic
IV,8.6 And Lets Capitalism Replace Catholic Sublimated Love
IV,8.7 With Work Rather than Prayer that Makes Life Sweet
IV,8.8 Loving Prayer for Enemies Predestined to Hell
IV,8.9 Makes no More Sense Than Loving Hell-Bent Neighbors

IV,9 The *agapeic* roots of modern economics, politics and law
IV,9.1 Are like the Roots, Trunk, Branches and Fruit of Descartes' Tree
IV,9.2 For the Seeds of Modern Health, Education and Welfare
IV,9.3 Were Planted by Calvin to Give Glory to God
IV,9.4 And the Pietist Roots of Sublimated Affection Sprouted
IV,9.5 As Did the Quaker Roots of Sublimated Friendship
IV,9.6 And the Catholic Roots of Sublimated *Eros.*
IV,9.7 And with Adam Smith the Trunk of the Wealth of Nations Grew
IV,9.8 And the Branches Were Seen as Growing out of Self Love
IV,9.9 And the Fruit of a Well Ordered Self Love Becomes Postmodern

Introduction

Two thousand years ago Jesus introduced
his new teaching and practice of *agape*
which loves all persons equally
each person uniquely
and all persons as interrelated
in the two natures of the one person of Jesus
and in the three persons of the one God.
This *agape* quickly made its way
throughout the Greco-Roman world
by becoming the foundation attitude
for the four natural loves or attitudes
of affection, *eros*, friendship and *agape*.
In our day as Nietzsche pondered
his own modern culture he saw that
its philosophy of love was not in keeping
with Jesus' love as our highest affirmation.
Thus, he rethought our history in terms of
Jesus' Yes and Amen for all of existence.
Surprisingly, one hundred years after Nietzsche
Bible Scholars came to his same insights
as they too picked out and explained
the original sayings of Jesus that next became
the judgmental sayings of that Christ
who stressed a Father's tough love of affection
for the few but a condemnation for the many.
To clarify the legacy of Jesus' universal love
we will show how through Western history
his *agape* transformed *storge*, *eros*, *philia* and *agape*.
To reflect on all this concretely I will with you
think of my father's life as he went through
his own stages of love and personal growth
in their moments of joy, sorrow and glory.

Agape and the Four Loves

At the age of five daddy was abandoned
by the death of his beloved daddy.
The reality of that abandonment's effects
and how best to cope with its tragedy
became a focal thread throughout his life.
Nietzsche too at the very same age
was abandoned by the death of his father
and his writings can to be understood
as attempts to explore and share with others
the gifts he received by being guided
through his tragedy with an holy artistry
whose glory took him through
realms of deeper and blacker sorrow
into an ever wider and brighter Joyful Wisdom.
The early Jesus community was abandoned too
when Jesus was crucified, died and was buried.
He returned in resurrection but abandoned
them again as he ascended into heaven.
But his Spirit came to them revealing
how to help take responsibility for tragedy
for by living seriously moral lives
of doing good and avoiding evil
we can not only transform but also decrease
the tragic dimension with responsible moral living.
Natural affection, friendship, *eros* and *agape*
can let us down and abandon us.
We can come to hate our families
our friends, our beloved and all humanity.
As we look into the abyss of tragic negativity
even with hatred for our enemies we wonder
if daddy, Nietzsche and Q1 might have similar
methods for coping with the tragedy of abandonment.

Introduction

Daddy:

> *My father bought a ranch in Tuttle.*
> *He raised sheep and milk cows.*
> *He died when I was five years old*
> *and is buried in the Shoshone Cemetery.*
> *I have never been able to find his grave.*

Thus at the age of five daddy began to know of *agape* when he,
his mother and five sisters began to go through the *agapeic*
mourning process that transformed their shattered affection into
an *agapeic* affection that let their dear lost father be present to them.
They prayed together for him daily and asked him to pray for them.
As Catholics they believed that he was alive in the spirit world
and that he could benefit from their prayer and intercede for them.
As daddy prayed both in the morning and in the evening he learned:
"*The Sign of the Cross*", "*The Angel of God*", "*The Hail Mary*"
and "*The Our Father*" and these prayers were an expression of *agape*.
The more he and his family prayed for their father the more
they loved him with an affection that was rooted in *agape*.
Thus in his very experience he had faith in an *agape* that
made possible a growing affection and in an affection that
gave a special content to his *agape* for God and his family.
Because of the successful mourning process daddy entered
into the shamanic realm of the presence of the absent spirits.
As soon as he met my mother's mother he and she were bonded
in the happy-go-lucky joy of that special shamanic presence.
He taught my mother and me his prayers when I was five.
I have said them ever since and taught them to my children.
Thus an agapeic affection can be passed on and it can let
a faithful hope in *agape* be real for those who live in its prayer.
The *agape* that let daddy's mourning process be so successful
not only gave him a transformed affection but also a transformed
friendship and *eros* the practise of which always deepened his *agape*.

Agape and the Four Loves

> *My five sisters and I went to school in Gooding.*
> *We were a poor family and all of us worked*
> *to help mother make a living . . .*
> *Your grandmother, Eulalia, was a very*
> *religious person, a real good Catholic.*
> *We lived close to the Gooding Catholic Church.*
> *My mother kept it clean and I helped her.*
> *I started the fire in the pot belly stove every*
> *Sunday morning when the priest came from Jerome.*

As we explore the relation between *agape* and the natural loves
we will have to distinguish transformed from sublimated loves.
In his family's agapeic mourning process for his lost father
his shattered affection was the occasion for his being gifted with
the faith of *agape* and a transformed kind of affection with his father.
However, as we reflect upon his friendships and *eros* we will have to
make distinctions for he will not have a sublimated *eros* as did
Nietzsche even though mother detected in him a Catholic reverence.
He had many good friends but he also liked the challenge of a fight.
Throughout high school he had many good sports' friends as
they worked so hard together for excellence and his gambling
friends in their excellence often were his hunting and fishing friends.
As the garbage man of Ketchum he cleaned up the town just as
he and his mother cleaned the church when he was in grade school.
A friend in need is a friend indeed and people could rely on him
to work with them and when Mary Hemmingway had to clean
the wall after Ernest spattered it with his brains she knew that
daddy could be a more reverent helping friend than anyone else.
Each of his four sons became friends with him as we ate our
peck of salt together cleaning up the town and as we became
his hunting and fishing friends as hunter-gatherers together.
But most of all his teaching us to pray initiated our agapeic friendship.

Introduction

> *On November 12, 1936, Joneva and I*
> *were married in Hailey.*
> *Uncle Pete and Claudia were there.*

Daddy's mother was a very religious person, a real good Catholic.
Her daughters and daddy identified with her in loving God and
her lost husband and their dead father made the world of *agape* real
as they prayed daily for him and asked Mary to intercede for them.
Just as daddy would later clean up the town just as he had cleaned
the church with his mother so he would always pray just as he
prayed with her and her prayer and the prayer of the Basque became his.
So his *eros*, given the context of *agape*, was always special and
mother could always feel it just as could her mother and just as could
his daughter-in-law, Annette, who spoke of his respect for women.
At church daddy and the Catholics were on their knees a lot
praying especially: "We love, praise, worship and adore you."
That Catholic agapeic prayer brought daddy to a kind of reverence
that Mormons and Methodists did not know with their different *agape*.
The fact that priests were celibate had a lot to do with each Catholic's
eros for just as Holy Mother Church is the Bride of Christ so she
is also the Bride of each priest as he sublimates his *eros* for her.
Daddy loved his wife and women with an agapeic *eros* like that
of Jesus as he loved the women who loved him and bridegroom
mysticism is a phenomenon of sublimated *eros* that can give
dynamic energy to any who are associated with the mystic.
Catholic agapeic *eros* can be felt especially at the sacrifice of the Mass
when the power of the celibate priest brings the body and blood
of the God-man into the bread and wine so that the real prescence
of Jesus is there with a presence to believing love that was
somewhat like the presence of daddy's absent-present father.
Thus daddy's experience of agapeic love gave him a special kind
of affection, friendship and *eros* that gave great content to his *agape*.

Agape and the Four Loves

Daddy's four noble truths
I. As a boy of five daddy first experienced
the universal suffering of all flesh
when his dear daddy died.
II. But instead of becoming detached from their desire
to be with him his mother lead her six children
through an agapeic mourning process
III. that let their absent father be present to them
in a way that motivated and energized daddy
with an agapeic affection, friendship and *eros*
IV. so that dialectically his natural loves
were given a special agapeic power just as
they gave a richer and richer content to his *agape*
throughout the nine stages of his life.

(1) Daddy's agapeic affection came into being
as he and his family prayed daily for
their lost father and asked him to pray for them.
(2) He was motivated to excellence with his sports friends
partly out of love for his father's athletic prowess.
(3) Mother and many women could feel the reverence
of his *agape* that was touched by erotic sublimation.
(4) As daddy began raising his family during war time
he embraced the many challenges in affectionate prayer.
(5) Brian who shot him remained his dear friend
and his other friends helped him raise his family.
(6) During his mid-life crisis he became Ketchum's
alcoholic garbage man but with pride as his
wife stood by him with her prayerful *eros*.
(7) For they shared an agapeic *eros* in every way
(8) just as he shared in an agapeic friendship
with each of his children's spouses
(9) and in an agapeic affection with his grandchildren
as he became even their fishing baby-sitter.

Introduction

Nietzsche

> *I have firmly resolved within me*
> *to dedicate myself forever to His service.*
> *May the dear Lord give me strength and power*
> *to carry out my intention*
> *and protect me on life's way.*
> *Like a child I trust in His grace.*
> *He will preserve us all*
> *that no misfortune may befall us.*
> *But His holy will be done!*
> *All he gives I will joyfully accept:*
> *happiness and unhappiness*
> *poverty and wealth*
> *and boldly look even death in the face,*
> *which shall one day unite us all*
> *in eternal joy and bliss.*
> *Yes, dear Lord, let Thy face*
> *shine upon us forever! Amen!*

When Nietzsche was but thirteen at the beginning of puberty he wrote this passage in his *Aus meinem Leben* and it reveals the universal love of his *agape* for God and all of God's creation. The death of his father and his family's pious love was the occasion for Nietzsche to receive his shamanic vocation to be a healer by being a prayerful lover and artistic philosopher of that love. Nietzsche's love went through a transformation or metamorphosis when at the age of five his father died and he went through the agapeic mourning process with his mother, grandmother, aunt and sister and his practice of agapeic prayer for his father and his family transformed his affection into a strong agapeic affection and his familial affection gave him the *agape* that we see in this passage. Already in this passage of the thirteen year old there are the themes of love, joy, the child, the mixed opposites, Yes saying to all woe and a sense for the eternal that develop as his mature themes.

Agape and the Four Loves

> *In your friend you should possess*
> *your best enemy.*
> *Your heart should feel closest to him*
> *when you oppose him.*

Nietzsche's concept of friendship is set in a dialectical interplay with his concept of *agape* or "eternal return" or "Amor Fati". The agapeic "Yes and Amen" prayer of Zarathustra's child brings Zarathustra to go out to each of his friends: Dionysus, Zoroaster, the Buddha, Socrates, Plato, Jesus, Kant, Schopenhauer and Wagner in a Yes saying to each that says No to each one's No saying. He wants his friends to be his best enemy and push him further into more agapeic excellence and he wants to do that for his friends. The *agape* which was given to him as he went through the agapeic mourning process for his father provided the context for this friendship that calls upon friends to be enemies to increase *agape*. *Agape* lets there be this new kind of Nietzschean friendship and the whole purpose of this friendship is to further increase *agape*.

> *Are you pure air and solitude*
> *and bread and medicine to your friend?*
> *Many a one cannot deliver himself*
> *from his own chains*
> *and yet he is his friends' deliverer.*

When one opposes his friend he can feel closer with him in the growth of *agape* for a friend can help deliver a friend. Even though we might not be able to lift ourselves up by our bootstraps out of ressentiment into *agape* we can help bring that gift of *agape* and its healing medicine to our opposed friend. Right in the middle of Part One of *Zarathustra* there is a discussion of chastity and then friendship as if he brings together *eros* and friendship for a kind of parallel consideration in relation to *agape*. And Nietzsche did know of a full fledged sublimation of *eros*.

Introduction

> *Now I shall relate the history of Zarathustra.*
> *The fundamental conception of this work,*
> *the idea of eternal recurrence,*
> *this highest formula of affirmation*
> *that is at all attainable*
> *belongs in August 1881:*
> *it was penned on a sheet*
> *with the notation underneath,*
> *"6000 feet beyond man and time."*

In 1881, Nietzsche was in love with Lou Solome but she left him for another and he went through the sublimation of *eros* as Plato describes it in the *Phaedrus* and his sexual energy was chanelled into the writing of *Zarathustra* and the books he wrote after that. As he tells us here he was fundamentally writing about *agape* or the Yes and Amen prayer of *Amor Fati* for the eternal return of all. In his chapter *On Chastity* in the middle of Part One of *Zarathustra* Zarathustra says:

> There are those who are chaste from the very heart:
> they are more gentle of heart and they laugh
> more often and more heartily than you.
> They laugh at chastity too, and ask:
> "What is chastity? Is chastity not folly?"
> But this folly came to us and not we too it.
> We offered this guest love and shelter:
> now it lives with us –
> let it stay as long as it wants.

Nietzsche was given the gift of erotic inspiration just as were Plato, Dante and Kierkegaard and the whole purpose of his life became to meditate on and write about *agape* or eternal recurrence and his celibacy enabled him to do that with a great creative energy. His sublimation of *eros* contributed to his project of expressing *agape* and his project of *agape* gave him the gift of sublimated *eros*.

Agape and the Four Loves

Nietzsche's ninefold path through the moments of sublimational reconciliation

(1) The affectionate child Nietzsche finds his lost father's *agape*.
    Reconciling all things with the child-like Jesus
    (From a physiology of reaction to one of proaction.)

(2) Finding the Dancing Dionysus in the Logos of the Socratic Apollo.
    Reconciling the Socratic Apollo with the Dionysian Jesus
    (From a physiology of the lost father to Star Friendship)

(3) Finding Zarathustra's *Amor Fati* in the *Eros* of his lost Lou Salome
    Reconciling Zarathustra with the eternally returning Jesus
    (From a physiology of guilt to one of innocence)

(4) A Camel ride with Plato's *eros* to the *agape* of Jesus
    Reconciling Plato with Jesus' Kingdom of Love
    (From a physiology of decadence to one of great health)

(5) A Camel ride with Luther's Christ to the good will of Jesus
    Reconciling Luther with the "Resist not evil" of Jesus
    (From a physiology of atonement to one of incarnation)

(6) To the Jesus of retarded puberty with the Enlightened Lion Kant
    Reconciling Kant's Enlightenment with Jesus as idiot
    (From a physiology of reason alone to one of loving appearances)

(7) To Jesus Eternal Wheel of Rebirth with the Enlightened Lion Buddha
    Reconciling the Buddha with the Evangel on the cross
    (From a physiology of mindfulness to one of perspectivism)

(8) To the mourning Jesus with the melancholic lioness Schopenhauer
    Reconciling romantic pessimism with the joyful Jesus
    (From a physiology of negation to one of affirmation)

(9) To the comic Jesus with the tragic lioness, Wagner
    Reconciling romantic tragedy with the playful Jesus
    (From a physiology of the unconscious to one of transference)

Introduction

The Gospel of Q[1]

> I am telling you, love your enemies
> bless those who curse you
> pray for those who mistreat you.
> If someone slaps you on the cheek
> offer your other cheek as well.
> If anyone grabs your coat
> let him have your shirt as well.
> Give to anyone who asks
> and if someone takes away your belongings
> do not ask to have them back.
> As you want people to treat you,
> do the same to them.

This first saying of the Jesus of Q[1] is momentous in that it announces the agapeic universal love that extends the command to love neighbors not only as the ones who are near or part of the chosen people, but it now includes all with special emphasis upon loving one's enemy. This all loving Jesus of Q[1] is the same Jesus that Nietzsche focused upon in the *Anti-Christ* as he distinguished the all loving Jesus from the judging Christ in order to center his philosophy on that Jesus. This universal *agape* that loves everyone especially enemies is explained in terms of the Father's affection for if you love the poor and your enemies:

> Your reward will be great
> and you will be the children of God.
> For he makes his sun rise
> on the evil and the good;
> He sends rain on the just and on the unjust.
> Be merciful even as your Father is merciful.

Do we have here a rewarder God but not a punisher God? Jesus urges us to imitate the Father's affection that seems to say Yes and Amen to the just and also to the unjust.

Agape and the Four Loves

Q²

> John appeared in the countryside
> along the Jordan river and said to the people
> who were coming out to be plunged (into the river)
> "You offspring of vipers! who warned you
> to flee from the coming fury?
> Change your ways if you have changed your mind.
> Don't say, 'we have Abraham as our father.'
> I am telling you, God can raise up children
> for Abraham from these stones.
> Even now the ax is aimed
> at the root of the tree.
> Every tree that does not bear good fruit
> is cut down and thrown into the fire."
>
> Q² sayings 3 and 4

Burton Mack in his wonderfully clear book: *The Lost Gospel: The Book of Q and Christian Origins* shows how the loving Jesus became the judging Christ in much the same way as did Nietzsche. In the Gospels of Matthew and Luke there are 62 sayings of Jesus which they share in common and they are called the Q sayings. Q is short for Quelle or source because they were a common source for Matthew and Luke just as was the Gospel of Mark. Mack and others, notably Kloppenborg, divide the Q sayings into three groups with group one belonging to the historical Jesus. So Jesus had a community in Galilee and they recorded the saying of the Agapeic historical Jesus but after he died and there were threats from the outside and from traitors the community attributed these harsh judgmental sayings to the Christ. These judgmental sayings about throwing the tree that bears bad fruit into the flames are part of revealed scripture and if we put the emphasis on the incarnation love theology of Q¹ it can let the atonement justice theology of Q² be secondary.

Q³

> Then Jesus was led into the wilderness
> by the spirit for trial by the diabolos...
> The accuser said, "If you are the son of God
> tell this stone to become bread."...
> Then the accuser took him to a very high mountain
> and showed him all the kingdoms of the world
> and their splendour, and he said to him,
> "All these I will give you
> if you will do obeisance and reverence me."
> But Jesus answered him, "It is written
> 'You shall reverence the Lord your God
> and serve him alone!'" Then the accuser left him.

Here in Q³ the transition is made to seeing Jesus as the son of God.
Q¹ saw him as the son of man and as a divine child of wisdom.
Q² expanded the son of man figure giving him an apocalyptic
context in which he would judge the just and unjust for eternity.
The Galilean community came to see Jesus as the Son of God
and as they were being persecuted and put to death they came
to see Jesus not as forgiving enemies with agapeic mercy
but as condemning them to eternal hellfire for persecuting them.
Jesus forgave those who were killing him because they knew
not what they were doing just as did St. Stephen who forgave.
But the voices of Q² and Q³ which seem to be lacking in *agape*
need to be harmonized with the voices of Q¹ and Jesus already
began that process with the hard saying of Q¹, 52:

> Whoever does not hate his father and mother
> will not be able to learn from me.
> Whoever does not hate his son and daughter
> cannot belong to my school.

To let our love become universal we must first root out
the self love in our affection, friendship and *eros* and
then when we love all persons equally we can love our own uniquely.

Agape and the Four Loves

Q's four noble truths

I The historical Jesus of Q^1 taught and practiced
a new unconditional love for all persons.

II. But his followers were persecuted as was he
and the Christ of Q^2 promised their punishment.

III The son of God of Q^3 showed more mercy
than did the Christ of Q^2.

IV But the Jesus of Q^1 and the Christ of Q^2 and ^{3}
can be reconciled in a higher truth.

(1) The Jesus of Q^1 gives us a clue as to how
to reconcile his all forgiving love with
the rewarder-punisher Christ of Q^2 and ^{3}.

(2) Any natural affection, friendship and *eros*
has a built in preferential self-love which
Jesus' *agape* can supernaturally transform.

(3) If by the help of Jesus's grace we move from
a self-realization ethics to the new agapeic
ethics that prefers even our persecuting enemy

(4) then we can get rid of self-centeredness by
hating mother, father, brother, sister and self
so that we can come to love all persons equally.

(5) Then with a primary love for neighbor
we can have a secondary love for our own
and our priorities will be agapeically ordered.

(6) This order of love was already prefigured
when God promised to David and his house
his everlasting merciful love of *hesed*.

(7) But he also warned that secondarily any sin
according to the natural law of justice
would be punished with the rods of men.

(8) So the Q^1 love of Jesus is primary and
the just punishment of Q^2's Christ is secondary.

(9) To imitate Christ we need this order of love.

The four loves need agape
Affection

> When family members in affection say: "I love you"
> their feeling has something within it of "the forever."
> And yet so many are so hurt by the break down
> of the affectionate union that it leaves them
> terribly wounded by love and even leary of it.

Every great work of art treats of love, death and religion.
That is so because love is the most important reality in our
lives and the death of love or the death of a lover brings us
to religion as we try to go through a healing, mourning process.
Each of the great religions has a special kind of religious love
at its core that is there to supplement the four natural loves.
The ancient Greek philosopher, Empedocles, saw love and hate
as moving the universe through its cycles of growth and destruction.
His word for love is *storge* which means affection and thus
he believed that a great power of affection would build things up
and then an equally great power of hate would tear them apart.
This necessary battle between the powers of affection and of hate
is a vicious circle that we cannot escape for all living things
follow this pattern of birth, growth, decline and destruction.
Affection is our first love and the other loves are influenced by it.
If mother, father and children grow together in a healthy, happy
affectionate love then friendship and *eros* will have a better chance.
Deep in their unconscious, physiological bodies children tend
to identify with their parents and if their parents agree upon
the basic hierarchy of values then they can become friends together.
Children might become best of friends with their parents and with
each other and even one's *eros* is given direction by one's parents.
The family tree has tremendous influence on all the offspring
and if from the beginning there is faith in an agapeic love
that will last forever then even death makes love grow stronger.
A breakdown of affection without *agape* might lead one to *agape*.

Agape and the Four Loves

Eros

> When lovers stand face to face
> enraptured in each other
> one might betray the other
> so that "Hell hath no fury
> like a scorned woman's wrath."

Eros can begin very early in a person's life for a boy might
fall in love with his teacher when he is only eight or nine
and boys and girls might be attracted to each other before puberty.
When we think of falling in love or of being in love that usually
has to do with *eros* for it is the most passionate of the loves.
Persons are so unique in their sexual passion or lack of it
that you cannot know another's concupiscible appetite unless
you share in that with him or her in the sexual experience.
All animals have a mating season and are controlled by *eros*.
Just as Empedocles saw affection and hate as ruling the universe
so Plato's philosophy centers on *eros* in the *Symposium* and *Phaedrus*.
Plato's philosophy of love has to do with a love of beauty that
proceeds through seven steps as we climb the ladder of love.
In the Symposium at 210A and following Diotima explains
to Socrates how we come to know *eros* by falling in love with:
(1) the beauty of an individual body (2) then the beauty of many
bodies (3) then the beauty of the soul (4) then the beauty of laws
and institutions (5) then the beauty of scientific knowledge (6)
then the beauty of philosophy (7) and finally the form of Beauty itself.
Eros is such a powerful passion that it can reveal values to us
and give to us the motivation to work for and attain them.
It is true that "the heart has reasons that the mind knows not."
As Plato explains in the *Phaedrus* at 245C and following
sexual energy can be sublimated and become a source of
enthusiasm and Divine Madness so that great creativity can
come from it and this has contributed to agapeic celibacy.

Introduction

Friendship

>When friends stand side by side
>enjoying the world together
>as the other half of each other's soul
>death might snatch one away
>and leave the other in mourning.

C.S. Lewis in his book on *The Four Loves* writes at the beginning of his chapter on *Friendship* on page 55:

>To the Ancients, Friendship seemed the happiest
>and most fully human of all loves;
>the crown of life and the school of virtue.
>The modern world in comparison ignores it.

This rings so true of Aristotle's *Nicomachean Ethics* in which he has two chapters on friendship and shows that it is the crown of life and the school of virtue for with a friend we can grow together in practicing prudence, justice, fortitude and temperance. By learning these virtues with friends we can achieve happiness which is the crown of life and practice the love of wisdom together. Philosophy or the love of wisdom has within it the word "philia" or friendship so the very word philosophy connects with friendship. We might wonder if it is true if the modern world does ignore friendship and if that is the case what is going on in modernity. Is friendship recovered with postmodernity so that Nietzsche and the other postmodernists might have a kinship with premodernists? In the Biblical world there are great friends like David and Jonathan. Aristotle centered his philosophy on friendship just as Empedocles did on affection and Plato on *eros* and Cicero, the Roman, wrote an essay, *De Amacitia*, on friendship and St. Augustine greatly praises friendship in his *Confessions* as did Aquinas. The incarnation love theology of the Middle Ages does promote friendship and perhaps the atonement justice theology of modernity demotes it and we must explore all this especially with Nietzsche.

Agape and the Four Loves

Agape's *four noble truths*
I For the pre-Biblical Greeks, *agape* meant
"to be content with something" and was not
a philosophical term like *storge, eros* or *philia*.
II The Septuagint used the word *agape* to translate
that *ahava* which is the love Jews are commanded
to have for God and for their neighbor.
III Then that *agape* of the Septuagint took another
qualitative leap forward in becoming
the unconditional love for all persons
even our enemies as we see in Q[1].
IV Under the influence of the Christian *agape*
Plotinus in about 250 AD used the term
to explain how things emanate from the One.

(1) The four natural loves can give us greatest gifts
but if they fail or our beloved dies
we can be plunged into deep despair.
(2) But when the union of our natural loves
is broken faith in the supernatural love of *agape*
can give us hope to be together forever.
(3) The theological virtues of faith, hope and *agape*
can heal any failure in the four natural loves.
(4) Fuller affection contributes to affectionate *agape*
and *agape* gives confidence for everlasting affection.
(5) Fuller *eros* contributes to erotic *agape*
and *agape* gives confidence for everlasting *eros*.
(6) Fuller friendship contributes to friendly *agape*
and *agape* give confidence for everlasting friendship.
(7) Any love wants to be forever and *agape* lets that be.
(8) Hence loving all with *agape* is our highest affirmation.
(9) To avoid love's suffering we do not need detachment
but rather the *agape* that guarantees success to love.

Part One

Joyful Beginnings

Agape and the Four Loves

I. Father

I.1 Of affectionate beginnings with his Basque family

I,1.1 Identification in mother-son bonding

Daddy was born on February 4, 1910 in Boise, Idaho which was one of the largest Basque settlements outside of Spain and France. Though the last half of January and the first half of February are the times of bitterest cold in that mountain desert valley, baby Jose Manuel was peaceful warm in his mother's serenity. Daddy was born into the quest of his mother, Eulalia Sabala, and into the dreams of his father, Eleuterio Goicoechea. Gramma Goicoechea, who grew up in that tiny seaport cove of Elanchove, Spain, lost her first husband in a fishing accident out on the North Sea when her two daughters were but babies. As a young woman in her mid-twenties, Gramma was sponsored by her brother, working in Boise to come join him in America. So with her four-year-old daughter, Claudia, and her two-year-old daughter, Mary, she took the boat to New York City and then traveled across the United States on the train out to Idaho. Without knowing any English she met Eleuterio and in 1907, a few months after she reached Boise, she and he were married. A year later their baby girl, Angelus, came to bless them and a year after that their first baby boy, little Jose, was born. During the nine months within his mother's womb baby Jose identified in the spirit of his physiology with his mother's great faith and strength and courage in anxiety before adversity. The Basques were hunter-gatherers from cave-painting antiquity and their shamanic culture became one with their Catholic faith. Gramma Goicoechea prayed through the day and God's presence let her be a fearless fighter as she adventured together with her new husband and received help from her first two daughters in caring for her two still nursing newest little babies. Already in her womb and through the first year of his life Daddy bonded with his mother and thereby was already becoming the fighter whose faith could meet any challenge.

Part One: Joyful Beginnings

I,1.2 Daddy's daddy and their Tuttle ranch

Daddy's daddy, Eleuterio Goicoechea, was born on a farm near Lekeitio,
that town where a young Basque dances on the casket as they carry it
from their beautiful church to the graveyard of their blessed dead.
He came to Boise all alone in his mid-twenties and like all Basques
was loyal and hardworking and thus experienced quick upward mobility.
Eleuterio was as proud as he could be of his little daughter and
of his new baby boy who basked in the constant affection, not only
of his mother, father and two older sisters, but of the whole
Basque community who lived in their part of town in boarding houses.
Many Basko men became sheepherders, but Eleuterio who was
nicknamed "legs" because of his long athletic legs was chosen
and chose to run a ranch in a tiny desert oasis called Tuttle.
Gramma Goicoechea's brother, who sponsored her to come from Spain,
was a cook for the big new construction company of Morisen-Knudson.
And just as he helped Gramma to come to Boise from Spain so
he helped her to find her husband and to get their Tuttle Ranch.
So out there in the desert just East of Gooding Gramma, Grampa,
Aunts Claudia, Mary and Angelus and Daddy as a two-year-old,
began to live their dream of running a farm in the new country.
They had a few milk cows, a few sheep, some chickens and
a team of horses that pulled them to town and helped with the crops.
The desert was unbelievably dry and desolate with lava rock
that flowed out from the craters of the moon across Southern Idaho.
Grampa became a rancher of the purple sage as he uprooted
the sage brush and made room to plant his crops of hay and grain.
Gramma worked constantly taking care of her household and she
showered her affection upon each member of her family according
to their own special needs and her hard-working husband was happy
to be her mate and to be so loved by her whom he loved so much.
His two adopted daughters felt so at home with him and he loved
to play with his little Angelus and rock and love his little Jose.

Agape and the Four Loves

I,1.3 Daddy's new little sister

On May 4, 1913, when Daddy was three, Maria Dolores, his new sister
was born into their family and since she had the same first name
as her older half-sister, they called her Dolores from the beginning.
Maria Dolores was a fond name for Basques because it had to do
with our *Mater Dolorosa*, our Mother of Sorrows, who suffered most
painfully with her son throughout his five sorrowful mysteries.
As Grampa worked daily with the cows, the sheep and the chickens,
he often thought of his wife and their children and he knew better
what affection was as he watched the mother cows with their calves,
the sheep with their lambs and the mother hen taking her little
yellow chicks under her wings to protect, warm and cuddle them.
He was raised on his parents' farm back there in Gizaburuaga,
right next to Lekeitio and his family had been farming there for
thousands of years in that high, rugged mountain region that
protected them from Romans, Goths, Franks, Moslems and from
all invading enemies, just as a mother hen protects her chicks.
That ancient tradition of the mountain protected Basque and
of the farm animal affection of mating, birthing, suckling,
of necking, licking, nestling and cuddling was inherited
by Grampa Goicoechea from centuries of passed on and developed
and nurtured and cherished and held dear affectionate love.
Deep in the unconscious physiology of his farmer's strong body,
the spirit of affection flowed through the blood, glands and mucosity
of his centuries old Basque Being and he strongly felt all of that
in his wife for her children and for him, her protecting provider.
Daddy was weaned as his mother's pregnancy had advanced and
he loved to be taught to eat and already his dancing brown eyes
were childish, playful joyous as he watched his older sisters
hold and love their new little baby sister and you would not know
that the name Dolores Dolorosa would fit her in any way.
And she learned to coo and to smile in her happy contentment.

Part One: Joyful Beginnings

I,1.4 Daddy's older sisters

When Daddy was four Aunt Claudia was ten and Aunt Mary eight.
They both sistered and mothered and played with him constantly.
They were both very proud of their cute, darling little brother and he
came to feel totally at ease with girls and not only to love them
with his playful affection but also to have for them a reverence.
Aunts Claudia and Mary lost their father when they were but babies
and they learned how to pray with their mother's heartfelt affection.
Aunt Claudia loved to pray and she helped her little brother
to begin to learn to pray and he began to memorize *The Sign of
The Cross* and to kiss his thumb upon completion in the Basque
way and he began to learn to pray at first only in Basque.
The family spoke only Basque together but Aunts Claudia and Mary
were going to school and were with their friends learning at English.
They started teaching Angelus and Jose a few words in English
and at bed time Aunt Claudia started praying *The Angel of God*
with them and she explained to them what angels were and told
little Angelus that she was so fortunate to be named Angelus.
After two years the little Tuttle ranch was beginning to flourish
and Aunts Claudia and Mary learned not only to be good mothers
and good cooks and good homemakers, but they even got to help
milk the cows and especially to feed the baby bum lamb whose
mother died and for whom they developed a special tenderness
as the sweet darling thing bleated and wagged its cut-off little tail
as they fed it with the same kind of bottle their little brother used.
Both parents of Aunts Claudia and Mary had been from fishing
rather than farming families and their own father dear
drowned at sea when they went out in their little six man,
almost canoe like fishing boat to harpoon the great whale.
It's almost as if there are two kinds of physiology in the ancient
Basques: the tall skinny mountain leapers like Grampa's type,
and the strong stocky valley lifters more like Gramma's type.

Agape and the Four Loves

I,1.4 Daddy's last little sister

When Daddy was five his sister, Simona, was born on Oct. 31, 1915.
Daddy was now the only boy right in the middle of five sisters.
The older ones loved and played with him as he began to love
and play with the younger ones and as the middle child, he developed
the responsibility of the older ones and the security of the younger.
He and his baby sister would in ways be most alike and have
as they grew up their father's Basque dancer's long and lanky look.
Thirty percent of the steps in ballet dancing originated from
the steps of the ancient Basque dancing and at Basque celebrations
Jose and his sisters watched the dancers and loved to imitate them.
As they grew up they loved to have their pictures taken together
and years later, at Dad's funeral, a lady told Tommy's wife
who also has that dancer's look that Dad was the best dancer ever.
Eleuterio called his little Jose by the affectionate name of "cho cho".
They loved to wrestle together and Grampa even took his five year old
horse back riding with him and he was already dreaming of how
he would fish and hunt with his son and watch him become
an excellent student and athlete in this new world of opportunity.
Back in the Basqueland there was lots of water and woodland.
All was always a luscious green but this Southern Idaho desert
was totally the opposite of what he knew and thought of as beautiful.
Tuttle was a tiny oasis in this most God-forsaken of deserts.
But for humankind there has always been the desert experience.
Moses was given the Law in the desert and the chosen people
grew to maturity as they spent their forty years in the desert.
Jesus spent his forty days in the desert and underwent his temptations.
St. Anthony, the hermit, became in the desert a saint of holy legend.
Slowly Grampa Goicoechea began to fall in love with the desert
from its starry night sky above to its rugged lava flow to
the delicate purple of its whispy sage to the song of its birds.
He was so happy that he and his family were living here.

Part One: Joyful Beginnings

I,1.6 Daddy's daddy dies

But then one day when Daddy was five a cow in the barnyard
charged seven-year-old Angelus who wanted to play with her calf.
Grampa Eleuterio in an instant and in a rage grabbed a heavy
hunk of lava and threw it at the cow with all his might.
Aunt Angelus backed away and was safe from the cow but Grampa
ruptured himself and fell to the ground in pain and began bleeding.
A neighbor took him to the doctor in Shoshone but to no avail.
He bled to death and his wife and children were left in a state
of disbelief and a numb and a traumatic shock as the older ones
tried to explain to the younger ones the meaning of his death.
What would they do now for they could keep their ranch no longer?
What would her children do now that her second husband had died?
On July 24, 1916, they went to Grampa's funeral and his mother
and sisters were crying and a lump formed in cho cho's throat
and he, too, began to cry and sob for he was told that his father
had gone to heaven and he would not see him until he, too, died.
But there was little time for mourning for the ranch had to be
turned over to another family immediately and Grandmother
and her children were moved into Gooding by the Catholic
Basque connection and Gramma and her two older daughters
would be the priest's housekeepers and take care of the church.
Each night before they went to bed Gramma and her children
would pray for her husband and their father and their Daddy
and they asked him to pray for them and to be always with them.
Devoutly on their knees with their eyes closed they would
pray *The Sign of the Cross, The Angel of God, The Hail Mary*
and *The Our Father* and ask God to care for their father dear
and from the age of five onwards Daddy began to live
in a world of five dimensions: 1. with the Father, Son
and Holy Spirit 2. and with Mary, 3. and with the angels,
4. and with the blessed dead, 5. and with all here on earth.

Agape and the Four Loves

I,1.7 Daddy's shame in the first grade

Years later his daughter, Bette Jo, would ask him why he
never taught them any Basque and he told the story that
when he went to school in the first grade he could not
speak any English and the kids made fun of him for
only speaking Basque and for being such an odd kid out.
He said that after that he tried his best to learn English
as quickly as he could and he would never thereafter
speak Basque with anyone who could understand English.
So Daddy had a handicap when he started the first grade,
but his older sisters helped him and besides learning
to speak and listen in English he learned to read and write
with the other children and his competitive spirit rooted
in a fear of shame and in the sorrow over his father's death
began to sublimate his negative passion into a quest for excellence.
He was not going to let anyone shame him anymore
and he was not going to let his father die for nothing.
He began to feel that he would make his father's dream come true.
He was the only boy in the family and already as a boy
of only seven a sense of duty began to become a competitive spirit
so that he would work and train extra hard to be the best.
And as they said the Rosary on Saturday evenings which
little Jose now becoming little Joe would pray a bit with
his mother and older sisters, he began to hear *The Creed*:

> I believe in the Holy Spirit,
> the Holy Catholic Church,
> the Communion of Saints,
> the forgiveness of sins,
> the resurrection of the dead,
> and life everlasting.

And they told him that his father was a Holy Spirit with
The Holy Spirit and that he was alive forever with the Saints.

Part One: Joyful Beginnings

I,1.8 Between the graveyard and the sea

When Daddy entered the second grade Gramma Goicoechea was
thirty-five and, as she took care of her six children she knew that
after loosing her first two husbands she would never marry again.
She often thought of her little home-town of Elanchove back there
on the North Sea as a little cove between the mountains and the sea.
Their saying was that it lay between the graveyard and the sea.
Her first husband was killed fighting the whale out at sea
and his body was buried in that graveyard and now her second
husband was buried at Shoshone between the oasis and the desert.
Death deepened her affection for she loved her children more than
ever as they lost their father love and had to struggle in his
absence which made his presence stronger in their feelings.
Death deepened their prayers as she and they prayed for their lost
father and asked their father to pray for them and Aunts Claudia
and Mary became more aware of their own father's untimely death
as they now suffered through their second father's early death.
Death deepened their *agape*, for it brought them to love God more
who taught them that their father would live and be with them.
They were frightened and anxious about how they would live.
Their affection was transformed through anxiety and prayer
into *agape* the love that believed in their father's presence.
Their deepening affection made possible by *agape* let them love
each other all the more as they tried to help each other better live.
Little Joe was in the second grade and Aunts Claudia and Mary
were helping their mother to look after him and he was well fed
and well cleaned and well clothed and his sisters' friends
became friends to him and his younger sisters there at school.
Through the presence of his absent father and through the special
affection from those around him little Joe began to be aware
of the other dimensions of the spirit world and he began to get
a kind of shamanic awareness that gave him a special presence.

Agape and the Four Loves

I,1.9 Love stronger than death

As Daddy prepared for his first communion he learned about
the real presence of Jesus in communion and everyone was devout
and from them he learned a reverence as they adored Jesus who
became present in the flesh and was now present in the bread.
And as the teacher asked him about the meaning of presence
Daddy even as a little nine year old thought about the presence
of his father whom no one could see but who motivated his passion.
Of course, he could not put all of this into words, but at the
unconscious level Daddy was living out agapeic affection.
His daddy was gone but not forgotten and with affection he
liked him so much that he wanted to hold on to him always.
Affection is liking and wanting to be with, but now Daddy had
to learn to let his father go and yet to never let go and
that paradox of submitting to the absence and yet being open
to the presence that was a two way street coming from his father
and being fostered so as to go out more and more to his father
was the essence of the agapeic affection that he was learning from
his mother and his Catholic tradition and from all his loved ones.
Both Nietzsche and my father lost their fathers when they were
only five years old and both their mothers were strong believers.
They both grew into a shamanic awareness that healed them
and that helped them to heal others with humankind's highest
affirmation that could say "Yes" and "Amen" to all of existence
and could even become aware of how the loser could take all.
They both lost that which was most important as the only boy
losing his father and yet they became aware of that presence
which could always be with them for if they were alone without
their mother or sister or some living person they would really
be alone without them, but their fathers could be more with them
in a certain strange powerful motivating way because
they would never be absent from them as a living person might be.

Part One: Joyful Beginnings

I,2 Of friendly success with his school mates

I,2.1 *Friendship with Basque boarders*

The beautiful oasis town of Gooding in which Daddy grew up
had its grade school, high school, a school for the deaf and blind
and even a four year college plus its own Basque boarding house.
Gramma Goicoechea began running that when Daddy was seven
and Aunts Claudia and Mary helped her and they dropped out
of high school in their junior year and to help support the family
they got jobs working as cooks and cleaners at the school for
the deaf and the blind where they made good money for a year.
Several Basque sheepherders would stay at the boarding house.
When Aunt Claudia was seventeen and Daddy was ten and
in the fourth grade, she married Pete Cenarrusa who met her
at the boarding house and shortly thereafter Aunt Mary also married.
The First World War ended and the Roaring Twenties began
and Daddy, as a boy of ten, had a great time with the Baskos
who stayed at the boarding house and they taught him how
to play Mus which is their Basque card game and before long
he came to savvy the game and to compete with the best of them.
Being a natural athlete he loved sports and they taught him
how to lift weights and play their special kind of Basque handball.
They called him their "cho cho" and standing side by side with
him they shared their world of dancing, singing and playing together.
With them he first began to develop hand-eye coordination as
they took him into their many games of strength and skill.
And their ballet type dancing gave his body a special agility.
In Gooding there was a tiny Basque community together with
Mormon, Episcopalian and Methodist communities and they brought up
their children in their culture and at school they became friends.
The Baskos at the boarding house were like a substitute father
for Daddy and as a playful youth he learned more from them
than he would have if he only had one mentoring father.
In the boarding house birds of a feather flocked together in *agape*.

Agape and the Four Loves

I,2.2 Friendship seeking New World success

In the boarding house Daddy was nourished by a strong
agapeic center which was alive with affection, *eros*, friendship,
and a natural *agape* that reached out to all with good will.
The Basques were like a family in that house with the same affection
for each other that they had had in their own families back home.
The name Goicoechea means "house on the hill" and in that
Goicoechea boarding house there in Gooding the Basques were
a family, and yet *eros* made for new families as Aunts
Claudia and Mary and others were drawn there to be together
with their mates as they stood face to face enraptured with each other.
And Daddy as an eleven year old, was already part of that atmosphere.
The *eros* of love between the sexes was a reality for him also.
He noticed pretty girls and they noticed him too and he even had
girl friends and the Baskos kidded him about certain pretty girls
and asked him questions about how he felt, and they talked about love.
But most of all Daddy was becoming friends with those at school
who liked athletics and already in the fourth grade he was
running races and starting to play basketball and football with
the Toone brothers from the Mormon community and with Clea
Prince and others as they loved to compete and grow with each other.
The Catholics, the Mormons, the Episcopalians and other religious
groups each had their church services and Sunday School or catechism
where children learned of the love of God and of neighbor.
In that little town of Gooding they worked together to be the best
and the best they were, as the five children in our family came to
know as we studied Daddy's high school and college Annuals.
From these stories and pictures in the Annuals it is easy to surmise
how already in the fourth and fifth grades Daddy and his friends
must have already been running races and playing football and
basketball together to become as good as they were for they won
many district and state championships setting new records.

Part One: Joyful Beginnings

I,2.3 *They ate their peck of salt together*

In Daddy's Annual, *The Toponis*, of 1927, when he was in his
third year of high school it says on page 50 about the track team:

HERE'S OUR 1927 RECORD

DISTRICT MEET	STATE MEET
McCrea—1st—440 yd. dash	Goicoechea—1st—880 yd. dash
Goicoechea—2nd—880 yd. dash	C.Toone—1st—100 yd. dash
C. Toone—1st—100 - 200 yd. dash	C.Toone—2nd—220 yd. dash
C. Prince—1st—Broad Jump	T. Toone, Shaw, C. Prince
C. Prince—3rd—High Jump	C. Toone—2nd—880 relay
T. Toone, Shaw, C. Prince	
C. Toone, 1st—880 relay	

Not only did they do this well in track, but their basketball
and football teams were equally excellent even for state championships.
Idaho is a large state and there were many cities far larger
than Gooding so the question is: "How did they achieve such success?"
Already in the middle grades of grade school they must have
been working hard together to become faster, stronger, better.
As Nietzsche, in his early essay *Homer's Contest,* reflected upon
the ancient Greeks of the classical period he saw their will to power
or will to prevail taking them into many contests of striving
against each other in athletics, politics, drama, debate and
even philosophy and Gooding must have been a little American Athens.
As Aristotle thought about friendship he saw it arising from
eating a peck of salt together and as Daddy and his friends
sweated it out together they must have licked their lips and
literally eaten that much salt together over an eight year period.
Years later when Daddy chose the name for his third son
it was Clifford after his great friend Clifford Toone with
whom he trained so hard and who must have befriended him
even more than others as a mentor who was a year older.
Clifford went on to Brigham Young University with a full scholarship.

Agape and the Four Loves

I,2.4 *On wonderfully coached teams*

In order for there to be several of the best athletes and several
of the best teams in one little area the coaches had to be excellent.
In that same *Toponis* Annual of 1928, at the beginning of the part
on ATHLETICS where there is a beautiful picture of a running
Indian Brave in colour above, and five sprinters drawn
below, it says:
"Fair competition, embodying high ideals, is a great teacher."
And then in the section on football where you see the pictures
of each player and a write-up on each, for Daddy, it says:

> Now fasten your optics upon Jose Goicoechea,
> the bounding Basque of the Senator squad.
> Goicoechea last year proved himself
> a clever field general
> as well as a shifty ball carrier.
> He has a disconcerting habit
> of leaping into the air when tackled
> and an uncanny ability
> to light on his feet still running.
> Joe will no doubt
> fill the quarterback berth next year,
> his senior year. p. 46.

In order for this sort of skill to be developed in a small town
both in the boys and the girls there must have been some
very excellent coaches who fit right into the poetry of this milieu.
The motto of "Fair competition, embodying high ideals, is a great teacher."
must have inspired the coaches even down in grade school to do
their best for their students and teach them with enthusiasm
how to throw the football, how to move your hips when running
through tacklers, how to block, how to tackle in various ways.
If Daddy could do this when he was seventeen he must have been
learning it well from a terrific coach already when he was thirteen.

Part One: Joyful Beginnings

I,2.5 Friendship in the physical, vital, intellectual, spiritual

As Daddy and his friends went though the eighth grade they had
together many dreams of excellence as they thought of high school.
Their teachers in grade school and their school spirit prepared them
not only physically to be the best athletes, but they worked equally
hard at their reading, writing, spelling and arithmetic and they were
already beginning to memorize poetry and read and discuss good stories.
They practiced singing, playing in the band, debating and public speaking
for they put on a school play each year and had fun in various parts.
They were getting a sense of history and of geography and as they
learned about the Mormons coming west, Daddy, as one of the few
Basques, took special pride in all he could learn and tell about his people.
They started each day together pledging allegiance to their flag
and each class began the day by praying aloud *The Our Father*.
In that same *Toponis* Annual of 1928, in the section on ACTIVITIES
GLEE CLUBS—DRAMATICS—DEBATE—ORGANIZATIONS:
"The Nucleus of Education is Social contact."
the first part is on DEBATE and under the picture of six
handsomely dressed students are the words:

> Having earned two decisions over strong Boise teams
> and one victory over Twin Falls, one over Buhl,
> and one over Hazelton, our debaters
> may well consider that they had
> a successful season this Spring.

They seemed to be winners in whatever contest they entered.
The plays through grade school prepared them well for high school
and in his junior year, Daddy was in the play: "*Adam and Eva*"
as James King, a rich man's business manager named Adam.
So by the end of the eighth grade Daddy and his friends were
an enthusiastic class well prepared for the pursuit of excellence,
not only in the physical realm of athletics, but equally well in the
realm of vital social values and the intellectual and the spiritual.

Agape and the Four Loves

I,2.6 A shining star in that constellation of friends

Already in his freshman year at the age of fifteen Daddy was
a rising star as can be seen on page 51 of *Toponis* (1926).
There is a picture of the fourteen best athletes of the high school
all wearing their G (for Gooding) sweaters and wearing a tie.
In *Toponis* (1927), on page 27 at the bottom, there is a picture
of Daddy and Clifford Toone and beneath it reads: "Food for Thought".
What that little prophecy indicates is that just as Clifford is
the star athlete of the school Daddy is the one to be that next.
Clifford Toone and his large Mormon community were very
healthy for they never smoked, drank, gambled or even touched
a cup of coffee or tea and as farmers they got exercise galore.
They were a loving people with their church at the center of their life.
The Basque community, on the other hand, was very, very small and
you can hardly find a student in the annuals with a Basque name.
So ominous things were on the horizon for this Basque star
as soon as he began to shine for he was already playing cards
with the Basques and the men all smoked and drank and he
already each morning had a cup of coffee there in the boarding house.
From the beginning as their written comments in the annuals show,
he was a favorite with many of the pretty young lady teachers
who wrote comments such as:

> Try hard, Joe, and there'll be
> no more special comp. for you. Pauline Bigham
> You kept away from my class this year.
> Will I have you in any next year? Fairy Sanger
> Do you think you'll like to sing next year
> as much as you did this? Marian Stevenson

By his Junior year Daddy did become the star athlete of Gooding High.
He was as popular as he was handsome and as a first-year student
he was fully inspired to train always to become faster and stronger
and he found a relation between mathematics and successful gambling.

Part One: Joyful Beginnings

I,2.7 Training up at the sheep camp with Uncle Pete

Daddy's oldest sister, Aunt Claudia, married Pete Cenarrusa and he
and his brother Joe ran sheep up at the head of Fish Creek where that
beautiful little trout stream first begins to form out of springs
and little streams from mountain lakes that add to it as it runs.
Right close to where Uncle Pete kept the sheep camp there were
some beaver ponds with many beautiful speckled brook trout
and by his sixteenth year Daddy was already a fly fisherman.
In the morning he would run up into the hills to check the sheep
and then run back down jumping over sagebrush and always
training for the Fall football season, the Winter basketball season
and the Spring track season and in late afternoon he would repeat
the same great exercise program and in the evening he went fishing.
By the time this highlander got back to Gooding for another year
of competition, he was in better shape than the farming lowlanders.
He just got better as an athlete and this artist of pleasure and
hero was a shining star of prowess and popularity as the
comments in the year books continued to show and *The Toponis*
of 1928, page 22, treats *The Juniors as Others Know Them* and
for Joe G, under *Favorite Occupation*, it says: "Doing everyone he can."
And under *Ambition*, it says: "Fire Sinclair." And under *Weakness*
it says: "Dating Teachers" and there appears to be a point to all this.
Bess Sinclair was an English teacher and she wrote a comment on
the first page of his '28 yearbook:

> Hope some day you'll be liking
> poor, weak English teachers. B Sinclair

Each of these three points can converge, for "Doing everyone he can"
points toward his being an opportunist who used people for his own
ends, and maybe, "dating teachers" had an element of that in it.
The faculty advisor for the *Toponis* Staff was H. F. Willmorth
and he must have agreed with the three points which again
point to something ominous on the horizon for the shining star.

Agape and the Four Loves

I,2.8 Training with farming friends on Silver Creek

When he was eighteen Daddy worked on the Purdy Ranch near Picabo.
The sheepmen needed hay for their large flocks for four months
and thus the farmers of Carey and Picabo could flourish not
only from their dairy herds, but also from growing and selling alfalfa.
Daddy told the story that one time, he was on top of the hay stack
arranging the hay and the fellows below told him a rattlesnake
was coming up hidden in the hay and he always liked rattlesnake stories.
That summer Daddy first started fishing on Silver Creek which
he would do for the rest of his life and it is one of the great fly fishing
streams of America and he began to learn how to match the hatch
with the kinds of flies that those rainbows were taking at a given time.
All was going so well in Daddy's second year of high school and
now that he was about to go into his third year he was also starting
to become a very good boxer and the farm work improved his strength.
Up at the sheep camp, the previous summer Uncle Pete would say
his prayers each morning with his cup of coffee and so did Daddy.
In Catholic culture there is a ritual of doing things over and over again.
Gramma Goicoechea always said the Rosary each day and during Lent
she and Aunt Claudia and later Aunt Dorothy would go to daily mass.
To do something religiously is to do it habitually out of a
programmed memory and Daddy learned that from his Catholic culture.
Daddy was an altar boy and he memorized the Latin prayers
and if he heard *Dominus vobiscum*-"The Lord be with you", he
would automatically respond *Et cum spiritu tuo* - "And also with you."
Our daily lives have rituals too with set ways of shaking hands
holding your fork and responding to a letter and even in athletics
Daddy learned each phase of basketball, football and boxing so that
he would have set ways of responding that were quicker than thought.
He was told how each Mass was Holy Thursday, Good Friday and
Easter Sunday made present at once in the ritual which he prayed.
And the deep *agape* of his family permeated his friendship and *eros*.

Part One: Joyful Beginnings

I,2.9 All the training pays off

In the *Toponis* Annual of 1928 we can read of the great success story.
Daddy was a star in football, basketball and track and field and
they won the State Football Championship and Daddy was the fastest man
in Idaho at the half mile and next year he hoped to break the state record.
He became very good friends especially with his fellow athletes.
He was well liked and looked up to for bringing glory to the school.
His annuals show that many beautiful young ladies found him
to be very attractive and lots of fun and yet you can sense
in many of their comments a tension that had to do with the way
in which the battle of the sexes was working itself out in the 1920's.
In Daddy's Basque culture there was gambling, drinking, smoking
and culminating in the late 20s and early 30s the puritanical
culture of Prohibition was strongly upheld, especially by ladies.
In the 1928 *Toponis*, on page 55, which is a totally blank page
there is this one beautifully written message:

> Dear Joe –
> I'm rather surprised, but guess I'll live.
> Mumm—you can kiss anyway.
> Vernita

So was Daddy just playing the field and did some girls become much
more involved with him than he was with them and were they a bit hurt?
She is surprised and yet there is the consolation prize of the kissing.
Since it takes two to have the mucosity of really good kissing maybe
she thought that she was just the right match for this Latin lover.
Maybe she was surprised that he was not as keen on her as she
was on him because in his kissing he seemed to be focused on her alone.
So was there something there in the Roaring Twenties that gave
the battle of the sexes a special uniqueness for us to explore?
In the annuals so many of the young men and young women
look as if they were so handsome and so beautiful that they came
from Hollywood with their lovely hairdos and beautiful clothes.

I,3 Of erotic exploring and finding his wife

I,3.1 Sex, death and religion at high school's end

Daddy never had and we never saw his Senior *Toponis* Annual.
But at Gooding High it is there to be seen and in the first part
of the athletic section it tells how they won the State Championship
in football, but then there is nothing about him in the rest of the section.
He was not on the basketball team or on the track and field team
and in that 1929 annual it says that he did not graduate and we
do not know what happened, but the newspaper says he graduated
and he must have done so for he entered Gooding College that Fall.
As he came to the end of his high school years with the help of his
mother and sisters and his friends he had to start getting serious.
The whole point of the Basques in coming to the New World was to have
a great new life in this land of prosperity and he did have a passion
that always let him evaluate situations and which motivated him
to put all of his energy, even with a religious fervor, into his work.
He wanted to be the best at whatever he did even that he might
fulfill the dream of his dead daddy dear who was always present to him.
When he said his prayers each morning and evening they had
a special devotion because of the intensity of his father's presence
and his religion whose passion had to do with death also touched
the whole realm of his sex and *eros* which was now becoming important.
Many of the young ladies as they were finishing high school were
strongly thinking of marriage and several thought of him as an
excellent possible husband for he was desirable in every way.
He, too, was focusing more and more on his deep down ideal woman
who would be his life-long wife and the mother of his children.
He wanted a wife like his mother and his sisters for whom
he had the greatest reverence and his girl friends felt that in him.
He needed to get a good job so that he could be a good provider.
So he applied to Gooding College, the four-year local college,
and he was accepted and his mother and sisters would help
earn the money so that together they could all pay for his tuition.

Part One: Joyful Beginnings

I,3.2 Starting college during the Great Depression

Just as everything looked wonderful when Daddy was a little boy before his father died, so now in 1930, when Daddy was twenty, everything looked equally full of promise and Daddy was optimistic. Even though Herbert Hoover was the new Republican president and the stock market came tumbling down and the Great Depression was hurting more and more each day, Daddy still felt safe and secure with a good summer job and total support from his mother and sisters he quickly became a hero again in his first year of college. On the first page of his college annual, *The Sagebrush Echo*, a young lady begins her best wishes with "Dearest Honey Joe". He is immediately the star on the basketball team and on the track and field team and it looks like things will only get better even though there are ominous clouds beginning to move in over his Basque culture for this is also the time of the Prohibition and in the Boarding House there would be a strange emptiness without wine and whiskey. Still in 1930 the beautiful look of the Roaring Twenties shines out at you as you look at all the well groomed, well dressed young people. Gooding College was established by the Methodists and other religious groups even though the Mormons would prefer to go to B.Y.U. Already in *The Burned-Over District* in Western New York, from 1800 to 1850, the purity of the Prohibition seemed more and more moral. Joseph Smith's family moved to Western New York in 1816 when Joseph was ten years old and he received his prophetic visions there and then quickly moved Westward and his Mormons settled especially in Utah and Idaho and their teetotalling purity was very strong in Gooding and Daddy's best friend was a Mormon. The Suffragettes helped Hoover get in and all, even in Gooding, was squeaky clean and lovely pure, just as it had been out there in the little oasis of Tuttle before calamity struck the Goicoecheas. It looked like Daddy had clear sailing right through college and then on to a wonderful job perhaps teaching and being a coach.

I,3.3 The Prohibition and being put in jail

During the Prohibition the producing and selling and drinking of alcohol was forbidden and the Basques could hardly believe it and many of them took to making their own whiskey and to bootlegging it here and there. Aunt Mary's husband, Uncle Telus, made it down in Nevada and then brought it up to the boarding house that Gramma ran and Daddy delivered it in the morning to certain persons' doorsteps the way the milkman delivers milk and it was obvious that he was lawbreaking. Then on April 23, 1931, four men and two women were taken in a liquor raid and handed over to the Federal Court and Joe Goicoechea was one of the men and Eulalia Goicoechea and Babe Taylor were the women. Gramma Goicoechea was sentenced to jail for five months and fined $100.00 and Daddy to six months and he was fined $200.00. They would not tell where they got the whiskey in trying to protect Uncle Telus, but some of the family worked it out that if Gramma would tell then she could get released early and that is what she did. Daddy was in the Mt. Home Jail until Oct. 1, 1931 and it was for him a great shock that at the age of twenty-one he was taken out of College where he was doing so well and put in jail over whiskey. Gramma, who was a totally holy woman and never got tipsy once in her life, made the whole scenario look totally absurd. For six months Daddy did his chain gang duties and played cards with his fellow inmates and he learned to really savvy the games of Poker and Pinocle and in that six month period, he made the transition from being a student and then a teacher to being a gambler for he knew he could never go to college again. The Boarding House was closed down and Gramma moved to Nevada where her younger daughters now lived and when Daddy got out of jail, he had no support system left, and except for Aunt Claudia and Uncle Pete down in Richfield, he had no family. Daddy felt that the Republican Party, with its Great Depression and its Prohibition could never be a party for him again.

Part One: Joyful Beginnings

I,3.4 Riding the rails with the bums to Omaha

While he was in jail for that half year his prayer life deepened.
Prisons are like seminaries and monasteries with a set time for
rising, an order of the day and a set time for lights out and going
to sleep and Daddy found that praying was the way to sleep in peace.
He would awaken sometimes an hour before get-up time and he would
pray and think about his plight as his mind moved back and forth.
Even though he did not pray the Rosary, he had prayed it at home
over the years with his mother and sisters and the structures of
the Joyful, Sorrowful and Glorious Mysteries were in his memory
in a programmed way, so that he could order his life in terms of them.
He was in great sorrow but he knew that the point was to turn
that suffering into something good and as he prayed *The Hail Mary*,
he thought of Mary at the crib with Jesus and then at the cross
with Jesus and then at Easter with Jesus and he asked her to pray
for his mother and take care of her and to guide him in this trouble.
He knew that if he really loved his mother he would have to be
healthy, happy, holy and wise for her sake or he would break her heart.
He saw that the first great tragedy in their life was connected with
his father getting angry and killing himself by throwing that big rock.
Now he saw that not really paying attention to the law and its
rules and regulations could take away your education and a certain future.
So, in jail, Daddy had a kind of solitude that took him away from
great activity and that solitude connected him in a deeper kind
of communication with his loved ones even his father and his enemies.
And, in jail, he knew that work was very scarce on the outside and
he and some of his fellow jail-birds talked about riding
freight trains for free and finding work from town to town.
When he got out he worked with Uncle Pete through the winter
and then in early summer he and a buddy snuck onto a freight car
in Shoshone and lived the adventure of exploring the world together
as handsome able-bodied workers who could help many needing help.

Agape and the Four Loves

1,3.5 *With family in Nevada and breaking wild horses*

Across Wyoming and into Colorado and Nebraska farmers needed
very good workers during the summer and even though they could not
pay much Daddy and his buddy were able to make it to Omaha,
which was the central city for the Union Pacific Railroad which went
through Idaho on its way to Portland, Oregon and they had a good time.
Daddy was arrested again in Omaha when he hopped off the
freight train, for really, stealing rides, too, was not within the law.
He had a skeleton key in his pocket and they thought it might
be a tool for breaking into people's houses but they soon set him free.
After doing dishes and cleaning out barns and banks he soon had
enough of the traveling bums' happy-go-lucky life, so, by Fall
he road the rails back to Shoshone and then made his way down
to Nevada to be with his mother and his sisters and their families.
He got a job on a ranch in Fallon, Nevada, breaking wild horses for
he was a wicked athlete and could excel at any sort of sport.
In Nevada there was also lots of gambling and boxing was a well
paid sport and he pursued both of these activities earning money
from both and being able to buy himself a car so that he could
move about in Nevada from fight to fight and deal poker games.
There is a picture of him and his sister Simona with their long and
lanky look having such a good time together and he loved to have
a bottle of beer in his hand as he stood by his car for a picture.
The Prohibition came to an end as a terribly failed experiment
and now it was as if Daddy and his kind liked to flout it.
He would love to go back to Gooding in his car and stand outside
the house of a prohibitionist woman teacher and drink a cool beer.
Daddy had gone through two great tragedies: the death of his father
and being thrown in jail and having his college career come to an end.
But now he was thriving again in the worlds of boxing and of gambling.
Several Basques owned Casinos in Nevada and he became friends with
them especially in Reno, Elko and in Fallon and he hoped for big things.

Part One: Joyful Beginnings

I,3.6 Getting his nose broken by the big black boxer

Daddy thought he might become a professional boxer and he was
moving up in the world of prize fighting having won many fights.
As he later told Tommy's wife, Annette, he thought he was the king.
But then in Reno, he had a ten-round fight with a "big black boy"
and he got his nose broken but good and that was the end
of any thinking about going on in boxing and the broken nose
was the third set back after his father's death and going to jail.
Ever after that Daddy's nose was slightly deformed and from then on
he never engaged in any contact sport such as football or boxing.
After that to earn his livelihood Daddy dealt cards in various places
and became better and better at knowing how to count the cards and
bluffing and knowing when someone was bluffing and letting little guys
win some so that they would keep coming back and he did succeed in this.
And his three younger sisters had husbands who found work
in saw mills and before long they went to Susanville, California
and then to Sonora, where they settled down and Grandma lived with
Aunt Dorothy and her husband Joe Goicoechea and their daughter Louise.
By the time he was twenty-four Franklin Delano Roosevelt was elected
president and they started big work projects in order to try to revive
the economy and get people back to work and Daddy heard that up
in Carey they were working on building the Fish Creek and Wood River
Damns and many workers and a lot of money was in the little town.
Nevada was sort of a tourist state and Daddy had not yet met a woman
whom he really wanted to marry and he remembered a certain young
lady whom he had met up Fish Creek and he had talked with her mother.
Even though she was not Catholic, he felt that she was a holy lady
like his mother and his sisters and Carey began to become a kind of
magnet for him and he did want to get back to his own kind of country.
So, in 1935, Daddy drove his car back to Idaho and went to see
his sister Claudia and Uncle Pete and they were doing very well for
through a government grant they had received 1000 acres of land.

Agape and the Four Loves

I,3.7 Coming back to Carey, Idaho and dealing poker

The little town of Carey had a population of about 500 people and
there was a tiny Basque population of the Arians and Cenarrusas.
The Taylor Grazing Act closed ten western states including Idaho,
to itinerant sheep herding and in Idaho, allotments were made,
letting each sheepherder with a certain size herd have 1000 acres.
Pete and Joe Cenarrusa each got their section and right next
to them, up Iron Mine, Levaur Coats, the father of Joneva, got his.
With workers coming in to help build the damns, Carey was
a boom town and right away Daddy got a job dealing poker
for Louie Arian who owned the only saloon in the town of Carey.
Carey was about 90% Mormon and they were opposed to drinking.
But Louie's little bar did a thriving business and Daddy was so
happy to be back where he could often fly fish on Silver Creek
and up Little Wood River especially with his new friend, Gary York.
Even though Daddy was a gambler and a drinker Gramma Coates
mentioned to her Joneva Mae when she was but seventeen that
this Joe Goicoechea was a very special sort of man and soon
those opposites were to attract with the help of Mother Cupid.
As they began to talk, Daddy told Joneva about the death of his father,
about his being put in jail and about his broken nose, and she
discussed this with her mother and Leona sensed some deep bonding
and she told Joneva about the early deaths of her own mother
and of Levaur's mother and there was some shamanic attraction.
In spite of the three major challenges that became opportunities
for some new way of life, Joe was an optimistic extravert and
he knew that the beautiful Joneva was a joyful, contemplative
introvert who would be a totally affectionate wife and mother.
Daddy did tell Joneva about all of his success as an athlete
but at the sub-conscious level what attracted her the most
was his ability to grow from any suffering and turn it into joy.
But most of all he had a reverence for her that she had never known.

Part One: Joyful Beginnings

I,3.8 He marries the near perfect lady, Joneva Mae Coates

Joneva Mae experienced in Joe something like the holy in a way
she had never felt it for there was in him a kind of *mysterium tremendum*.
He was somehow fascinating and yet frightening for he did so many
things she really did not like such as smoking, drinking and gambling.
She even asked him about these bad habits and he acted as if it was
totally normal for he told her how Basques would stroll from bar
to bar, stopping briefly for a drink and in Boise they would socialize
by going from boarding house to boarding house and even stop to gamble.
He thought that it was cool to smoke like Humphrey Bogart in *Casablanca*
and he loved to drink in front of prohibition ladies, even out in public,
now that their laws that punished him were stricken down as failures.
But he also told her that at Basque dances priests often served as
stifling chaperones and there were no waltzes but only dances that
allowed for no physical contact between men and women and she felt that.
She could feel the presence of the Basque women within him who often
went to daily mass and that reverence was strongly attractive to her.
He was a mix of the mysterious tremendous that nearly made her tremble
and she did not know that sort of passion in Mormons or even Anglicans.
In other words he swept her off her feet and he could feel in her
that kind of holiness that was in his mother and sisters and he knew
that she was the one for none of the other ladies he met were like her.
Joe had suffered his three trials patiently and that gave him
a charm that is not there except in those who have suffered and
she could appreciate this which both her parents had gone through.
Joe had a joy that could say "*Yes*" to all sorrow and, in fact, it was
so strong that he seemed to go out and raise a little hell almost
as if he were inviting the rods of men and sorrow to come his way.
Not in the least did she want to raise a little hell and she did
not want him to either and maybe she thought she could redeem him.
And maybe he thought she could too, for her love did give him
a new kind of patience and gentleness that was strangely new to him.

Agape and the Four Loves

I,3.9 A Democrat forever with Franklin Delano Roosevelt

On November 12, 1936, Joneva and Joe were married in the Hailey Catholic Church by Father Dougherty with Aunt Claudia and Uncle Pete as their witnesses and that was mother's first real Catholic experience. She thought that he might stop smoking, drinking and gambling, but what happened most was that she started moving more in his direction. She very much liked Father Dougherty, who, in some way that had never quite happened before was the face and mind and heart of Jesus for her. This celibate Irish priest with his kindness and good humor seemed to love her and focus on her with a new special love that she could feel. Even though she was not a Catholic their wedding had something of a sacrament about it for her such that her husband and Claudia and Pete and Father Dougherty all prayed in a special powerful way. It was as if her wedding was an outward sign instituted by Jesus to give special graces and those gifts she could begin to sense and she knew that they would grow in significance as she lived her marriage. Joneva loved to read and Father Dougherty gave her a little prayer book because he could sense something special in her and she already thought of him baptizing her children just as he married her. And she had already told Joe, as she was going through her last year of high school, how she was reading a book called *Just David* and she wanted to name her first son David and her daughter Bette Jo. And the thought even crossed Joe's mind that she already loved those names and the strong persons they stood for and she wanted a son and a daughter so she could give them those names she loved. And Roosevelt's work programs were starting to help people in 1936 and 1937 and she wanted Daddy to get a good job and to stop working in the pool hall, as she called it, and he did move in her direction and he helped Joe and Pete Cenarrusa with the lambing. And the farmers and even sheep men became Republicans because the bankers gave them loans and knew they would pay at harvest time and when the lambs were shipped but Daddy would be a Democrat forever.

II. Nietzsche

II.1 The affectionate child finds his lost father's *agape*

II,1.1 Becoming a pietistic Jesus shaman

We might think of Nietzsche as a postmodern shaman who, in questing
after health, education and welfare, was able to bring it to many others.
When he lost his father and became a semi-orphan, three big things
happened that took him into the realm of Jesus' healing *agape*
and let him become a healed healer, an educated educator and
a parented semi-orphan who could help parent all other orphans.
With the women of his family, he prayed for his father and asked
his father to pray for them, and through his successful mourning,
he got in touched very strongly with the spirit world, so that his
father's spirited embodiment was always with him in presence-absence.
Secondly, he was like Demosthenes, the great orator of Ancient Greece.
Demosthenes was an orphan who, without his father's voice to teach
him speaking, developed a speech impediment which, in overcoming,
he was enabled to become the greatest orator of all, and thus to be
the model teacher for all those who would learn the art of persuasion.
Thirdly, Nietzsche was taken to the Pforta Schule when he was young,
and just as Holy Mother Church and Holy Mother Mary can be
additional mothers for the Catholic, so the Pforta Schule became
a surrogate father for the orphaned Nietzsche, and he learned
far better from that group of fathers than he would have from
his own and, of course, this school had his father's Lutheran spirit.
Nietzsche, as the little boy who lost his father, was very loved
by his family of women, by those who looked after his welfare
in helping him overcome his impediments and by his teachers.
He received a great health from his family, great welfare from his
community and great education from his teachers, and all of this
healing-learning was accomplished in the atmosphere of Pietism's
heartfelt love for Jesus which would always remain at the center
of the healing-caring-teaching heart of Nietzsche from the time
as a five-year-old, he sobbed in prayers and tears for his father
until he broke down insane in prayers and tears for the beaten horse.

Agape and the Four Loves

II,1.2 *The Anti-Christ describes Nietzsche's life-long Jesus*

In *The Anti-Christ*, sections 28 through 35, Nietzsche describes the psychological type of the redeemer by contrasting Jesus with other types that have been suggested, such as that of hero and genius. Of course, all along, Nietzsche wants to show that the loving Jesus is not the blaming Christ, which is the main point of the book. If we consider our two bookend quotations from *Aus Meinem Leben*, and from *The Intoxication Song*, we will see that this fits right in. Nietzsche writes:

> The incapacity for resistance here becomes morality
> ('resist not evil!'; the profoundest saying of the Gospel,
> Its key in a certain sense) blessedness in peace,
> in gentleness, in the *inability* for enmity.

This Jesus at the center of Nietzsche's heart does not resist any evil. He is a gentle pacifist and peacemaker who does not even have the ability for enmity, a physiological state Nietzsche will ponder. As he learned to become a shamanic follower of Jesus, Nietzsche was healed from the deep habit of resisting with negative reactions. In that way, like Jesus, he came to have an automatic affirmation of his father's death, and for the departure of Lou Salome and other ills to which his ill-constituted decadence tended to succumb. Nietzsche became the teacher of a non-resisting *amor fati*, as he philosophically learned to revalue all values and, in joy, to welcome all sorrow by seeing how joy wanted all forever, even all sorrow. His vocation was to bring welfare to all the needy as he received the same in a peaceful gentleness that could love all of existence with humankind's highest affirmation for their eternal return. For Jesus to be a hero, he would have to win in resisting the enemy. But from the core of his heart, Jesus loves his enemy and Nietzsche learns to do the same in a strange paradoxical way that we will have to understand as he came to love death, hatred and even resisting, which is in the hero's contesting, especially for the Greeks.

Part One: Joyful Beginnings

II,1.3 Jesus' Kingdom of Love is here and now

As Nietzsche goes on in Section 29 to describe his dear Lord and the joy that thirsts for this world, he writes:

> What are the 'glad tidings'?
> True life, eternal life is found –
> it is not promised, it is here,
> it is *within you*:
> as life lived in love,
> in love without deduction
> or exclusion, without distance.

Nietzsche's love let him believe in an eschatology that saw Jesus' Kingdom as imminent and as right here and now, wherever there is the true love of *agape* which can pray: "Thy will be done, on earth as it is in heaven", as Nietzsche did when he was thirteen. Because Nietzsche loves an incarnate Jesus in the flesh, heaven is not an immaterial realm where the extracted soul is able to escape its punishment of being placed in a body of bad karma. If one really loves all, even our enemies, as Jesus taught us, then there will be no evil to resist, for good will be seen in all. This Kingdom of love within is without any exclusion, for its logic is one of mixed opposites, which sees the lovable, and the so-called unlovable, in a realm that is beyond good and evil. Good and evil are the moral categories of the Judging Christ, but Jesus always *resisted* being called the Christ, for there were at least seven different meanings of the Christ or the Messiah and his Kingdom with which people could misinterpret Jesus. The Zionists thought that the Messiah would overcome Rome and Jesus did not want to be identified with that anymore than he wanted to be only an apocalyptic Christ who would come after the anti-Christ and save the good but condemn the bad. Nietzsche himself became the Anti-Christ to say "*No*" to that anti-Christ, in order to say "*Yes*" to the Kingdom of Jesus's love.

Agape and the Four Loves

II,1.4 Jesus as a child of God loves everyone equally

Going on in section 29, Nietzsche writes:

> Everyone is a child of God –
> Jesus definitely claims nothing for himself alone –
> as a child of God
> everyone is equal to everyone else.

In our first study on *Agape* and personhood, we focused on the three essential traits of persons as belonging to the Kingdom of *agape*. Each person is equal in worth to all others and each is unique an no person is an island, but we are all related in the body of Jesus. Nietzsche's Jesus, who resists not evil, is a peacemaker and all peacemakers are recognized as children of God and this notion of the child is a key concept, because the drama of Zarathustra leads up to the child and his or her perfect love in joy for all. If any idea is at the center between the two book-end passages, it has to be this one about the loving child Jesus, loving all equally. When Nietzsche goes into dialogue with all the ill-constituted higher men of his authorship, we will have to see how he loves all of them equally and yet resists and contests their *No*-saying. In *The Anti-Christ*, when Nietzsche treats the Hebrew Bible, he says "*Yes*" to all of it until the priests make their distinction between the sacred and profane, and he says "*No*" to saying "*No*" to the profane. We can begin to understand the relation between Nietzsche's *Yes*-saying with Jesus and yet his *No*-saying if we consider II Samuel 7, in which David is told that Yahweh will always love him with his everlasting merciful love or *hesed*, which becomes *agape*, and yet David will be punished with the rods of men. Any resistance on David's part will meet with natural resistance. Any *No*-saying will be met with a *No*-saying, but all of this is secondary for the sake of a higher *Yes*-saying, so, for Jesus, who loves his enemy, any resistance from the enemy will not be resisted, but loved, but Christ's *No* will resist any resistance.

II,1.5 Jesus' love is not that of a genius, but of an idiot

Whereas a hero is a resisting winner of contests, like Homer's Greek heroes, the genius is a builder of the real world, and all of its wonderful institutions of health, education and welfare. So whereas Renan would picture Jesus as a genius, Nietzsche following Dostoyevsky thinks he can better picture him as an idiot. Jesus, who is at home

> in a world undisturbed by reality of any kind,
> a merely 'inner' world,
> a 'real' world, an 'eternal' world . . .
> The Kingdom of God is within you.

is called by Nietzsche an idiot, for not wanting to be touched by the outer world as outer reality, which sees no inner reality. So Jesus and his idiot followers will live in the world, but be not of it, and this paradox came up in our Zarathustra bookend:

> So rich is joy that it thirsts for woe,
> for Hell, for hatred, for shame, for the lame,
> for the world—for it knows,
> Oh, it knows this world!

The joy of the idiot savant will know this world, and yet thirst for it, just as it thirsts for Hell, for hatred, for shame, for the lame. Nietzsche thinks that already the idiot Jesus saw the world as being like Hell in its hatred and shame, and yet Jesus loved it in its 'inner', 'eternal' reality as a Kingdom of God within. So the world has two aspects and a genius will build up its outer aspect, which without agapeic love, we see as the real. But the idiot Jesus will thirst for the 'inner' aspect of the world and not want to be touched by or to touch 'reality' of any kind. This idiot Jesus will not want to be disturbed by that aspect of the world which geniuses like Socrates, Plato, Kant, Schopenhauer and Wagner might be building up and yet Nietzsche, for Jesus, will love them all as equally lovable.

Agape and the Four Loves

II,1.6 The loving idiot Jesus shrinks back from "reality"

In *Twilight of The Idols*, Nietzsche writes about

> HOW THE 'REAL WORLD' AT LAST BECAME A MYTH
> History of an Error

He sees this history as having six stages: (1) From Plato (2) to the Christians (3) to Kant (4) to the positivists (5) to Free Spirits running wild (6) to Zarathustra, so that this distinction between two kinds of real world is central for Nietzsche. The physiological type of the idiot has an ultimate logic

> an instinctive hatred of *every* reality
> as flight into the ungraspable,
> into the inconceivable,
> as antipathy towards every form,
> every spatial and temporal concept,
> towards everything firm,
> all that is custom, institution, church.

So Jesus, as an idiot, while resisting nothing, did not want to be touched by any 'reality'; in fact, he had instinctive hatred for it, insofar as it was conceivable and graspable as Platonic form, or as Kantian spatial and temporal concept, or insofar as it was made real by church, institution, custom or anything fixed. This is Nietzsche's way of protecting each unique singularity. Platonists disregard unique individuals, as they stress forms that are ultra real and Kantians argue that we know and love only appearances and never persons, places or things in themselves. Aristotelian realists, while emphasizing the reality of individuals, still treat them scientifically in classifications of genera and species. It is the nominalists who argue that universals are only names to remind us to attend to the single individuals and Nietzsche sees Jesus and himself as idiot nominalists who love individuals and shy away from formal reality, which looses touch with the lovability of the children of God in all their happy joy.

Part One: Joyful Beginnings

II,1.7 With a loving idiosyncratic capacity for suffering

In Section 30, Nietzsche further elaborates Jesus' idiotic recoil from 'reality' into his inner world of love in terms of an extreme capacity for suffering, which no longer wants to be 'touched' at all because it feels every contact too deeply, so that he writes:

> Instinctive exclusion of all aversion, all enmity,
> all feeling for limitation and distancing:
> consequence of an extreme capacity
> for suffering and irritation,
> which already feels all resisting,
> all need for resistance
> as an unbearable displeasure:
> and knows blessedness (pleasure)
> only in no longer resisting anyone or anything,
> neither the evil nor the evil-doer –
> love as the sole, as the last possibility of life.

So Nietzsche is like Pascal in thinking that "The heart has its reasons that the mind knows not." And he is trying to understand the heart of Jesus which feels displeasure or pain in any resisting of evil and which feels a blessed pleasure in not resisting evil, or the evil doer. Jesus not only takes a blessed pleasure in loving his enemy, but he would feel a great pain if he hated or resisted his enemy. Now this idiotic Jesus, who is so unlike your normal person, has an extreme capacity for suffering and irritation, which lets him feel the pain of others in an extraordinary fashion and would give him great pain if he did not love that person in his pain. So Nietzsche sees Jesus as not dwelling in the world of detraction, but he simply has proactive affirmations for all creatures and especially insofar as they may be trying to inflict pain on him. He is able to love those who persecute him and it would greatly pain him not to love them, so that his religion of love is like that of Epicurus who also was motivated by a decadent pleasure.

Agape and the Four Loves

II,1.8 Dostoyevsky's sublime, sick, and childish Idiot.

In Section 31, Nietzsche goes on to write:

> one has to regret that no Dostoyevsky
> lived in the neighbourhood of
> this most interesting *decadent*;
> I mean someone who could feel
> the thrilling fascination of such a combination
> of the sublime, the sick and the childish.

It is to be expected that the coarsened first followers of Jesus would reduce him to familiar forms ... The Prophet, the Messiah, the judge who is to come, the moral preacher, the miracle-worker, all of which underestimated the proper character of their Jesus whose unfamiliar traits and idiosyncrasies were overlooked. Dostoyevsky was an astute enough physiologist to be able to see the sublime, the sick and the childish in this all-loving Jesus. Nietzsche thinks that this childishness is related to his sickness or his decadence, for as he writes in Section 31:

> The 'glad tidings' are precisely
> that there are no more opposites;
> the kingdom of heaven belongs to the children;
> the faith which here finds utterance
> is not a faith which has been won by struggle—
> it is there, from the beginning ...
> The occurrence of retarded puberty,
> underdeveloped in the organism
> as a consequence of degeneration,
> is familiar at any rate to physiologists.

So Nietzsche sees Jesus as having a retarded puberty that would let him retain a childlike way of seeing and loving all things. There would be something sublime in this most interesting decadent. There would be a sublimation that could transform degenerated others, such as the thief on the cross, to be childlike like Jesus.

Part One: Joyful Beginnings

II,1.9 The Evangel died as he ived and taught

In Section 35, Nietzsche ends his description of the loving Jesus, whom he knew as a child and knew even better after his own sublimation process with Lou Salome, by writing:

> His words to the thief on the cross
> contain the whole of the Evangel.
> 'That was verily a *divine* man,
> a child of God' - says the thief.
> 'If thou feelest this' - answers the redeemer
> 'thou art in Paradise, thou art a child of God.'
> *Not* to defend oneself, *not* to grow angry,
> not to make responsible . . .
> But not to resist evil man—to love him . . .

Nietzsche selected this consistent symbolic picture of the loving Jesus out of the Gospels and as he began in Section 29, he wrote:

> What I am concerned with is
> the psychological type of the redeemer.
> For it *could* be contained in the Gospels.
> in spite of the Gospels, however much
> mutilated and overloaded with foreign tracts:
> as that of Francis of Assisi is contained
> in the legends about him
> in spite of the legends.

Now it is our task to meditate on the place and role of this Jesus in the thought of Nietzsche as he went out with Jesus' love to meet the higher ill-constituted men and to heal them as he was healed. Just as there was *The birth of Tragedy* so there was *The Birth of the Gospel*; but soon there was the death of the Gospel just as there was the death of Tragedy for Socrates overemphasized Apollo just as the Christ was overemphasized bringing about the forgetfulness of Dionysius as well as of Jesus and it is Nietzsche's task to recover for all the Dionysian Jesus and his *amor fati*.

II.2 Reconciling the Socratic Apollo with the dancing Dionysus
II,2.1 From the Dionysus to Jesus

As a physiologist and philosopher, Nietzsche looked into Christianity and the Gospels and ferreted out the loving Jesus, and in a similar way, he studied the birth and the death of tragedy and came to evaluate the proper and the improper relation between Dionysus and Apollo. Living out the right relation between the loving Jesus and the judging Christ is the key to Nietzsche's life and philosophy, and that pattern of letting Apollo be subordinate to Dionysus lets Tragedy be born, just as the pattern of subordinating Dionysus to Apollo kills tragedy. With the death of his father, Nietzsche knew tragedy, but he distinguished between two kinds of tragedy: (1) that of Sophocles and Aeschylus, in which Apollo was subordinate to Dionysus and (2) that of Euripides in which Dionysus became subordinate to the moralizing Apollo. So in *The Birth of Tragedy*, Nietzsche spells out the type and traits of Dionysus, just as he does with the type of Jesus in *The Anti-Christ*. Nietzsche will be an Anti-Socratic Apollonian, just as he will be an Anti-Christ in order to give primacy to Dionysus and to Jesus. To think about Nietzsche's meditation on the history of these relations, we can see him work it out in *Thus Spake Zarathustra* with its Prologue and four parts, and *The Prologue* is like *The Birth of Tragedy*. Nietzsche, as a shamanic healer, teacher, caregiver, had his own experience as his criterion, for writing his *Prologue* in the form of *Homer's Contest*, *The Birth of Tragedy* and *Philosophy in the Tragic Age of the Greeks* and always he was watching to see how the contest of the natural and the moral worked out. In Section One, paragraph one, Nietzsche writes about the duality of two art forms, and he uses the word "reconciliation" twice in discussing how Dionysus and his music come together with Apollo and his sculpture and there is perpetual strife between them. It is as if they are involved in the battle of the sexes, and only periodically are there intervening reconciliations as they always incite each other to new and more powerful births, an in tragedy.

Part One: Joyful Beginnings

II,2.2 Are the 7 traits of Dionysus similar to those of Jesus?

So, in the beginning of *The Birth of Tragedy*, Nietzsche writes of the Apollonian-Dionysian duality and their:

> perpetual strife with only periodically intervening reconciliation . . .
> which perpetuates an antagonism only superficially reconciled..
> till eventually, by a metaphysical miracle of that Hellenic "will",
> they appear coupled with each other, and through this coupling
> ultimately generate an equally Dionysian and Apollonian
> form of art—attic tragedy.

So, in the tragedy of Aeschylus and Sophocles, according to Nietzsche, there is a reconciled set of opposites which work together as

Dionysus	Apollo
The Art of Music	The Art of sculpture
intoxication and springtime	dreams
unification	individuation
truth	appearance
natural	ethical
excess	restrained proportion
mystery	naivety

In the first four sections of *The Birth of Tragedy*, Nietzsche tells us how the beautiful plastic arts of Apollo enabled the Greeks to find joy in their suffering by putting between themselves and the terrors and horrors of existence the radiant dream birth of the Olympian. The Greek Pantheon of Zeus, Hera, Aphrodite, etc. were figures that came from the dream world to provide order, solace and courage. Then, at the end of Section Four, he writes:

> Here the sublime and celebrated art of Attic tragedy,
> and the dramatic dithyramb presents itself as
> the common goal of both these tendencies, whose
> mysterious union, after many and long precursory struggles,
> found glorious consummation in this child, Antigone Cassandra.

This image of the child throws light on all the Dionysian traits.

II,2.3 Tragedy is born from the epic and the lyric
Homer, the great Epic poet, gave us a world of vivid Gods and heroes
whom Nietzsche argues came to him in dreams of restrained proportion.
On the other hand, Archilochus, the great lyric poet, would be taken
up into a musical mood and then sing out our primordial pain.
The sweetest songs of lyric poets tell of our saddest experience.
The great cultures had the epic poems of their history and the
lyric poems, which sang out the glory of their joys and sorrows,
but only the Greeks were inspired to bring forth the tragic drama.
It was the dancing chorus that gave birth to Tragedy, as that sacred
dance of the satyrs broke forth into a sacred lyric song, out of which
the masked figures of Dionysus stepped forth as Oedipus or Prometheus.
The satyr was half human and half goat and, of course, the goats
were symbolically put down in comparison with the useful sheep.
The Billy with his Nanny and Kid never have the place of the lamb.
Jesus, who was half man and half God, was seen as the lamb of God.
Dionysus, as half man and half goat, is a very funny erotic
creature who, of course, is the God who brings cheerfulness.
In Section 8, Nietzsche writes of the satyr:

> The satyr, like the idyllic shepherd of more recent times,
> is the offspring of a longing of the primitive and natural . . .
> The satyr was something sublime and divine: thus he had
> to appear to the painfully broken vision of Dionysian man.

The Dionysian, the satyr and the chorus belong together in the
realm of the lyric which is the beginning of the tragic drama,
and also is supplemented by the epic dream figures of Apollo.
In Section 7, Nietzsche tells us that the Dionysian man, like Hamlet,
has looked into the essence of things and seen the horrible truth
of our tragic condition that brings a nausea that inhibits action.
Everywhere he sees the horrible absurdity of existence, but
the art of the satyr approaches as a saving sorceress,
who is expert at healing in the shamanic way Nietzsche knew.

Part One: Joyful Beginnings

II,2.4 Does Nietzsche link the "sus" of Jesus and Dionysus?

From the day his father died when he was only five, Nietzsche knew
the horrible absurdity of existence, and as Sartre would say, following
Nietzsche, existence is like rotting newspaper in a mud puddle.
It is absurd and it is nauseating, even to the point that it can
paralyze you, leaving you unable to love and unable to produce.
But, with his grandmother and mother and aunt and sister,
he prayed to the Lord Jesus and he was energized and thought that
he would not let his father die for nothing and he was taken into creativity.
As he reflected upon Greek Tragedy, he detected there a similar pattern.
Finding Dionysus in the Greek Chorus, with the half man-half goat,
could do for the Greeks what finding Jesus, the half man-half God, had
done for the young Nietzsche, for the satyr poet, by expressing the truth
of nature, instead of the lie of culture, brought magical transformation.
As Nietzsche puts it in Section 8:

> Such magic transformation is the presupposition of all
> dramatic art. In this magic transformation, the Dionysian
> revealer sees himself as a satyr, and as a satyr, in turn,
> he sees the god, which means that in his metamorphosis,
> he beholds another vision outside himself, as the
> Apollonian complement of his own state.
> With this new vision, the drama is complete.

Just as St. Augustine built his Christian Philosophy around Plato
and Aquinas built his around Aristotle, so also Nietzsche builds
his philosophy of the love of Jesus around Greek Tragedy.
His entire philosophy is about these transformations or
metamorphoses, as we will see in *Zarathustra*, which is a drama.
True Tragedy, with its metaphysical comfort of a great cheerfulness,
is born when the Dionysian satyr music, in its artistic poetry,
gives birth to the Apollonian figures who step out of the chorus
as masked figures, and the *prosopon* mask is the persona
through which the cheerful vision of a direction sounds forth.

Agape and the Four Loves

II,2.5 Socrates is to Dionysus as Christ is to Jesus

Aeschylean-Sophoclean tragedy gave the primacy to the Dionysian satyr chorus, with is musical mystery of natural excess and subordinated the Apollonian actors and the naïve plastic art of their proportion and restraint in a reconciliation of opposites. But with Euripides and Socrates, the mixing shifted, so that Euripides, as a poet, is essentially an echo of his own consciousness. The focal point shifted from the primacy of celebrating in joyous dance, which was in union with all, even the present blessed dead, to the primacy of reasoning that now individuated, the masked figures who came whirling out of the ecstatic chorus to be persona on their own. Dialectical optimism destroys tragedy and dialogue annuls poetry. Euripides, as a poet, essentially echoes his own conscious knowledge. The Euripidean prologue exemplifies the productivity of the rational. As Nietzsche puts it concerning this method in Section 12:

> So long as the spectator has to figure out the meaning of this or that person, or the presuppositions of this or that conflict of inclinations and purposes, he cannot become completely absorbed in the activities and sufferings of the chief characters or feel breathless pity and fear.

Nietzsche participated fully in the tragedy of his father's death. He was absorbed completely in the activities and sufferings of the women of his family and he felt their breathless pity and fear. With his father and Dionysus and Jesus, he totally felt the musical mystery of the truth of unification, and in a kind of intoxication from the time he first listened to the funeral music for this father, he knew that all flesh and all persons were united. But as he reached the age of reason and left behind the natural truth of the child, he moved from synthetic unity to analytic separation. As he matured as a philologist and philosopher, he saw how Socrates emerged out of tragedy with Euripides, as Christ emerged out of Jesus.

Part One: Joyful Beginnings

II,2.6 From the affectionate child to star friendship

As Nietzsche grew through the four loves in the *agape* given to him through the love and tragedy of his family, he discovered Star Friendship. As an affectionate child breathing in constantly all that female affection for the one little boy, he was one with Dionysus as the childlike Antigone and Cassandra were one with him and he was a member of the body of Jesus in a preconscious way as united with his father. As the semi-orphan, he got in touch with the spirit-world in affection with his family, and then at Pforta Schule, his teachers became his friends as he stood side by side with them in learning Greek and of Greek heroes. As his affection was always haunted by tragic death, so was his friendship and while he became friends with Socrates, Plato, the Christ and Luther, he began to sense his necessary departure from them that he might be totally with Dionysus and Jesus, and in *The Gay Science*, Part Four, Section 279, he wrote:

> Star friendship.—we were friends and have become estranged.
> But this was right, and we do not want to conceal and obscure it
> from ourselves as if we had reason to feel ashamed.
> We are two ships, each of which has its goal and course;
> our paths may cross and we may celebrate a feast together,
> as we did—and then the good ships rested so quietly
> in one harbor and one sunshine that it may have looked
> as if they had reached their goal and had but one goal.
> But then the almighty force of our tasks drove us apart
> into different seas and sunny zones,
> and perhaps we shall never see each other again;
> perhaps we shall meet, but fail to recognize each other!
> Our exposure to different seas and suns has changed us.

Nietzsche's love for Jesus and in Jesus Dionysus was the sun of his sea that guided his ship and it would bring him into contest with the Christ and Socrates and yet they were his star friends. Throughout *Zarathustra*, he will go from them to the child Jesus.

Agape and the Four Loves

II,2.7 From Socrates to Dionysus and from Christ to Jesus

When Nietzsche went to university and began to ponder the Greek world, in many ways, Socrates brought him to better understand Dionysus. In Nietzsche's day, Socrates was greatly admired by philosophers. We might recall that Kierkegaard's *The Concept of Irony: with Constant Reference to Socrates* was the beginning of Kierkegaard's long, ambivalent relation to Socrates, which was not unlike Nietzsche's. "If Jesus lived and died as a God, Socrates lived and died as a Philosopher" was a saying that revealed how Socrates was revered by Classicists, as Jesus was adored and worshipped by pious, believing Christians. As Nietzsche looked at the Christ of the Christians and became an Anti-Christ, so he looked at Socrates and became anti-Socratic. When Socrates and Plato looked death in the face and saw tragedy, they set up the after life of the extracted soul and denied this life. But in comparing and contrasting the Dionysus of Aeschylus and Sophocles with Socrates and Euripides, Nietzsche came to see that the Dionysus of the satyr chorus did not deny this world. Tragedy was given a *Yes* and *Amen* saying in the dancing chorus. So Socrates and Christ were star friends with Nietzsche, and thus going on, he writes:

> That we have become estranged is the law *above* us;
> by the same token, we should become more venerable for each other—
> and the memory off our former friendship more sacred.
> There is probably a tremendous, but invisible stellar orbit
> in which our very different ways and goals may be *included*,
> as small parts of this path; let us rise up to this thought.
> But our life is too short and our power of vision too small
> for us to be more than friends in the sense of that sublime possibility.
> Let us then *believe* in our star friendship, even if
> we should be compelled to be earth enemies.

This shows us the very essence of Nietzsche's *Yes* and *Amen* saying to many of his great friends, which must also say "*No*".

Part One: Joyful Beginnings

II,2.8 Jesus—the unknown God—Dionysus

Nietzsche's prayer at puberty, which he wrote out, never died but rather deepened as he grew in the wisdom of love:

> I have firmly resolved within me
> to dedicate myself forever to His service.
> May the dear Lord give me strength and power
> to carry out my intention
> and protect me on life's way.

His prayer, of course, was answered and he was protected on life's way. Six years later, when he was twenty, he wrote another prayer:

> I life up my hands to you in loneliness –
> You, to whom I flee,
> to whom in the deepest depths of my heart
> I have solemnly consecrated altars
> so that your voice
> might summon me again.
>
> On them glows, deeply inscribed,
> the word: To the unknown god
> I am his ...
>
> I want to know you, unknown One,
> You have reached deep into my soul.

From 1864, when he was twenty, until 1881, when he was thirty seven, the God remained hidden, but then Jesus and his love began to dawn on Nietzsche, as he was inspired with humankind's highest affirmation of an eternal recurrence that called for a *Yes* and *Amen* for all existence. Slowly, Nietzsche's Zarathustra formed in his mind as the mix of Jesus and Dionysus, for Zarathustra will love only a God who dances and who is natural and not moral. Nietzsche's prayer to the unknown God was answered and he let us all come to know him in his beautiful *Zarathustra*.

Agape and the Four Loves

II,2.9 The way to reconcile Christian Platonism with Jesus

Greek Tragedy was a magic reconciliation of Apollo with Dionysius
that could powerfully transform the beholders of this dramatic art
so that they could live their tragic lives with a cheerful *Yes* and *Amen*.
The sculpted individuals of inspiring dreams were reconciled
in their very physiology with the music of unity of intoxicated song.
Homer and the ethical restraint of Socratic-Platonic-Aristotelian
Proportion were reconciled with Archilochus and the natural
excess of the satyr of Aeschylus and Sophocles in springtime mysteries.
The pattern for Nietzsche's vision of loving reconciliation is here
in the tragedy of Aeschylus and Sophocles and it began to be
very clear for him as he studied the death of tragic reconciliation
in Euripides and Socrates as they subordinated physiology
to logic and took flight from the physical into the immaterial.
As long as Socrates is subordinated to Dionysius there can be
loving reconciliation but when Socratic logic takes the upper hand
then physiology of tragedy in all its physical love and suffering
is driven off the stage so that judging blame drives away love.
So also with Christian religion and theology for as long as
the incarnation theology of Jesus with all its physiological implications
is given priority the atonement theology of the Christ can be there
in its important subordinate role, but as soon as Christ and
his atonement theology predominate Jesus's *agape* is forgotten.
This model that Nietzsche sees so clearly and lets him in
the primacy of Jesus's *agape* be star friends with Christian
Platonists and enlightenment humanists and Romantics
is the Model that was revealed to David in 2nd Samuel 7:
There God promised David that he would always be with
him in his everlasting merciful love and if he sinned
he would be punished with the rods of men but that is secondary.
Of course, ethics and justice are important just as are Socrates
and Christ but what is most important is the love of the Unknown God.

Part One: Joyful Beginnings

II,3 Reconciling Zarathustra with the eternally returning Jesus

II,3.1 *The erotic agape of Nietzsche's Zarathustra*

Nietzsche, like Kierkegaard, experienced a great erotic sublimation that gave him the inspiration to write his gloriously beautiful *Zarathustra*. Nietzsche was possessed of a robust sex drive, but his total lack of experience resulted in a frustration that transformed into creativity. On April 11, 1876, he wrote a letter to Mathilde Trampedach, whom he had just recently met:

> My dear Miss Trampedach: - You are going to write
> something for me today? Well, then, I too shall write
> something for you. –
> Please gather all the courage your heart is capable of
> in order not to become frightened by the question
> I herewith put to you: will you become my wife?
> I love you and I feel as if you already belong to me.
> Not a word about the suddenness of my affection.

Soon after his moment of inspiration came to him in August, 1881, he was smitten with Lou Salome, just as Kierkegaard was smitten with Regina when all his sexual energy was channeled into his renewed religious fervour and the creative writing it brought forth. Since his puberty, when he piously wrote of his love for his Lord, Nietzsche had moved further and further from his Lutheran religion. He became totally disenchanted with the rewarder-punisher God and with the fear mongering that Christianity employed in trying to persuade persons that they become obedient and faithful followers. Nietzsche's Pietism was already a great step toward an incarnation love theology and away from the primacy of atonement justice theology. From the time he was fifteen until he was thirty-five, Nietzsche went through stage after stage of secularism and the death of God. But when he fell in love with Lou, a great love, joy, peace and patience took over the deep fundamental attitude of his body. Now, beginning in April of 1882, he knew that he must write his *Zarathustra* in order to express his agapeic *eros*.

Agape and the Four Loves

II,3.2 An erotic agape born out of modernity's God

Nietzsche claims that Christianity gave *eros* poison to drink but it never killed him; it only transformed him into a vice. For Nietzsche, *eros* has often been and should be a virtue and throughout *Zarathustra*, the agapeic *eros* which he felt for his dear Lou Salome and for all of existence is portrayed in poetry and in song as humankind's greatest gift. In *Ecce Homo*, in his chapter "Why I write such Good Books", Nietzsche begins by saying that if anyone really experienced even six sentences of his *Zarathustra*, that

> would raise one to a higher level of existence
> than "modern" men could attain:
> Given this feeling of distance, how could I
> possibly wish to be read by those "moderns"
> whom I know!

Throughout his drama *Zarathustra* and the prose books that explain it, Nietzsche shows us how, throughout modernity, Christian Platonism and then Enlightenment Humanism and even Romanticism made of *eros* a vice that killed its God. Nietzsche could not be read by these modernists anymore than he could be fully loved by his ideal Lou Salome, and yet from the distance of his heights, he could love them more and more. He became a born again lover of Jesus in all the fulfilled affection, friendship, *eros*, and *agape* that Jesus practiced. It became Nietzsche's passion and mission to bring this highest affirmation of humankind to all dear humans and that is why he had to write such good books in order to create a new audience who would eventually learn how to read him and to grow into that love of Jesus with which he was gifted. Nietzsche, speaking through his *Zarathustra*, in "The Prologue", comes down from his mountain heights to bring his love to the modern secularists, for whom God and love are dead.

Part One: Joyful Beginnings

II,3.3 An erotic agape that emanates like the Sun

In "The Prologue", part one, we learn that Zarathustra has lived high in his mountains with his eagle and serpent for ten years.

> And one morning, he rose with the dawn
> stepped before the sun, and spoke to it thus:
> Great star! What would your happiness be,
> if you had not those for whom you shine!

For Plotinus, the many emanated from the One as light and warmth do from the Sun, but Plotinus questioned this cycle. Why should things emanate into suffering, only to return to the same source and be no different than when they started? This is also the strange story of the Hindu and Platonic cycle. But, Zarathustra's sun is happy in giving warmth and light to others and Zarathustra, like this sun, now longs to share his love and wisdom with all the people down in the lowlands. Love, for Zarathustra, is creative and not merely emanative. It moves the lover, as God is the prime mover of all things. The sun would have grown weary of his light if he did not have Zarathustra and his eagle and serpent with whom to share it. After ten years of loving wisdom, Zarathustra is weary:

> Behold! I am weary of my wisdom,
> like a bee that has gathered too much honey;
> I need hands outstretched to take it.

Of course, the modern masses are not ready to receive it. But, like Jesus, Zarathustra will try to prepare them for it. Zarathustra is going out to the poor and to the worldly wise.

> I should like to give it away . . .
> until the wise among men
> have again become happy in their folly
> and the poor happy in their wealth.

Zarathustra has a love beyond wisdom that lets poverty be wealth, and his love is aching to love others with this gift.

Agape and the Four Loves

II,3.4 *In a confrontation of friendship with the old saint*

As Zarathustra comes down out of his mountain peaks that are above the timberline, he meets the old saint who remembers him. He asks Zarathustra why he is coming down and Zarathustra says:

> I love mankind.

After responding to the forest dweller's challenges, he says:

> What did I say of love?
> I am bringing mankind a gift.

Zarathustra's love does not want something from mankind, but his *agape* is a giving of gifts, just as he has been gifted by the inspiration he received in August of 1881, of which he writes in *Ecce Homo* at the beginning of the part on *Zarathustra*:

> The text, to say this expressly
> because a misunderstanding has gained currency,
> is not by me:
> it is the amazing inspiration
> of a young Russian woman
> who was my friend at that time,
> Miss Lou von Salome.

The old saint advises him:

> Do not go to men, but stay in the forest.

And Zarathustra asks:

> And what does the saint do in the forest?

The saint answered:

> I make songs and sing them,
> and when I make songs
> I laugh, weep, and mutter
> and thus I praise God.

Zarathustra wonders if he knows that God is dead and

> They parted from one another,
> the old man and Zarathustra
> laughing as two boys laugh.

Part One: Joyful Beginnings

II,3.5 Teaching the overman to the people of the first town

As Zarathustra leaves the forest and arrives in the first town, the people are in the market square to watch a tight-rope walker. He spoke thus to the people:

> I teach you the Superman.
> Man is something that should be overcome.
> What have you done to overcome him?

He tries to inspire them to go beyond themselves, just as he was inspired to go beyond himself in August of 1881.
Again, in section 3 of that same chapter of *Ecce Homo*, he writes:

> Has anyone at the end of the nineteenth century
> a clear idea of what poets
> of strong ages have called inspiration?
> If not, I will describe it. –
> If one had the slightest residue
> of superstition left in one's system,
> one could hardly reject altogether
> the idea that one is merely an incarnation,
> merely mouthpiece, merely a medium
> of overpowering forces.

Nietzsche became a superman or overman by overcoming his *No*-saying to Christianity, when he was given the *Yes*-saying of Jesus. He became an incarnation of the overpowering forces that made of him a medium to bring the message of eternal return to others. This incarnate, shamanic medium also said to the people:

> The Superman is the meaning of the earth.
> Let your will say:
> The Superman *shall be* the meaning of the earth.

Incarnation lets the flesh or the body or the earth have a new meaning and it *shall be* the gift and the task of the people to will that meaning, for their will to power should affirm the eternal return of all incarnate creatures and not have contempt for the body.

Agape and the Four Loves

II,3.6 Loving the overman who in going under goes across

The people of the town want the tight-rope walker, and are not
the least interested in Zarathustra's overman, so with a litany
of love, he tells them that:

> Man is a rope, fastened between animal and Superman.
> A rope over an abyss. A dangerous going-across,
> a dangerous wayfaring, a dangerous looking-back,
> a dangerous shuddering and staying-still.

Nietzsche and Daddy both went under when the undertaker buried
their fathers and they and their loved ones kept going under with
an eternally recurring suffering that always made life dangerous.
But, they became childlike supermen with their first going under
and by being inspirited and inspired, any sorrow thereafter became joy.
Their joy let them pray *Yes* and *Amen* for life and all of its sorrow.
Now, Zarathustra wants to bring this gift of love to the people,
and he tells them how he loves them with his litany of
18 "I love you" declarations:

> I love those who do not know how to live
> except their lives be a going down,
> for they are those who are going across.

Those who go under if they are but shamanically graced will be
the ones who overcome and cross over the tight-rope walker's abyss.
There is no doubt that *Thus Spake Zarathustra* is a book about love.
These 18 "I love you" statements are its heart, mind, body and soul.
They are the perfect Prologue for what will be poetized throughout.
Zarathustra, a book for all and none, is a love poem for all
who suffer, perish and go under, for their sorrow, in its glory
of inspiration, can become that joy that wills deep, deep eternity.
We are never here and gone tomorrow, nor are we drops of water
that lose their singularity by merging back into the great ocean.
The suffering of each will let them be loved with eternal recurrence.
But this is a book for none and they reject Nietzsche's *Zarathustra*.

Part One: Joyful Beginnings

II,3.7 And he even loves the mediocre last man

The crowd does not have ears to hear Zarathustra's litany of love.
He tells them that they and their culture are going under, but they
can be born again if they but have the daring of the tight-rope walker.
But that walker, with his danger, is not to be a symbol of themselves.
Since they reject the overman, Zarathustra tells them of the last man.
He still speaks to them with love as he sees them perishing:

> Behold! I shall show you the *Ultimate Man.*
> 'What is love? What is creation? What is longing?
> What is a star?' thus asks the ultimate man and blinks.

These last men simply stare and blink when he speaks to them
of a creative love that, in suffering, longs to go beyond itself.
They cannot hear him when he speaks with contempt for their
present culture and a longing to create a new culture of love.
For them, the great health is avoiding indigestion, and they are
clever with no end to their mockery, so what can Zarathustra do?

> And here ended Zarathustra's first discourse
> which is also called 'The Prologue':
> for at this point, the shouting and mirth
> of the crowd interrupted him.
> "Give us this Ultimate Man, O Zarathustra—'
> so they cried—'Make us into this Ultimate Man!
> You can have the Superman!"
> And all the people laughed and shouted.
> But Zarathustra grew sad.

Seeking to bring his gift of creative love and longing to be greater
to this crowd, he appealed to them with the image of the tight-rope walker.
Then he tried to shock them with the image of the Ultimate Man.
But just as no one really appreciated Nietzsche's writings,
so no one appreciated Zarathustra's love beyond their wisdom.
But before he begins his discourses on camel, lion, lioness and child,
he must still care for the tight-rope walker and learn from his animals.

Agape and the Four Loves

II,3.8 And saves the tight-rope walker from the devil's hell

As the crowd was ridiculing Zarathustra, the tight-rope walker was going across, high above the middle of the market square, when all of a sudden, a little fellow came running out on the rope behind him and, crying out like a little devil, jumped over the walker's head. He landed perfectly on the rope and, all flustered, the walker fell in a broken heap on the market floor and the crowd ran away. Zarathustra rushed to him, and kneeling beside him, waited for him to become conscious, and the broken, shattered man said:

> I've known for a long time
> that the Devil would trip me up.
> Now he's dragging me to Hell:
> Are you trying to prevent him?

Zarathustra answered:

> On my honour, friend,
> all you have spoken of does not exist:
> there is no Devil and no Hell.
> Your soul will be dead
> even before your body;
> therefore, fear nothing anymore.

The poor tight-rope walker wants deep, deep eternity and he asks Zarathustra if this is all there is and Zarathustra praises him for his heroic, dangerous life and promises to bury him.

> When Zarathustra had said this,
> the dying man replied no more,
> but he motioned with his hand,
> as if he sought Zarathustra's hand
> to thank him.

So in Zarathustra's eschatology, there is no hell, and since the soul dies before the body, perhaps the incarnate body will continue to live on in love into deep, deep, eternity. Zarathustra ends his Prologue by burying his companion with love.

Part One: Joyful Beginnings

II,3.9 He loves his proud eagle and wise serpent

Modern protestant Christianity, with is rewarder-punisher God
and its atonement justice theology, saw pride as the root of all evil.
And the serpent was hated as the fork-tongued tempter of Eve.
But Zarathustra goes beyond good and evil, as if pride and
serpents could be exclusively evil, for creators don't make junk
and his most beloved animals are the proud eagle and the wise serpent.

> The proudest animal under the sun
> and the wisest animal under the sun . . .
> May my animals lead me! . . .
> I wish I were wise . . . like my serpent!
> But I am asking the impossible:
> therefore I ask my pride
> always to go along with my wisdom!
> And if, one day, my wisdom should desert me –
> Oh, it loves to fly away!-
> then may my pride fly with my folly.

Of course, wisdom is highly esteemed, so Zarathustra praises folly.
His love, which he shares with Jesus, is full of folly in loving all.
As we follow the unfolding of the Drama of Zarathustra, we will
see how traditional wisdom leaves him as he attains a joyful wisdom.
Guided by his animals, Zarathustra will seek fellow creators.

> The creator seeks companions.
> They will be called destroyers
> and despisers of good and evil.
> They are harvesters and rejoicers.

By going under, like the seed, he will bring forth a rich harvest.
By despising the exclusive opposites of good and evil, he will
show how to love all as good: the masses, the last man and
the corpse which he buried with love, which was not yet dead.
His love will go beyond that wisdom that avoids pride
to a folly of joyful wisdom that children share with animals.

Agape and the Four Loves

III. Q¹

III,1 The Q¹ agape sayings of Jesus

III,1.1 Burton Mack's 7 clusters of 21 love sayings

On page 109 Mack gives the following outline which can guide us through our meditations:

1. JESUS' TEACHING
   - QS8   On Those who are Fortunate
   - QS9   On Responding to Reproach
   - QS10 On Making Judgments
   - QS11 On Teachers and Students
   - QS12 On Hypocrisy
   - QS13 On Integrity
   - QS14 On Practical Obedience

2. INSTRUCTIONS FOR THE JESUS MOVEMENT
   - QS19 On Becoming a Follower of Jesus
   - QS20 On Working for the Kingdom of God

3. CONFIDENCE IN THE FATHER'S CARE
   - QS26 How to Pray
   - QS27 Confidence in Asking

4. ON ANXIETY AND SPEAKING OUT
   - QS35 On Speaking Out
   - QS36 On Fear

5. ON PERSONAL GOODS
   - QS38 Foolish Possessions
   - QS39 On Food and Clothing
   - QS40 On Heavenly Treasure

6. PARABLES OF THE KINGDOM
   - QS46 The Mustard Seed and the Yeast

7. THE TRUE FOLLOWERS OF JESUS
   - QS50 On Humility
   - QS51 The Great Supper
   - QS52 On the Cost of Being a Disciple
   - QS53 Savorless Salt

Part One: Joyful Beginnings

III,1.2 Jesus loves especially the poor, hungry and crying

Whereas Matthew has the Eight Beatitudes Luke has only the three of Q¹.
The main theme that runs throughout the Synoptic Gospels is given
in the first Beatitude which Matthew and Luke share so that
at Luke 6:20 Jesus says:

> How blessed are you who are poor:
> the Kingdom of God is yours.

And at Matthew 5:3 Jesus says:

> How blessed are the poor in spirit:
> the kingdom of heaven is theirs.

So with Matthew it is the poor in spirit and not literally the poor
and it is the kingdom of heaven and not the kingdom of God but
in both cases those who are poor or hungry or crying can belong
to the kingdom of love which is coming with Luke and is here with
Matthew but in either case belongs to those who love and pray for all.
The kingdom of this world has the territorial imperative for wealth
at the centre, pleasure at the display point and power along the borders.
But the poor without wealth, the hungry without satisfaction and those
who cry without power are invited by Jesus into his kingdom of love.
He teaches them how to pray for themselves and especially for those
who mistreat them to their Heavenly Father that his kingdom will come.
However, the bookend saying at the other end of the Q¹ sayings is:

> Whosoever does not hate his father and mother
> will not be able to learn from me.
> Whoever does not hate his son and daughter
> will not be able to learn from me.

This is the challenging saying that Kierkegaard picked out as an
opportunity in terms of which he could work out his philosophy of love.
It has to be our challenging saying too for how can we reconcile
the love sayings at the beginning of Q¹ and throughout with
these hate sayings at the end so that we can understand how
this Jesus is thinking when he says love enemies and hate family.

Agape and the Four Loves

III,1.3 Jesus sends out his workers as lambs among wolves

After Jesus gives his seven teachings on how to love he instructs
those who say they want to follow him and work for the Kingdom.
He began teaching by saying: "How fortunate are the poor; they have
God's kingdom." And his fellow workers will be poor for while foxes
have dens and birds nests the son of man has nowhere to lay his head.
It will be like this for those who want to follow him for they too must be
foot-loose and fancy-free to go out and bring others to the kingdom.
If they want to work with him they should leap in and not procrastinate.
Once they begin they should be totally committed and never look back.
Very few will want to become itinerant preachers with and like Jesus
so they should pray that the master of the harvest will send workers.
Here again prayer is central to loving and if Jesus is like a Cynic
teacher he is also very different with his emphasis on constant prayer
for enemies, for fellow workers and in the words of the *Our Father*.
These teachers should have no money, bag, sandals or staff.
They should not greet anyone on the road. Why should this be so?
They should hate their mothers and fathers, their wives and children
and should not greet anyone on the road. Does this mean that
they should have total commitment to teaching the kingdom of *agape*
and not get caught up in family affection and friendly greetings?
His workers should say: "Peace be to this house!" whenever they
enter someone's house and if a child of peace is there their peace
will rest upon him, but often they will be resisted without peace.
Are these resisters the ones the disciples should especially pray for?
But then Jesus tells them that workers deserve to be fed so they
should eat at the house in which they teach, however, in a puzzling
way he then tells them that they should "not go from house to house."
Within Q^1 we will notice many of these difficult sayings and it
will be our task to reconcile them with each other and then with
the more contrary statements of the Judging Christ of Q^2 and we will
have to reconcile the child of wisdom, the Son of Man and the Son of God.

III,1.4 Jesus teaches them how to pray and be confident

Being strongly resisted even to the point of being lambs among wolves
made the disciples frightened and anxious and Jesus' main method
for bolstering their confidence was to teach them how to pray and
to give them good reasons for knowing that their prayers would be heard.
He taught them "The Our Father" which summed up everything important
about his teaching of the coming of the Kingdom of love and how to be
in that kingdom here and now on earth by totally loving with *agape*.
If as the lambs of God they would resist the wolves by going after them
with the negative reactions of the sword as Augustine would say
then that sword would have to go through their own bodies first
before it could touch anyone against whom they were aiming it.
If they would totally forgive others they would be totally forgiven.
As the Jesus of Q^1 put it in Q saying 27:

> If you, although you are not good,
> know how to give good gifts to your children,
> how much more will the father above
> give good things to those who ask him?

Jesus tells them that the prayer of petition is very important
because it will just naturally take away their anxiety "for
everyone who asks receives, and the one who seeks finds,
and to the one who knocks, the door will be opened." If they
but learn the habit of constant prayer they will live in
the realm of blessed peace for prayer is the language of love and
a totally pure love that seeks the good of others automatically
brings a confidence with its faith that all is good with the world.
As William James put it in his *Varieties of Religious Experience:*
"If you want faith and do not have it then get down on
your knees and pray and it will come to you." It will come
to you with all the confidence and peace that belong to
frisky, happy, playful lambs and to all children of God who,
if they pray as Jesus teaches them, will no longer be anxious.

Agape and the Four Loves

III,1.5 Jesus tells the anxious to speak out in love

To overcome their anxiety the disciples could pray for their enemies but Jesus tells them that they could also receive confidence and peace from performing the works of love and in QS35 he says:

> Nothing is hidden that will not be made known,
> or secret that will not come to light.
> What I tell you in the dark, speak in the light.
> What you hear as a whisper, proclaim on the housetops.

So they should go out and bravely tell everyone to sell their possessions and give to the poor and to seek the kingdom first. These very works of love by which they tell everyone of the kingdom of love and proclaim it from the housetops is a way of loving that together with their praying will strengthen them in their love. Again in QS 36, Jesus returns to the theme of fear:

> Don't be afraid of those who can kill the body,
> but can't kill the soul.
> Can't you buy five sparrows for two cents?
> Not one of them will fall to the ground
> without God knowing about it.
> Even the hairs on your head are all numbered.
> So don't be afraid.
> You are worth more than many sparrows.

The whole point of Jesus' teaching is to bring out the great worth of each unique being and here he tells them why they should not be afraid because each one is so loved in every detail. They are each immortal and so in the long run have nothing to fear. God loves each sparrow and every hair on a person's head and it is this all loving God that the all loving Jesus is revealing. If we have faith and hope in this kingdom of God's love we will not fear but we will want to contribute our loving to it. What seems so worthless to the everyday worldling such as five sparrows and two cents is precious in the heart of God forever.

Part One: Joyful Beginnings

III,1.6 Seek ye first the kingdom of love

Jesus teaches his disciples that first of all they should put first
things first and thus they need to go through a transformation
and become children of God in his kingdom of love and then they will
no longer be anxious which comes from being possessed by possessions.
The shamanic Jesus is not only healer-teacher-caregiver
but he is also an exorcist who drives out evil spirits that good
spirits might replace them and prayer for others lets that happen.
If evil spirits are our enemy then if we but pray for them
they will become good spirits for prayer exorcises us and
lets us see the good that is there in creatures including evil spirits.
In the fifth cluster of Q^1 sayings (38, 39, 40) Jesus teaches his
followers how not to be foolish toward possessions but rather
wise by seeking first the kingdom of love in such a way that
all these other things: money, food and clothing will be added.
After telling them how God feeds the birds of the air and
clothes the flowers of the fields and that surely he will care
for them even more Jesus says:

> So don't worry, thinking 'What will we eat'
> or 'What will we drink' or 'What will we wear?'
> For everybody in the whole world does that,
> and your father knows that you need these things.
> Instead, make sure of his rule over you,
> and all these things will be yours as well.

Perhaps, this gives us the clues for interpreting the conflicting
sayings of Jesus such as "love your enemy" and "hate
your father and mother." Does the loving Jesus really teach hate?
Or does he mean by hate put second what we usually put first
and then it will be added unto us? If Nietzsche as a child
loved his mother and father above all else and then his father died
then Nietzsche could be very miserable; but if he prayed for his
father and put God's will first then he could pray *Yes* and *Amen*.

Agape and the Four Loves

III,1.7 *The kingdom of love is like a mustard seed or yeast*

In Q[1] Saying 46 we see how the practice of love increases love.

> He said: "What is the kingdom of God like?
> To what should I compare it?
> It is like a grain of mustard
> which a man took and sowed in his garden.
> It grew up and became a tree,
> and the birds of the air made nests in its branches."
> He also said, "The kingdom of God
> is like yeast which a woman took
> and hid in three measures of flour
> until it leavened the whole mass."

If we are transformed and move away from the restricted economies of the territorial imperative where we live for wealth, satisfaction and power to a general economy of love it will be a good investment. One little seed will make a big tree and it will bring forth not only many seeds but it will provide for birds' nests and other good things. If disciples go out and offer themselves as lambs to wolves and pray constantly for the wolves many of them will become like lambs. Once a hungry wolf learns to love he will be like the wolf of Gubbio whom St. Francis saved and who then lived peacefully with the people who had wanted to kill him and his love reminded them of St. Francis. The yeast parable tells us how powerful a little bit of love is in being able to transform a whole mass of dough and give it power to rise up and be light and fluffy like good home made bread. Jesus and his followers can transform the world with such down-to-earth and homey stories for when the farmer plants his seeds he can remember this parable and pray while he works and his loving prayer and work will plant seeds of growing love. And from now on when his wife is making her bread she too can pray *The Our Father* and she too can make good bread and at the same time be giving great increase to the Kingdom of love.

III,1.8 Whoever loves Jesus will carry his cross

This last cluster of Q¹ Sayings (50, 51, 52, 53) gives us that hard saying:

> Whoever does not hate his father and mother
> will not be able to learn from me.
> Whoever does not hate his son and daughter
> cannot belong to my school.

This saying is followed by:

> Whoever does not accept his cross
> and so become my follower
> cannot be one of my students.

So here we get the context for the hard saying because it is immediately preceded by the parable of the great wedding banquet. Those invited had many reasons for not coming: "I've bought a farm and I must go and see it." "I've just bought five pair of oxen and I need to check them out." "I just married a woman and so I can't come." All people have their own priorities and for many the kingdom of love and the love supper are not worth while. To work for Jesus and his Kingdom we need transformed priorities. If we love our possessions or family or friends most we cannot seek first the kingdom just as these people cannot because they have preferences and priorities that exclude love's primacy. So the hard saying in this context has to do with being totally committed to belonging to the love school of Jesus and other loves must be secondary if we are really going to be a follower of Jesus. Hating our family members has to do with not letting any of them detain us from putting the God of love first and loving them in accord with the universal love for God and all equally. So the hard saying need not be that hard for it is also said: "Seek ye first the kingdom of heaven and all these things will be added unto you." If we make the love of Jesus first we will love all persons equally and then also our family.

Agape and the Four Loves

III,1.9 An our Father summary of Jesus' love teaching

There are 5 clusters of sayings by the Q^1 Jesus and seven petitions in *The Our Father* so let us see if his prayer does give a summary of his key ideas in the seven clusters.

1. Father, may your name be holy.
   The poor, the hungry, the crying who come to love the holy loving father will be blessed and will love his name as holy.

2. May your rule take place.
   The key theme of Jesus is that this kingdom of love will come and his followers are instructed to bring this rule of love to all.

3. Thy will be done.
   In teaching his followers this prayer he gives them the way of loving prayer and they see that loving all is the love of God.

4. Give us each day our daily bread
   For those who spend their life working for the kingdom of love they trust God will provide but they still need to pray for God's help.

5. And forgive us our trespasses
   as we forgive those who trespass against us.
   This is the key revolutionary idea of Jesus for we do need to forgive our enemies and love them and pray for them and forgive those who are indebted to us as we want God to forgive our debts. This petition reveals to the person praying it the natural law of love that was not easily seen but which makes perfect sense for if we do have a loving, forgiving heart, then we are blessed.

6. And do not bring us to trial (into a trying situation).
   Jesus teaches his disciples to pray always as if God does everything and to work always as if they do everything and the prayer and the works of love will give them security and keep them from any trial.

7. But deliver us from evil. Amen.
   If we get our priorities right and seek first the kingdom of love then all else will be added unto us and even when we carry our cross it will be with Jesus and this suffering servant delivers us all from evil.

Part One: Joyful Beginnings

III,2 The Q² judgment sayings of the Christ
III,2.1 Mack's first 7 clusters of Q² sayings

1. JOHN'S PREACHING
   QS3   The Appearance of John
   QS4   John's Address to the People
   QS5   John's Prediction of Someone to Come

2. JOHN'S AND JESUS' THOUGHTS ABOUT EACH OTHER
   QS15 The Occasion
   QS16 John's Inquiry
   QS17 What Jesus Said About John
   QS18 What Jesus Said About This Generation

3. AGAINST TOWNS THAT REJECT THE MOVEMENT
   QS21 The Unreceptive Town
   QS22 The Galilean Towns

4. CONGRATULATION TO THOSE WHO ACCEPT IT
   QS23 On the One Who Receives the Worker
   QS25 On the One Who Hears and Sees

5. CONTROVERSY WITH THIS GENERATION
   QS28 On Kingdoms in Conflict

6. MAKING SURE WHOSE SIDE YOU ARE ON
   QS29 Those For and Those Against
   QS30 The Return of an Evil Spirit

7. JUDGMENT ON THIS GENERATION
   QS32 The Sign of Jonah

The Jesus of Q¹ emphasizes loving the enemy and non-resistance.
With this Jesus the *agape* of love for all is clear and unadulterated.
Bust as soon as we come to this son of man of Q², everything
totally changes, for now there is hatred instead of love for the enemy.
Since there are fourteen clusters of Q² sayings we will divide
our meditation on them into two parts and do the first 7 here.
In the Hebrew Bible, there are at least seven understandings of
the Messiah and the coming of his kingdom and with Q²
the apocalyptic view predominates instead of the various love views.

Agape and the Four Loves

III,2.2 *The Christ of John will burn the chaff*

As John the Baptist comes on the scene he preaches a message of apocalyptic judgment against those who frustrated the mission of the Jesus people and were threatening the Jesus followers. Thus according to QS 2 John the Baptist says:

> You offspring of vipers!
> Who warned you to flee
> from the coming fury?
> Change your ways
> if you have changed your mind.

Here there is no longer a gentle, peaceful, love for all especially enemies. Now the enemies are called a brood of vipers and compared to the evil serpent who is a symbol of the hated for blaming, judgmental types. Those people who are against the Jesus community or, perhaps, tempted to leave it as they see their own people being killed by the likes of the Pharisees, as was Stephen, are given warning to be loyal to Christ. They are called upon to repent and live a new life style if they have really had a conversion or change of mind about fundamental values. John tells the people that one stronger than he is coming who will gather the wheat into his barn and

> the chaff he will burn
> with a fire that no one can put out.

This hellfire and brimstone preaching of Q^2 brings us to the question of how to reconcile the all-loving Jesus of Q^1 with the judgmental Christ of Q^2 for what is the Holy Spirit doing by inspiring Holy Mother Church in the assembly of the Q people to come forth with two such seemingly contradictory views? All through church history it has been the task to reconcile this double message of the Incarnate Jesus and the Atonement Christ. Through the early centuries of Christianity and the Middle Ages a priority was given to the incarnational forgiving love and the punishment of the rods of men of the Christ was secondary.

Part One: Joyful Beginnings

III,2.3 The reconciling interplay between John and Jesus

In QS18 Jesus says what he thinks of this generation for they think one thing about John and the opposite about Jesus:

> To what shall I compare this generation?
> It is like children sitting in the marketplace
> and calling to each other:
> "We played the pipes for you and you did not dance.
> We sang a dirge and you did not wail."
> For John did not come eating or drinking,
> and they are saying "He is demon possessed."
> The son of man has come eating and drinking
> and they say, "Look at him, a glutton and
> a drunkard, a friend of tax collectors and sinners."
> But in spite of what they say,
> wisdom's children show that she is right.

John is a prophet and a messenger coming out of the desert to prepare a way for Jesus and he introduces Jesus as an apocalyptic judge. Jesus says of John that no one born of woman is greater than him. Yet Jesus also says that the least in God's realm is greater than John. Jesus is the child of wisdom and the son of man and all who love with him are wisdom's children and they know that dancing to the pipes of joy and eating and drinking and being a friend of tax collectors and sinners is what Jesus has taught them about how to love and live in accord with that love; but they are also beginning to see that John as an ascetic is also most lovable. So how is the Jesus of Q^1 who does not judge others but loves all to be reconciled with the Christ of Q^2 who judges all who are against the Q community and finds them worthy of punishment and hellfire? Q^2 already seems to be answering this question or working toward an answer by saying that wisdom's children show that she is right in presenting Jesus as a non-judging friend of tax-collectors and sinners. The all loving Jesus can show that John is not demon possessed.

Agape and the Four Loves

III,2.4 Condemnation of towns that reject the Jesus movement

In this third cluster of Q^2 sayings towns that reject the Q community and do not want to welcome it are condemned with great harshness:

> Woe for you, Chorazin! Woe for you Bethsaida!
> If the forceful deeds performed among you
> had been done in Tyre and Sidon
> they would have changed their ways long ago,
> sitting in sackcloth and ashes . . .
> And you, Capernaum, do you think you
> will be praised to high heaven?
> You will be told to go to hell.

This judging Christ of Q^2 is very angry and he is proclaiming
the wrath of God against any who reject the loving followers of Jesus.
So how does the message of loving even enemies without resistance
and this angry message of resisting enemies with hateful threats
fit together as revealed by the same Holy Spirit in Sacred Scriptures?
The formula for reconciling these opposite views as we have said
goes back to 2nd Samuel 7, where God promises David his everlasting
merciful love (*hesed*) but also says that any of David's wrongdoing
will be punished with the rods of men or with a natural punishment.
Jesus did perform a forceful set of deeds by being the God who
emptied himself out of love and became flesh and thus suffered,
died and was buried out of love for sufferers and then was resurrected.
That message should win over Chorazin, Bethsaida and Capernaum
just as it won over Stephen who loved in the same way so that
Paul was won over to this life of non-resisting universal love.
But the truth is that if anyone hates or resists they will receive
a natural punishment for the sword must pass through their own body
first before it can ever touch the enemy at whom they are angry.
Alright, so these cities will suffer earthly punishment but each
person in them should be loved with an everlasting, merciful love.
But, is it becoming of this son of man to be so angry at these cities?

Part One: Joyful Beginnings

III,2.5 Loving praise for those who accept the movement

This Christ of Q² as Nietzsche would say is a rewarder-punisher God.
He tells those who persecute the early church that they will go to hell and
he tells those who welcome the Q community that they will be rewarded.
Q²S 23 says:

> Whoever welcomes you welcomes me
> and whoever welcomes me
> welcomes the one who sent me.

This Christ as the son of man is an apocalyptic judge who tells
the people of Capernaum that they will go to hell because they resist
the people of Jesus and he tells those who welcome him and his
community that the heavenly Father will love and welcome them.
Burton Mack and the Q scholars are very helpful in making
distinctions about the apocalyptic attitude and on page 134
of *The Book of Q* Mack explains how:

> The apocalyptic imagination served only one purpose for the people of Q
> and that was to guarantee the threat of judgment that they wanted
> to bring down upon the people who had frustrated their mission.
> It is obvious that the people of Q were distressed and incensed
> and that they had targeted certain people like the Pharisees for fire.

But they were not in the process of becoming an apocalyptic community.
They did not think of a glorious kingdom at the end of time.
The last judgment does not vindicate a sectarian group by picturing
all other enemy groups as being condemned to eternal hell fire.
There is no imagination that is fascinated on how the kingdom
of the righteous might look once it is saved from all its enemies.
So the eschatology of how the last judgment will look or how
hell will look and how heaven will look is not worked out
by the community of Q² who like to threaten their enemies
by saying that the son of man will judge them as fit for hell
and who promises rewards to their friends from the son of man Judge.
The Community of Q² does not love the enemy or turn the other cheek.

Agape and the Four Loves

III,2.6 *A physiology of exclusively opposite kingdoms*

QS 28 tells of Jesus exorcising a demon that had made a man mute.
When the demon left the man and he began to speak someone said
that Jesus cast out demons with a demonic power of Satan.
But Jesus said to them that if a Kingdom is divided against itself
it will self-destruct as will the Kingdom of Satan if he is against himself.
Jesus said:

> Every kingdom divided against itself is destroyed
> and every house divided against itself will not stand.
> And if Satan also is divided against himself
> how will his kingdom stand?
> But if I exorcise demons by the finger of God,
> then God's rule has caught up with you.

So there is the kingdom of God and the kingdom of Satan and it is our task
to see the meanings of the concept of kingdom and those concepts differ
between Q^1 and Q^2 which needs to be clarified and Burton begins
this on page 124 when he lists 7 Q^1 passages on the kingdom of God:
1. How fortunate the poor; theirs is God's kingdom. (QS 8)
2. No one who puts his hand to the plow and looks back
   is fit for God's kingdom. (QS 19)
3. If you enter a town and they welcome you, eat what they set before you;
   attend to the sick, and say that "God's kingdom has come near to you."
4. But if you enter a town and they do not welcome you . . . say
   "Nevertheless, be sure of this, that God's rule has come to you." (QS 20)
5. When you pray, say: "Father . . . may your kingdom take place,
   give us each day our daily bread." (QS 26)
6. Make sure of his rule over you
   and these things will be yours as well. (QS 39)
7. What is God's kingdom like? It is like a grain of mustard. (QS 46)

None of these conceptions of the kingdom has any apocalyptic viewpoint.
In each case the rule stands for something that can be accomplished.
Q^1 has to do with an imminent *parousia* or coming of the kingdom.

III,2.7 From a kingdom of nomos to a kingdom of physis

On page 125 as Burton Mack is discussing the notion of the kingdom in Q^1 he writes:

> The terms were set by classical Greek philosophy
> and its discussions of politics and governance.
> The issue had finally settled on the difference between
> *nomos* and *physis* as alternate foundations for society.
> *Nomos* meant legislation or social convention, understood
> as the laws enacted by the city's council of citizens.
> *Physis* meant the divine order reflected in the cosmos.

As an insurrectionist Cynic Jesus of Q^1 is speaking against
a political kingdom of laws and penalties which threaten persons.
Roman law ruled over the Jewish people of Galilee and in terms of
religion they were enabled by the Romans to have their kings
and prophets and priests with all their laws and ordinances.
But Jesus spoke against putting one's total trust in politics
and he preached a kingdom of love within each of their hearts
that could come now would they but follow him in loving everyone.
The Jesus of Q^1 is revealing a new divine order in the cosmos.
His new *physis* or nature of things has to do with an unheard-of
love of the enemy that is unlike any love ethics before and
it reveals a new understanding of the God who also loves all.
"Be merciful, even as your Father is merciful." This insight
into God which Jesus used to motivate his followers was what
caught their attention and explains why the movement caught on.
Greek law, Roman law, Jewish law all aimed at a justice
that spelled out a whole system of rewards and punishments.
But this Jesus told them to leave behind the emphasis on *nomos*
and put a new physiological focus on a totally loving heart.
The people could feel that Jesus was this absolutely new kind of lover
and he did reveal to them an absolutely new notion of God as love.
Jesus took his people from law and justice to love and mercy.

Agape and the Four Loves

III,2.8 From a kingdom of physis to a kingdom of nomos

As soon as we come to the Q^2 texts there is an immediate shift from this new realm of physical love back to the old *nomos* or world of law and its order of justice and of reward and punishment. In the sixth cluster of Q^2 sayings the apocalyptic Christ warns the people to be sure whose side they are on and at QS 29, he says:

> Whoever is not with me is against me
> and the one who does not gather with me scatters.

There is no love of enemy here for the enemy is condemned for scattering and not gathering, and the enemy is judged as guilty. At first Jesus was understood as a child of wisdom and those who followed him were children of wisdom in love's kingdom now. But once he was gone after his Ascension it was difficult for them to understand how to love the enemy that was destroying them. So they began to interpret him according to the old *nomos* model as the Apocalyptic son of man who would condemn the scatterers. The Apocalyptic sayings of Q^2 are so predominate and forceful that at first scholars wondered how to fit the love texts into the judgment texts and it was assumed that Christ was at first an apocalyptic prophet who then started giving some love teachings. But with much critical thinking as Burton Mack explains in ordered detail they come to see that the sayings of the child of wisdom were there before the sayings of the Son of man and so the problem is to understand how to reconcile an attitude that loved without judgment with an attitude that seemed to have judgment without love. As Mack puts it on page 38:

> The assumption had been that preaching
> an apocalyptic message of judgment
> could attract people to a movement
> that promised salvation from that judgment.

But if the wisdom message of love is first with its own motivation how did the Q people reconcile apocalyptic judgment with that love?

Part One: Joyful Beginnings

III,2.9 Judgment on this generation by the Son of Man

The seventh cluster of Q^2 sayings has to do with the sign of Jonah.
In QS 32 it is said:

> For as Jonah became a sign to the Ninevites
> so will the son of man be to this generation.

Mack treats the development of the son of man theme on pages 160
to 164 and shows the step by step slow development from Q^1 into
Q^2 and beyond and already in Q^1 there is an innocent son of man saying:

> Foxes have dens, and birds of the sky have nests
> but the son of man has nowhere to lay his head. (QS 19)

This sounds like a Cynic saying for those political insurrectionists
did choose poverty and the life of a wandering wisdom figure in order
to not only preach their message of equality for all but to live it out.
Burton Mack does not primarily treat the Jesus of Q^1 as a love teacher
rather for him Jesus is primarily this cynical insurrectionist figure.
So the transition for Mack is from Jesus, the wise Cynic, to
the son of man who develops into an apocalyptic judgment figure.
The second significant son of man saying is in Q^2:

> How fortunate you are when they reproach you
> ... because of the son of man. (QS 8)

This is still a transition saying because it takes the form of
Q^1 sayings about "How fortunate you are" and nothing yet
spells out the son of man figure to be a judge as he is in Daniel.
The third occurrence is this statement that connects the sign of Jonah
with the son of man who will be harsh against this evil generation
because it does not repent the way the Ninevites did for Jonah.
So it is a problem for us to reconcile the loving Jesus of Q^1
with the judging Jesus of Q^2 but Mack will show us how that
was also a problem for the writer of the Q document and for
the community of Q so in our next meditation we will follow
Mack's reconstruction of how he and the Q scholars think
the Q community saw the loving Jesus becoming a judging Christ.

Agape and the Four Loves

III The Second Stage of Q² Judgment Sayings
III,3.1 Mack's second set of 7 clusters of Q² sayings

8. TRUE ENLIGHTENMENT
   QS 33   The Lamp and the Eye

9. PRONOUNCEMENTS AGAINST THE PHARISEES
   QS 34   O You Pharisees

10. ON ANXIETY AN SPEAKING OUT
    QS 37   On Public Confessions

11. THE COMING JUDGMENT
    QS 41   The Hour
    QS 42   On Faithfulness
    QS 43   Fire and Division
    QS 44   Signs of the Times
    QS 45   Settling Accounts

12. THE TWO WAYS
    QS 47   The Narrow Gate and the Closed Door
    QS 48   Exclusion from the Kingdom

13. COMMUNITY RULES
    QS 54   When to Rejoice
    QS 55   Either / Or
    QS 57   On Scandals
    QS 58   On Forgiveness
    QS 59   On Faith
    QS 60   The Day of Separation
    QS 61   Squaring Accounts

Mack points out how there are two stages in the Q² sayings.
At first the problem is dealing with traitors and persecutors
who threaten the Jesus Movement once Jesus is not with them.
But as they proceed they develop an epic-apocalyptic myth
that tells the story of the Jewish people throughout their history
and up to the final judgment and this mythical story turns
Jewish history against the Jews who do not accept Jesus
and it shows the favor of God to those who are loyal to Jesus.

Part One: Joyful Beginnings

III,3.2 True enlightenment: the lamp and the eye
Burton Mack shows how the Jesus people of the Q community were
persecuted by the Pharisees very soon after Jesus ascended into heaven.
The stoning of Stephen by Pharisees like Saul was a danger that
threatened all Christians and some out of fear began to leave the group.
The Q^2 sayings have to do with a judgmental attitude against both
these persecutors and the traitors and the sayings of Jesus now
show the difference between those who truly love and those who do not.
Thus the Q community will think it fitting of Jesus to have him say:

> The lamp of the body is the eye.
> If your eye is good
> your whole body will be full of light.
> But if it is bad
> your whole body will be full of darkness.

So the loyal followers of Jesus who love God and each other have
an eye that sees the good in all that is and thus loved everyone.
But those who betray the people of Jesus and persecute them have
an eye that is bad or an evil eye and thus their individual
and communal bodies will be full of darkness and misery.
True enlightenment is to live in the kingdom of love with Jesus
and to love especially the traitors and the persecutors and to let
them know that they are wretched in proportion to their lack of love.
Jesus says to his beloved Q community:

> No one lights a lamp
> and puts it under a bushel basket,
> but on a lampstand.
> And those in the house see the light.

And Jesus is that light and all of his people see with it.
But those who prefer to live outside the house of David and
Jesus who has brought the Davidic promise of blessedness
for all mankind will only bring misery to themselves and others.
There is a natural punishment for all who prefer to live in darkness.

Agape and the Four Loves

III,3.3 Pronouncements against the Pharisees

At this point the Q people begin their rewriting of the Biblical story against the Pharisees and for themselves:

> Shame on you Pharisees!
> Shame on you lawyers!

they repeat over and over to show what hypocrites they are. After the Pharisees are denounced they get to their point:

> For this reason the wisdom of God said,
> I will send them prophets and wise men
> some of whom they will kill and persecute,
> in order to hold this generation accountable
> for the blood of all the prophets
> shed from the foundation of the world,
> from the blood of Abel to the blood of Zechariah.

So they begin at the beginning of the human story according to the Hebrew Bible with the sons of Adam and Eve, Cain and Abel. Cain killed Abel just as the Pharisees of their day are killing the Christians and so also Zechariah, a Godly man, was killed. The Jesus people see themselves as fortunate in being like the prophets who were persecuted and the connection between Cain and all the persecutors is meant to warn their own persecutors. This figure, the Wisdom of God, knows the whole sweep of history and Jesus, the child of wisdom, is seen as the Wisdom of God and soon he will be seen as the son of man who knows of the end of time. The Jesus people of Q come to see themselves at the center of history. Jesus who is the Wisdom of God, teaches them of all that has happened and of all that will happen in a great new epic-apocalyptic story. This great new story is the legacy of the Q^2 community as they sought to understand what will happen now that Jesus has gone. They think of him as saying to them just how to understand their place in history as they remain true to the love community. They will be followers of Abel and Zechariah who suffer for love.

Part One: Joyful Beginnings

III,3.4 On anxiety and speaking out

The Q² saying 37 is *On Public Confessions* and it says:

> When they bring you before the assemblies
> of the people (synagogues or town meetings),
> don't be afraid about what you are to say.
> When the time comes, the holy spirit
> will teach you what you are to say.

Jesus tells his people that they need not be afraid because his Holy Spirit will be there to guide them in all that they will say. All they have to do is spontaneously say that they love God and each other and even their very questioners and they will not go wrong for loving all is the whole message of Jesus. But again there is warning here in Q²:

> Whoever makes a speech
> against the son of man will be forgiven.
> But whoever speaks against
> the holy spirit will not be forgiven.

So the Jesus of Q² is the son of man and if the persecutors of the Q community do not understand him and speak out against him they will not be punished, but they will bring down punishment upon themselves if they speak against the Holy Spirit. In reality the Holy Spirit will come to be seen as the very love which is the love between the father and the son so the Q people are just beginning to learn of this spirit of love as God himself. So the son of man is the apocalyptic judge and he says:

> Everyone who admits in public
> that they know me, the son of man
> will acknowledge before the angels of God
> (heavenly court).

If the people of the Q community witness to Jesus they will be witnessing to love in a loving way and the kingdom of love will be theirs but if they disown it then it will not be theirs.

Agape and the Four Loves

III,3.5 *The coming judgment*

Now we come to the heart of the problem in understanding the son of man in Q^2 in relation to the all loving Jesus of Q^1. These five Q^2 sayings are strong and explicit and make us ponder the meaning of unconditional *agape* for all. Q^2 43 says:

> Do you think that I have come
> to bring peace on earth?
> No, not peace, but a sword.
> For I have come to create conflict
> between a man and his father,
> disagreement between a daughter
> and her mother, and estrangement
> between a daughter-in-law
> and her mother-in-law.
> A person's enemies
> will be one's own kin.

We have already seen something like this at the end of the Q^1 sayings when Jesus said we cannot be his disciples unless we hate our mother and father and our wife and child and ourself. So how can this kind of conflict and hatred be reconciled with the unlimited, unconditional *agape* that must love even enemies? When persons follow Jesus and seek first the kingdom of his love they will be persecuted by those who pursue self interest and their own family could easily be strongly opposed to their Jesus life. Those who leave the love community might be against them, their own Jewish people and especially the Pharisees are against them, and their very own family might be against them and even hate them. They, of course, must fully love and forgive and not even resist any who persecute and hate them just as did Jesus and Stephen. Of course, those who persecute and hate will receive natural punishment but after their purgatory they too will be forgiven.

Part One: Joyful Beginnings

III,3.6 The two ways

Burton Mack explains in convincing detail how the Q community worked out the great epic-apocalyptic story to warn their enemy and to assure themselves that they were on the right side of history. After introducing the epic of those who have been, are and will be for God and of those who are persecutors of the holy ones Q^2 now tells us of the apocalyptic judgment of the good and of the evil. QS 2, 48 says:

> Many will come from the east and west
> and sit at table in the kingdom of God.
> There will be wailing and clenching of teeth
> when you see Abraham, Isaac, Jacob
> and all the prophets in the kingdom of God
> and you yourselves excluded.
> Look, the last will be first,
> and the first will be last.

Here we hear more about the great epic and see how Abraham, Isaac and Jacob are one with Abel and Zechariah and now we hear how Cain and all the persecutors will be excluded from the kingdom of God. So we now have the big picture of history and its apocalyptic end. It seems pretty clear here that this exclusion will last forever or in other words there will be eternal punishment for all the persecutors. So what is the logic of love and punishment as we see it in Q^1 and Q^2? Jesus loved his enemies in thought, word and deed and the Jesus of Q^1 taught his disciples to do the same but now it seems that the Judge at the end of time that is, God himself, will not forgive the enemies of love. So Jesus forgives, the members of the Q community should forgive but the apocalyptic judge and God will not practise forgiveness. Jesus came to reveal the father as a loving, forgiving father God. So it is a gigantic transition to shift from the forgiving God of Q^1 to the non-forgiving rewarder-punisher God in Q^2. This apocalyptic judge works with a clear logic of exclusive opposites.

Agape and the Four Loves

III,3.7 Community rules

The five Q² sayings in this cluster on community rules continue
to complicate the question of loving forgiveness and punishment.
QS 55 again stresses the logic of exclusive opposites:

> No one can serve two masters.
> Either he hates the one and loves the other,
> or he is loyal to one and despises the other.
> You cannot serve God and wealth.

So the followers of Jesus tend to practise poverty, celibacy and obedience.
If they are the disciples of Jesus they should love every person and
hate no one for that is what it means for them to serve God.
They can love all persons and at the same time despise wealth
as did their master for focusing on self-centered wealth could keep
them from attending to persons as their attitude focuses on having.
They can become possessed by their possessions and not love all persons.
QS 58 is on forgiveness and it says:

> If your brother sins, warn him.
> If he listens to you, forgive him.
> Even if he sins against you
> seven times in a day,
> you must forgive him.

So even here in Q² the emphasis is still on total forgiveness.
Q² is warning the brother with its epic-apocalyptic story
but even though God and the son of man might not forgive
that is not the least reason for an excuse on the part of the Jesus follower.
The Q community of Jesus people has its rules and the main
one is to forgive anyone who offends you, but Jesus also said
"resist not evil" and do not these Q² sayings resist evil?
In so far as they do not simply love but warn with all kinds
of threats is there not a resisting of evil that is not loving forgiveness?
However, if it is obvious that any evil deed is going to receive
a natural punishment do not lovers have to warn all sinners?

Part One: Joyful Beginnings

III,3.8 The final judgment

QS 2, 60 on The Day of Separation and QS 2, 61 on Squaring Accounts are both very harsh in their judgment which will happen all of a sudden when the son of man appears at end time. At the end of the QS 60 section it says:

> This is how it will be on the day
> when the son of man appears.
> I am telling you, on that night
> there will be two in the field.
> One will be seized and the other left.
> Two women will be grinding together.
> One will be taken and the other left.
> Where the corpse is,
> there the vultures will gather.

According to the apocalyptic vision the end of the world will come very unexpectedly and the Jesus people will be taken up in rapture and all the non-loving, non believers will perish. The last of the Q^2 sayings ends with a parable on squaring accounts that seems to be even unjust let alone non-loving. That they might invest for him the master gives to one servant five talents, to another he gives two and to another he gives one. The first two do very well with their investment, but the servant who received only one talent protected it and gained nothing. His talent was taken away and given to the servant with more. The parable ends by saying:

> Everyone who has will receive more,
> and from the one who does not have,
> even what he has will be taken away.

This seems like a predestination approach in which those given great grace will flourish and those given little grace will perish so that apocalyptic approach is not very loving. The Q^2 sayings end with a stark contrast between Jesus and this judge.

Agape and the Four Loves

III,3.9 The epic-apocalyptic story

These last two sayings of the Q^2 text give a summary
of the epic-apocalyptic story and QS 60 says:

> Just as it was in the days of Noah
> so it will be on the day of the son of man.
> They ate, they drank, they married,
> they were given in marriage
> right up until the day
> when Noah entered the ark.
> Then the flood came and took them all.

So we return to the epic story of the Jewish people by going back
to Noah and the flood and again the point is that the Jesus people
will be on the ark and their persecutors will be left to drown.
Now at the end the epic and apocalyptic parts are put together
insofar as Noah and the son of man are linked together in terms of
a final judgment which will save the good and let the wicked perish.
This final Q^2 story also links Lot and the son of man.

> In the days of Lot it was the same –
> they ate, they drank, they bought, they sold
> they planted, they built.
> But on the day when Lot left Sodom,
> fire and sulfur rained down
> from heaven and destroyed them all.
> This is how it will be on the day
> when the son of man appears.

So the Q^1 Jesus of unconditional love for all is now the son of man
who comes right out of the Jewish justice worldview and
you are left to wonder if the Q^2 people have lost what is new
and unique about the *agape* of Jesus by reducing it to justice.
In fact this atonement justice view may not seem so just
insofar as the servant who got only one talent seems mistreated
and were all the people of Sodom unlovable in the eyes of Jesus?

Part One: Joyful Beginnings

The coffin dancing of Lequeitio

Elanchove

IV. The Four Loves

IV,1 Why the four natural loves need *agape*

IV,1.1 Must affection and wrath give rise to hatred?

Empedocles thinks of the affection of *Storge* as caught by necessity
in a vicious circle with all devouring wrath, so that at noon
on the circle of time, love will unite all in the accord of harmony.
But by three o'clock, hatred is already starting to raise its head
and the elements are beginning to be painfully torn asunder.
By six o'clock, hatred is totally in power and the cosmos has
fallen into utter chaos through a great turmoil of sorrowful hate.
By nine o'clock, affectionate love starts to regain its strength
and by high noon, once again the cosmos is born in utter joy.
And besides this circular cosmology, Empedocles also gives
a theory of epistemology in terms of the cycle of love and hate
for in Fragment 109, it is written:

> We see earth by means of earth,
> water by means of water,
> divine air by means of air,
> and destructive fire by means of fire;
> Affection by means of affection
> hate by means of baneful hate.

Empedocles seems to have a Gnostic universe in which evil
hatred is primordially there with good love and that it always
has been that way and always will be in our natural universe.
Even if we do come to know love by love and hate by hate
it will not in anyway help to break the power of necessity
and give love and joy any special advantage over their opposite.
In the Hebrew creation account at the very beginning of the Bible,
an anti-Gnostic world view is set up in which good is primordial
and evil comes later as a result of the Fall of Adam and Eve and
the detail of the Fall Story is not in the Priestly Creation Story
in chapter one, but is in the account given in the Book of J in
chapters two and three of Genesis, so you wonder if family
affection is fated to imply hatred or can that be spared?

Part One: Joyful Beginnings

IV,1.2 Can agape heal affection becoming hatred?

This view of Empedocles concerning the war of the opposites is strong with Greek philosophers and Heraclitus is like Empedocles:

> God is day-night, winter-summer,
> war-peace, satiety-famine. Fragment 57

So as the Greeks thought of the battle of the sexes and familial affection, they did come to the final teaching of the Jesus of Q¹ about hatred. They seem to say that people come to hate their mother and father and their wives and their children and given love there will be hatred. Jesus seems to say that if this were not the case, there would be no need to become his disciple and to take up the love of *agape* that can overcome hatred with its attitude that forgives and reconciles all. When Nietzsche and Daddy lost their beloved fathers when they were only five, *agape* was there to make them stronger through their loss. But all through history, many have lost their fathers in the past through war and in our day through divorce and even in unbroken families there can be failures of affection so that security is weak. As Freud listened to his patients, even under hypnosis, he often detected an Oedipal complex at work, making sons want in some symbolic way to kill their fathers and marry their mothers. And daughters might want to kill their mothers and marry their fathers. Freud, who never had the agapeic solution, worked with patients who didn't have the methods of confession, forgiveness and reconciliation. So the Greeks, the Jews and the Christians all see the treachery of love and they each try to get different solutions to the problem by going back and meditating on Adam and Eve and Cain and Abel and by going back to Empedocles and Heraclitus and they can go back to the hard saying concluding Q¹. Everyday affection can break down as brothers kill brothers and thus a higher love is needed as a solution to the treachery of love for it will be found in natural affection as well as in *eros* and even in friendship and also in any natural *agape*.

Agape and the Four Loves

IV,1.3 Must natural eros always betray the beloved?

The battle of the sexes seems to increase the hatred between lovers. If *eros* has to do with lovers standing face to face, enraptured in each other, then we know how prolonged proximity can end the rapture and hell will have no wrath like a scorned woman's fury. Each great religious philosophy has its way of providing a remedy for the hurt and hatred that can arise from out of erotic desires. Plato's Ladder of Love in *The Symposium* is such a mystical remedy for he describes how a lover (1) falls in love with someone with a beautiful body and then (2) falls in love with many beautiful bodies. On the third rung of the Ladder, (3) he falls in love with someone with a beautiful soul and then (4) the lover climbs higher to love the beauty of laws and institutions and then (5) he comes to love the beauty of mathematics and science and next (6) he falls in love with philosophy "that most fruitful discourse and loftiest thought" and finally Diotima tells Socrates (7) how the lover comes to fall in love with the universal Beauty

> that wondrous vision which is the very soul
> of the beauty he has toiled so long for.
> *Symposium* 210e

The lower *eros* which seeks to have children of the body can be transformed into this higher *eros* seeking children of the mind. But even this beautiful, mystical *eros* has its shortcomings and thus Plato's student, Aristotle, pointed out how this loving of the immaterial form by the immaterial soul devalues the body and the material which is the principle of individuation, and thus individuals have no place in this mystical philosophy as they are swallowed up like drops of water in the ocean of Beauty. So the Higher Aphrodite as well as this Lower Aphrodite has her problematic dark side and Plato writes his *Phaedrus* as an answer to the Aristotelian criticism, arguing that all things do not merely participate in the forms, but are their mixture.

IV,1.4 Can Plato's sublimated eros help agape?

> There are two kinds of madness,
> one resulting from human ailments,
> the other from a divine disturbance
> of our conventions of conduct . . .
> and in the divine kind we distinguish four types,
> ascribing then to four gods:
> the inspiration of the prophet to Apollo,
> that of the mystic to Dionysus,
> that of the poet to the Muses,
> and a fourth type which we declare to be the highest,
> the madness of the lover, to Aphrodite and *Eros*.
> *Phaedrus* 265a-b

The sublimation process described in The Myth of the Charioteer
is the fourth kind of Divine Madness, which is even more wonderful
than the inspiration of prophecy, mysticism or that of poetry.
It can bring about a transformation of one's whole physiological
attitude, mood and set of feelings, as it did for Dante and Nietzsche.
Augustine could pray for years: "Oh Lord, give me chastity, but not yet."
Then in a miraculous moment he is given the surprising grace that
lets him be free from all the irascible and consupiscible negativities
that haunted him for so long and became free for a loving creativity.
Augustine, Kierkegaard and Nietzsche are erotics like Plato, whereas
Aquinas, Kant and Hegel worked more with Aristotelian *Philia*.
The Buddha and many Buddhist monks and nuns, as well as Jesus,
Paul and many Catholics live out a sublime celibacy that lets
them have a special shamanic energy for health, education and welfare.
So the Higher *Eros* can contribute to *agape* just as *agape* can
contribute to it by letting sexual energy be used for spiritual purposes.
Plato's *Phaedrus* with its erotic sublimation and inspiration
has been a spiritual reading for many down through the years
and its enthusiasm and Divine madness have gifted *agape*.

Agape and the Four Loves

IV,1.5 Why is friendship in need of agape?

Friendship might be thought of as two persons standing side by side appreciating the world together and a friend might say to a friend:

"You are the other half of my soul."

In the 8th and 9th books of his *Ethics*, Aristotle gives his treatment of *Philia* or friendship and he shows how we can be acquaintances with many, but true friends with only a few, for true friendship can take place only when:

"Two persons eat a peck of salt together."

They have to work very hard on the same thing, even so that they perspire so much as it were that in licking their sweaty lips they take in that much salt, even as Plato and Aristotle worked together on philosophy for twenty years, so that Plato was a friend. While Plato thought of the love of wisdom that came from *eros*, the name "philosophy" itself is connected with *philia* or the friendly pursuit of wisdom or of knowing all things or the big picture together. But, Affection, *eros* and friendship are each limited to only a few beloveds, even though they can intermix, so that a pair of erotic lovers can have great affection for each other and also be the best of friends, if they should deeply have a common focal interest. There can be an affectionate personality who has affection for many or perhaps for all and a friendly personality, friendly to many but that special friendship, as Aristotle defines it, is limited to one or a few, just as *eros* must be to prevent terrible jealousy. There are erotic personalities, but if erotic activity is not limited to one's one and only beloved, adultery will cause great problems. So *agape* differs from affection, *eros* and friendship in their strict senses because it is not limited to a few but seeks to love all others, even if they do not love in return or are enemies. Aristotle defines friendship as mutual goodwill that is recognized. *Agape* on the other hand need not be mutual for it is goodwill in the sense of prayer and affirmation even though not recognized.

IV,1.6 Can Aristotle's friendship contribute to agape?

Just as Platonism and Platonic *Eros* contributed greatly to the tradition
of Christian *agape*, so has Aristotelianism and Aristotelian friendship,
as we will see as we meditate further into *agape* and the four loves.
Origen, Bernard of Clairvaux, the Victorines and the Carmelites
were very Platonic in their approach toward becoming one with God.
But Thomas Aquinas is very Aristotelian and his love of God
and of all creatures is explained more in terms of friendship than
of *eros* and the Franciscan love of Francis, Bonaventure and Scotus
is more of an Aristotelian friendship for all of God's creatures
than a desire for an erotic union of enthusiasm and Divine Madness.
True friendship for Aristotle sees friends as becoming virtuous together
that they might be happy together and thus they come to love
the moral and intellectual virtues together by practising those virtues
together and they even discover contemplation of the good together.
For Christian Aristotelians, there are added the three theological
virtues of faith, hope and charity or *agape*, which makes friends
of those who pursue them as one soul, growing within two bodies.
A virtue for Aristotle has to do with the golden mean between extremes.
Courage, for example, is the golden mean between the extremes of fear
and foolhardiness, and this balance is the opposite of the passion
that arises out of the enthusiasm and Divine Madness of Platonic *Eros*.
Thus, even the theological virtues of faith, hope and *agape* will
be very passionate for Platonic erotics, and have to do with
the kisses of the feet, the hands, the mouth and of the breasts.
Erotic Christians will grow through sexuality and suffering
and theirs will be more the logic of the heart than of the mind.
Aristotelian Christians have more of a balance of the mind
and the heart of love and theirs is a friendly heart of love.
Platonic Christians are more like Hindu and Islamic Mystics
whereas Aristotelian Christians are more like Buddhists
in their calm illumination without passionate, erotic madness.

Agape and the Four Loves

IV,1.7 How do natural and supernatural agape differ?

The word "*agape*" that is used in *The New Testament* was borrowed from the Greeks and it had more to do with a universal love for all than did affection, friendship and *eros* with their limited directions. Plotinus, even though he lived around 250 A.D. in Alexandria and no doubt knew of Christian *agape*, was a non-Christian and yet in writing of the Greek philosophers and their concepts of love he did bring in his concept of *agape* in a very significant way. *Ennead* III, 5 is on *Eros* and it treats *eros* as affection and makes the distinction with Plato between lower and higher Aphrodite. *Eros* is the mixture of poverty and wealth so that it desires and overflows and Plotinus builds on that to get his concept of *agape*. Love as *agape* is the Alpha and the Omega, the beginning and the end and it is from the superabundance of love which is the One that everything emanates, and it is back to this Love, the One, that all things return, for it is their goal and fulfillment. This *agape* of Plotinus is the creative principle and it is the Principle of unification for only "like can know like" or only love can know love by bringing all back to the source. In *Ennead* VI, 8, Plotinus distinguishes *Agape* from *eros* because *eros* is connected with desire, but when the Intellect flows forth from the One, there is only a superabundance of love. This natural *agape* on the part of the One gives without any cost, a love which is beyond choice and choosing, a love which is so great that it is simply spontaneous in its outpouring love. So time is a circle for Plotinus and what comes forth from the One by way of *agape*, as it makes its way back in its last stage, will make a leap of love beyond knowing and its duality and thus beyond *eros* in an *agape* of pure giving. So time as circular implies that *agape* flows into the realm of the problematic and then must get out and Plotinus wonders if it might have been better if *Agape* had never emanated.

V,1.8 Can natural agape contribute to Jesus' agape?

In a certain sense, the Stoic universal, cosmopolitan respect for all humans having reason has an element of *agape* about it in that it is not restricted as are affection, *eros*, and friendship. So Paul was able to use many of his Stoic concepts to explain both to himself and others the agapeic attitude he found in Jesus. The Stoic ethic based on conscience and transforming negative reactions into positive proactions became central for Paul's understanding of the love that transforms sorrow into joy. Of course, Plotinus was very influential on Augustine and many other Christian mystics who experienced and wrote about the stages of purificational catharsis, illumination and then unification. Augustine said that St. John's Gospel, in its beginning, is just like Neo-Platonism until it gets to "And the Word was made flesh." So the *agape* that is there in the spirit of Stoicism and in the vocabulary of Plotinus is a wonderful and holy *agape*. But because of its circularity that has not been redeemed by the reality and the concept of the Incarnation, it can have only a limited love of equity universalism and cannot get to the difference universalism of incarnational *agape* that goes out to all unique beings and loves them eternally in their differences. Plotinus did write a tractate against Gnosticism, but he had a hard time escaping the idea that from the first moment of emanation, there was something lacking or evil that should not be. For only the One is completely good and all else, though it flows from the Good, is tainted with negativity, so that Plotinus is ambivalent about the duality of knowing and of *eros*, even though it might be the higher Aphrodite which desires because it lacks. So all four of the natural loves, when viewed from the aspect of Jesus' *agape*, are good and can help us to love better. But if their self-centered preferences are not purified by the sword of the *agape* of Jesus, they will not really love others.

Agape and the Four Loves

IV,1.9 Reconciling the four loves in Jesus' agape

For the sake of completeness, it should be said that there are five Greek words for love: *storge, eros, philia, agape* and *elios*. *Elios*, meaning "mercy" or "compassion," is the term used in the Septuagint to translate *hesed*, or the everlasting, merciful love promised in II Samuel 7 to King David and his house. This notion of *elios* has been enshrined in the saying "*Kyrie Eleison*" or "Lord, have mercy." and in the Hebrew Bible's history, it was at the heart of the Kingdom of David which, with a qualitative leap, became the *agape* of the Kingdom of Jesus. When Jesus, the Son of God, became incarnate within Mary, whose husband-to-be was from the family of David, he performed that act of *agape* which became the heart of his teaching and practice and this *agape* has been, is, and will be reconciling all the other loves with itself with a "*Yes*" and "*Amen*" for their higher and lower forms. Jesus told us that whatever we do to anyone that we do unto Him. So anyone who loves anyone with the affection of *storge* is already loving Jesus with his *agape* and if affection should become hatred, then the *agape* of Jesus can give it a saving perspective that can transform its hatred into a love that gets beyond hatred. Affection, *eros* and friendship are directed to a special beloved and in that they are good and part of *agape* and when that limited love begins to become self-destructive, *agape* can save it. So *agape*, which loves all five of the loves, sees them as part of itself, and if any of them begins to suffer from their limitations, then *agape*, by showing them a universal love that sees all differences and limitations as lovable, can save them by taking them into its attitude which loves the good in all. All five loves contribute to *agape* insofar as they are loving. And insofar as they are not loving of all and thus not fully loving of any, since all are related, *agape* can come to them and show them that in loving all they will be able to be fulfilled.

IV,2 The four loves of the pre-christian Augustine

IV,2.1 Can Nietzsche and Q help clarify Augustine?

In *Beyond Good and Evil*, Nietzsche claims that:

> Christianity gave *Eros* poison to drink:
> he did not die of it but degenerated into a vice.

In Nietzsche's view, this poisoning began with Paul as he focused
on Eve as the first sinner but Augustine went further and saw
sexual desire as originating with Adam and Eve's original sin.
In Augustine's *Confessions*, he tells the story of how he lived with
the four loves and how they each became more and more poison
until finally the grace of his conversion regenerated them with
a new and marvelous *agape* that delivered them of their poison.
To follow Augustine's story, we can first see how he treats
each of the four natural loves and then see how, from a
Christian viewpoint, they could be seen as becoming poisoned.
As we meditate on Augustine's understanding of his own experience,
we can ask if Nietzsche and Q can help us better understand him.
According to Nietzsche, the pattern of poisoning began with the
Jewish priests, as they belittled the profane to favour their sacred.
Then Paul connected sex with sin by demoralizing the natural.
Augustine became the pivotal figure in the poisoning process
by viewing all four of the natural loves as corrupted by sin.
Finally, Luther's exclusivistic logic denied the value of good works.
Is Nietzsche ambivalent toward Augustine as he is toward Socrates,
who contributed to the poisoning of Dionysus and Tragedy's death?
If Nietzsche is ambivalent toward Augustine, does he see him as
also revealing the way to a healthy, inspiring Platonic *Eros*?
Can meditating on Augustine in terms of Q also help us to better
understand Augustine, for in his poisoning process, is it not
the case that Augustine can show how the Q community moved
from the all-loving Jesus to the Judging Christ and once we
see this, can we not see Augustine as giving a primacy
to the Incarnate loving Jesus over the wrathful, judging Christ?

Agape and the Four Loves

IV,2.2 *Augustine's praise for affection*

In his *Confessions*, Augustine tells us how he appropriated the theory and practise of the four loves from the classic Greco-Roman world. Immediately after the introduction to his *Confessions*, in the first five sections of Book I, in which he presents his most basic thesis:

> Man is one of your creatures, Lord,
> and his instinct is to praise you ...
> The thought of you stirs him so deeply that
> he cannot be content unless he praises you,
> because you made us for yourself
> and our hearts can find no peace
> until they rest in you.

He goes on to describe the affection that his mother and nurses had for him as his mother carried him in her womb and as she and his nurses grew in love with him as they each nursed him. He examines his early life as an infant and then as a boy and then as a youth, and he tells how his father loved him so and how he was very concerned about his education and how he worked hard and saved that Augustine might go away to a good school in Carthage. Right from the first words of his *Confessions*, we see that these very *Confessions* are primarily works of praise and thus are prayers. Confession, thanksgiving and petition let us grow in our praising. The essence of love is to praise with a *Yes* and *Amen* and Augustine is praising the God who loves and is love and he praises first of all the affection which brought him into existence and sustained and nourished him, as his parents gave themselves to each other for him in such a sweet and joyous way, and you can feel his love for the flesh as he describes being nursed at the breast. Augustine was an affectionate infant, boy and youth and with praise for his childhood, he confesses his childlike affirmations. But as with Nietzsche, his Yes-saying for affection also includes a No-saying, for he did not love his many, many enemies.

Part One: Joyful Beginnings

IV,2.3 Augustine discovers affection's poison

The Jesus of Q[1] said:

> Whoever does not hate his mother and father
> will not be able to learn from me.
> Whoever does not hate his son and daughter
> cannot belong to my school.

While Augustine loved love and had great affection for affection, his experience did bring him to the poison, tragedy and evil which he suffered in his affection, even from his early days. He tells us how he and other children are evil from the beginning in that they throw tantrums when they do not get their way and when they do not get affection in just the way and when they want it. Augustine came to define evil as a lack of what should be and his definition is like Nietzsche's in saying *Yes* to all that is and yet, in saying *No* to all that is negative and lacking in love. Augustine came to love *agape* in the sense of Jesus and Nietzsche who love all beings, even the enemy, because he came to see the poison in the four natural loves if they were simply left as natural and non sublimated loves, as affection was for Empedocles. As that first philosopher of love reflected on the *Storge* that makes the world go around, he saw love as bringing harmony to all and yet it was naturally connected with an equally destructive hate. The wisdom of that insight that affection and hatred are a pair of mixed opposites, could help one tolerate the evil, knowing that this, too, will pass and love will return after the dark night of tragedy. Augustine discovered the down side of affection, especially when his teachers would beat him at school and his parents approved. They seemed to have no sympathetic affection for his plight. Augustine felt a great hatred toward his teachers as they beat him and that extended to his parents who did not protect him. The hatred there in the relation between children and parents could bring the young Augustine to seek a power greater than his parents.

Agape and the Four Loves

IV,2.4 Augustine's praise for eros

Augustine did not go to school for a year when he was sixteen because his father was saving money to send him to Carthage. For Augustine, idle hands were the devil's workshop and he found how much he loved sex and his father encouraged his sexuality. At the beginning of Book III, when he writes of going to Carthage, he shows how he loves sexual and erotic love so much:

> I had not yet fallen in love
> but I was in love with the idea of it . . .
> To love and have my love returned
> was my heart's desire
> and it would have been all the sweeter
> if I could also enjoy
> the body of the one who loved me.

He describes how he abandons himself to a life of pleasure and at the beginning of Book IV, he goes to Thagaste to teach rhetoric and he takes a mistress:

> In those days, I lived with a woman,
> not my lawful wedded wife,
> but a mistress whom I had chosen
> for no special reason
> but that my restless passions
> had alighted on her.
> But she was the only one,
> and I was faithful to her.

Even though he read Cicero's *Hortentius*, and knew his vocation was to love wisdom and be a philosopher, he was focused on *eros*. In Virgil's *Aeneid*, he loved the love story of Dido, and at the Theatre, he was fascinated with the allure of erotic allure. In Book VI, section 15, he describes the love he had for his mistress who bore him a son, Adeodatus, given by God. This story tells of how Christianity gave *eros* poison to drink.

Part One: Joyful Beginnings

IV,2.5 Augustine's eros is poisoned

Augustine was eager to attain fame, wealth and marriage and his dear mother, Monica, totally encouraged him in this. She arranged a marriage for him with a girl who was two years too young to marry, and he was pleased with her and her family. If he were to marry, he could be baptized and not have to worry about being a great sinner after his baptism, so he dismissed his mistress in the saddest story of his *Confessions*, Book VI, Part 15:

> The woman with whom I had been living
> was torn from my side
> as an obstacle to my marriage.
> And this was a terrible blow
> which crushed my heart to bleeding
> because I loved her dearly.
> She went back to Africa
> vowing never to give herself
> to any other man
> and left me with the son
> whom she had borne me.

If Christianity ever gave *eros* poison to drink, it must have been at this moment, for surely Augustine's *eros* became vice as he hurt this woman, and his son and himself so much and he goes on to tell us how, as a result:

> I was sinning more and more.

He took other mistresses after his first love was taken from him for he could not wait for two years, given his robust sex drive. So why did he not marry his first mistress whom he loved so much, for he and she and their son could have had a family with such affection that they could have lived happily ever after? Did it all have unconsciously to do with his philosophical vocation, because there was friction with his mistress, not only because of his mother and the church, but his friends too opposed the marriage?

Agape and the Four Loves

IV,2.6 Augustine's praise for friendship

From his study of the Greek and Roman classics, Augustine knew that one of our greatest treasures is that of a rare and true friendship. As he finished his studies and began to teach, Augustine found that he had just such a friend, as he tells us in book IV, section 4:

> Yet in a moment before we had reached
> the end of our first year of friendship
> that was sweeter to me
> than all the joys of life,
> You took him from this world.

Of course, absence makes the heart grow fonder, but here, Augustine does praise friendship, and show that it can be just as lovely as affection and *eros* and he even seems to say the sweetest of all. In describing his grief, he brings out its special kind of value.

> My heart grew somber with grief,
> and wherever I looked, I saw only death.
> My own country became a torment
> and my own home a grotesque abode of misery.
> All that we had done together
> was now a grim ordeal without him.

Friendship is a standing side by side, appreciating the world together in such a way that each shared thing that is loved together becomes a pain, reminding you of our lost friend when he is gone. Augustine goes on to have other dear friends, such as Alypius and Nebridius, and it is as if his vocation to philosophy is connected with his love for friends and they are necessary, that they might philosophize together in a way they could not alone. Aristotle could say that Plato is a friend, but truth is greater than friendship and Augustine, from his experience, knew that you would not even come to that wisdom without friendship. Augustine and his friends loved and praised their friendship because their love of wisdom gave them such a wisdom of love.

IV,2.7 Augustine discovers friendship's poison

Augustine's *eros* poisoned Christianity, for since he lived
in fornication, he could be consistent only if he denied God.
His fornication poisoned his affection with his mother and
made of him a child of so many prayers and tears and he
became a Manichean because that kind of Gnosticism was
a cosmological, psychological and ethical determinism, and he
could tell his mother that he was just determined to fornicate.
His friend shared all these views with him, but then, when
he became ill, he and his family asked a priest to baptize him.
Then, for a while, his friend got better and Augustine thought
he would renounce his baptism and rejoin Augustine in atheism.
But, his friend basically told Augustine: "Get behind me, Satan."
In his unconscious mind, Augustine must have seen that, yes,
truth and true love are greater than friendship, and so even
before he died, his friend was already separated from him and
thus Augustine really mourned two separations from his friend.
In an odd way, Christianity did poison Augustine's friendship,
for when his friend became a Christian, friendship was a vice.
In Book VI, section 12, Augustine writes:

> It was Alypius who prevented me from marrying
> because he insisted that if I did so,
> we could not possibly live together
> in uninterrupted leisure
> devoted to the pursuit of wisdom,
> as we had long desired to do.

So Augustine was torn between *eros* and friendship and
his friendship and love of philosophy wanted to give *eros*
poison to drink so that it might just die and Alypius
could not understand Augustine's sex drive and turmoil.
Augustine also had an *eros* and affection that wanted to give
his deep philosophical friendship poison that it might die.

Agape and the Four Loves

IV,2.8 Augustine's praise for neo-Platonic agape

With his friends Alypius and Nebridius, Augustine philosophized together and they worked their way through the self-contradictions of Manicheanism and Epicureanism and moved beyond these philosophies of materialism and determinism, and by pondering the problem of evil, they discovered Neo-Platonism and the idea that evil is a lack of what should be and not a substance.
In Book VII, section 20, Augustine writes:

> By reading these books of the Platonists,
> I had been prompted to look for truth
> as something incorporeal
> and I had caught sight of your invisible nature
> as it is known through your creatures.

Augustine, with his friends, became convinced intellectually of the realms of the physical, the vital, the intellectual and the spiritual, but he could not yet mystically appropriate them in a catharsis, sublimation, enlightenment and unification that he saw others such as Valentinius, Plotinius' translator, living out. Intellectually with Plotinus and Nietzsche, Augustine could see that all things are loveable because they derive their being from the one source that is the Beautiful, Good, True and Holy. Augustine's *eros* poisoned his capacity to become a Platonist. He prayed: "O Lord, give me chastity, but not yet."
Ironically, the wild *eros* of his sex drive, which was not yet sublimated, let him appreciate the universal love of natural *agape*. Just as the double loss of his first, last, fast friend helped him to better love and praise friendship, so his inability to attain the Neo-Platonic *agape* which he intellectually appreciated, let him love that *agape* all the more as a value out of his reach. Augustine found that the Neo-Platonists gave *eros* poison to drink and it turned the black horse of vice and his energy into a new sublimated power to be used in loving holy wisdom.

IV,2.9 Augustine discovers natural agape's poison

Augustine greatly desired the celibacy of the Platonists and he
wondered why they were able to be celibate while he was unable.
Then, before his conversion, he began to read St. Paul, and he saw
a certain poison right at the heart of the mystical way to unification.
There is poison in its origin and its goal, for it is narcissistic
in its pride that I can lift myself up by my bootstraps
without any need of a gifted grace from a power greater than myself.
St. Paul led Augustine to see our radical weakness and our need
for grace which the Pelagians of Augustine's day denied.
But the main poison of the universal love of natural *agape*
is that it has no qualms about eradicating each single individual
in a unity in which each ray of the sun becomes part of the sun.
At the end of Book VII, Augustine writes:

> None of this is contained in the Platonists' books.
> Their pages have not the mein of the true love of God.
> They make no mention of the tears of confession . . .
> nor do they speak of the salvation of your people.

Aristotle had already criticized Plato on that vital point
that the extracted soul becoming one with the World Soul
wiped away any trace of this individual's unique survival.
That is a deadly poison which mystical *agape* administers
to anyone who goes through illumination and especially unification.
Paul let Augustine begin to believe that his lost friend and
his father dear and all of the blessed dead could live forever.
Augustine now begins to intellectually believe in Christian *agape*
and from this viewpoint, he sees the poison of each of the four
natural loves, each of which must suffer the loss of the beloved.
But he is not yet converted to being able to live out the life
of Christian *agape* which can restore virtue to the four loves
which are each self-poisoning and which poison each other.
Augustine loved the four loves, but he could not yet revive them.

IV, 3 Augustine's conversion to agape heals his bipolarity

IV,3.1 Can Augustine help clarify Nietzsche and Q?

Augustine was born into the bi-polar tension between his mother's
Christian culture and his father's more worldly ways, and as he grew,
the tension increased within and between his four kinds of relating.
His *Confessions* is the story of one crisis after another within
and between his family affection, his sex life, his circle of friends
and with all humans as he went from the Manichees, to the Epicureans
to the Platonistis in his quest for peace rather than bi-polar torture.
At the end of Book VIII, as he approaches his conversion, he tells
of his tension as it reaches its final climax:

> I probed the hidden depths of my soul
> and wrung its pitiful secrets from it,
> and when I mustered them all
> before the eyes of my heart
> a great storm broke within me,
> bringing with it a great deluge of tears.

Augustine began to see through his own self-deceit, as he saw
the love-hatred bi-polar mix with each of his four loves.
He was constantly being punished by the rods of men, just
as he had been by his early teachers, for all the self love
hidden in the affection, *eros*, friendship and *agape* of his first
thirty years and thus, in Book VIII, section 12, he writes:

> Lord, will you never be content?
> Must we always taste your vengeance?
> Forget the long record of our sins.

As we consider Augustine's fourfold love conversion, we can
think about this pattern and ask if its is not also Nietzsche's and Q's.
The main theme of Nietzsche's writing has to do with resolving
the bi-polar flip-flopping between the loving Jesus and the Christ.
This is the same tension between Dionysius and the moral Apollo.
The main question concerning Q also has to do with relating
the all-loving Jesus with the harshly judging Son of Man.

Part One: Joyful Beginnings

IV,3.2 Agape heals Augustine's bi-polar affection

Concerning the moment of his conversion, Augustine writes there at the end of Book VIII:

> I was asking myself these questions,
> weeping all the while
> with the most bitter sorrow in my heart,
> when all at once, I heard
> the singing voice of a child . . .
> "Take it and read, take it and read."

He opened at random the book of Paul's epistles and read:

> Not in reveling and drunkenness,
> not in lust and wantonness,
> not in quarrels and rivalries.
> Rather, arm yourself with the Lord Jesus Christ;
> spend no more thought
> on nature and nature's appetites.

He shared this with his friend, Alypius, and they went in and told his mother, who was overjoyed:

> For she saw that you had granted her
> far more than she used to ask
> in her tearful prayers and plaintive lamentations.
> You converted me to yourself,
> so that I no longer desired a wife
> or placed any hope in this world,
> but stood firmly in the rule of faith.

In this little page, he describes the healing of his Affection, *eros* friendship and *agape* as he and his mother were reconciled, as he was given celibacy and taken beyond bi-polar sexuality. He and Alypius needed no more excuse-making questions. His *agape* was no longer self-interested in worldly matters. All of a sudden, he came to love God with a peace that surpasses understanding and he loved himself and all others.

Agape and the Four Loves

IV,3.3 *Giving mother and son a mystical agapeic affection*

In book IX, chapter ten Augustine describes a mystical experience he and his mother had together which took them into the realm of a new joy brought about by what he calls "the flame of love". Shortly after his conversion and shortly before Monica's death mother and son were alone

> leaning from a window which overlooked
> the garden in the courtyard of the house
> where we were staying at Ostia.

As they conversed together they were graced to go ever more inward and ever more upward so that

> As the flame of love burned stronger in us
> and raised us higher towards the eternal God
> our thoughts ranged over the whole compass
> of material things in their various degrees.

First, they saw that bodily pleasure is not nearly as fulfilling as the happiness of the life of the saints who can appreciate the whole compass of material things up to the heavens themselves. Secondly, they beheld in joy the spiritual realm of their own souls. Thirdly, in a moment of awesome wonder they passed beyond to the realm of eternal Wisdom

> and while we spoke of the eternal Wisdom
> longing for it and straining for it
> with all the strength of our hearts
> for one fleeting instant
> we reached out and touched it.

This new flame of agapeic love which Augustine received at his conversion now burned bright and lovely for mother and son. No longer were all the trials and tribulations of their bipolar affection tormenting them but in love for God and each other their hearts were no longer restless for now they could rest in God in a peaceful joy and excitement that surpassed even the joy of sex.

Part One: Joyful Beginnings

IV,3.4 And gives great peace to all as Monica dies

Up until now Augustine had undergone many tearful separations. He wept and was depressed when his friend died as he did when he and his mistress were separated and when his son and his son's mother were torn apart that Augustine might please his mother. Monica had wept and prayed for him for twenty years and now she was dying and now again Augustine felt like crying. Augustine's brother, about whom he has hardly written, was there also and he was concerned that she he buried next to her husband. On the ninth day of her illness, when she was fifty six and Augustine was thirty three, her pious and devoted soul was set free from her body:

> I closed her eyes, and a great wave
> of sorrow surged into my heart.
> It would have overflowed in tears
> if I had not made a strong effort of will
> and stemmed the flow . . .
> As she breathed her last,
> the boy Adeodatus began to wail
> and only ceased his cries when
> we all checked him.

But now Augustine had the faith and hope of his new *agape*.

> She had not died in misery
> nor had she wholly died.
> Of this we were certain, both
> because we knew what a holy life
> she had led and also because
> our faith was real and we had
> sure reasons not to doubt it.

Because *agape* was so strong in healing all the wounds of affection there was a self evidence to its worth as mankind's highest affirmation and because of the power of this love there was no reason to weep.

Agape and the Four Loves

IV, 3.5 Agape leads to a politics of friendship

Greek and Roman classical thinkers like Aristotle and Cicero
were clear that true friendship is a rare and exclusive love
between two or a few based upon their unique, kindred spirit.
But step by step from the moment of Augustine's conversion to *agape*
his friendliness was renewed as it moved out more and more
to all until as the Bishop of Hippo all were his agapeic friends.
For Augustine the essence of friendship was to share the inner life
of ideals together as he did with his early friend who died and
with Alypius and Evodius and in his *Confessions* he does that with
anyone who reads him so that we can become friends with Augustine.
As a Bishop he not only had a fatherly affection for all but by
sharing the Judeo-Christian religion with his flock he was leading
his flock into a deeper and deeper friendship with him and each other.
As a Bishop he was always performing the works of love by saying
the Mass and praying for and working with his flock in friendship.
The writing of his *Confessions* was an exercise of holy friendship.
In his *Confessions* he is always appropriating the Jewish and
Christian scriptures and especially the psalms and reconciling
them with his own and other's Neo-Platonism so that in his writing
friendship was forged of the Judeo-Christian, Greco-Roman worlds.
It was in the 8th and 9th books of Aristotle's *Politics* that he
wrote about friendship and its value for ethics and politics and
now in Augustine's *Confessions* he is creating a new Politics of love.
In the language of our day we would call the broken hearted
failures of all Augustine's love a bi-polar psychotic disorder.
His conversion brought him to a healing of his self-centered
affection, friendship and erotic religiosity so that by continuing
to become more and more friendly with others he was more healthy.
His conversion gave him a turn-around but still he was
tempted to weep and wail when his mother died and still he was
tempted to self-centered friendship but by loving he kept growing.

IV,3.6 And to a celibacy that still dreams of sex

Concerning the 10th Book of the *Confessions* Peter Brown in his *Augustine of Hippo* writes on page 177:

> The amazing Book Ten of the *Confessions*
> is not the affirmation of a cured man:
> it is the self-portrait of a convalescent.

In the great sexual conversion story of Plato's Phaedrus 245c, one gets the impression of a complete healing of the bi-polarity of the black and white horse as they fight each other in misery. When the soul falls in love with just the right soul all the great energy of the black horse is transferred to the noble creativity of the charioteer and the white horse for their project of loving wisdom. This Platonic conversion story goes into Neo-Platonism and the great mystical way inward and upward which Augustine describes so well in his experience with his mother and in this great treatment of loving God who is above the body with its external senses and even above all the kinds and levels of memory is what classical thinkers would expect of a mystical conversion. But Augustine tells us of another conversion story in which he is always convalescing and not completely cured of his sexuality. As he concludes his great treatment of memory Book X, 30:

> You commanded me not to commit fornication,
> and though you did not forbid me to marry,
> you counseled me to take a better course.
> You gave me the grace and I did your bidding,
> even before I became a minister of your sacrament.
> But in my memory, of which I have said much,
> the images of things imprinted upon it
> by my former habits still linger on.

Augustine is not a pure soul and mind as the Platonists thought but he is an incarnate person so that if he really examines his conscience he finds in some way he will be what he has been.

Agape and the Four Loves

IV,3.7 So that in sorrow he continues confessing

Augustine's agapeic world is so different from Plato's erotic world that their transformations from sexuality to celibate sublimation are also unalike in many ways that seem to surprise Augustine. Thus he goes on to write about his sexual images:

> When I am awake they intrude themselves upon me,
> though with little strength.
> But when I dream, they not only give me pleasure
> but are very much like acquiescence in the act.

He mentions that sometimes in sleep he resists the attraction of the image and he remembers his chaste resolutions, but at other times he gives in, but upon awakening his conscience is clear. For there is responsibility when awake but not when he is asleep. However, he still must write and confess that:

> Although I am sorry
> that by some means or other
> it happened to me.

With Augustine a new type of agapeic spirituality has been born. With Jesus, the apostles and Paul there was the spirituality of the witness for they and the Christians of the first three hundred years were such a challenge to Romans and Jews that they might be martyred. But once with Constantine the empire became Christian the spirituality of the witness shifted to the background and the figure of a new kind of holiness began to emerge with the great church fathers and for Augustine the struggle for chastity was right at the center. He very much is drawn by Platonic sublimation but in his *Confessions* as we see here there is a belief in the value of the body and the memory of bodily images that is not just dismissed. Plato's notion of the eternal extracted soul is not Augustine's belief in a resurrected body which will retain its bodily relations. They do have to be further purified and they can lead us to greater praise, petition and repentance which is the meaning of confession.

Part One: Joyful Beginnings

IV,3.8 For Augustinian sublimation is not Platonic

Plato moved from a lower *eros* to a higher *eros* and Augustine
tried to do that for three or four terribly bi-polar years.
But the black horse of lust, frustration and anger kept winning.
Then finally he read St. Paul and was given the grace that he
might be celibate and that was the key point of his conversion.
That, by the way, is what the Augustinian monk, Luther, was
never graced to do and thus began five hundred years of modernity.
The Platonist fell in love with a beautiful soul in a beautiful
body and that brought about a sublimation that Augustine wanted.
But that method of falling in love to receive the sublimation was
not the same for him as it was for Plato and for Kierkegaard,
for Dante and for Nietzsche and for some other Catholic celibates.
Jesus according to Catholics was celibate and those who will be
to be priests, nuns or monks seek to imitate him in his celibacy.
Paul in his first letter to his Corinthians at the beginning of Chapter 7
tells them that it is better to marry than to burn and then at verse 6
he goes on to write:

> I should still like everyone to be as I am myself;
> but everyone has his own gift from God,
> one this kind and the next something different.

Augustine was inspired first by the Platonists and then by Paul
to be a celibate in imitation of Jesus that he might become free
from self indulgence in order to serve God and the church of Christ.
For the Platonists there is vulgar and noble *eros* but there is no
noble vocation to marriage as Paul spells it out and thus
Augustine and his Catholics will come to believe in the seven
sacraments one of which is Holy Matrimony which Monica
wanted for her son and which will never be a vulgar *eros*.
Luther and all the protestants will not believe in Platonic celibacy
but they are not really following the whole of the Bible when
they ignore Paul and his celibacy which was also Augustine's.

Agape and the Four Loves

IV, 3.9 So is his conversion a Christian sublimation?

In order to reflect upon the ways of relating *agape* and the four loves throughout our Western history from Augustine, until our time it will be very helpful to consider Anders Nygren's great book *Agape and Eros*. He points out three major models in which *agape* is related to *eros*: (1) by the Gnostics and (2) by Catholics from Augustine to Luther who synthesize *agape* and *eros* and thereby destroy *agape* and (3) by the Lutherans and Reformers who protect *agape* from *eros*. Augustine's conversion was not a Platonic sublimation in which he moved from vulgar *eros* to the higher *eros* by falling in love with a beautiful soul in a beautiful body so that he loved Beauty itself. Rather when he read Saint Paul he was so touched by grace that he was freed from the slavery of lust that he might be free to serve others. That could be taken in a Lutheran direction in which we have faith in God's grace alone that can then let us go out to love our neighbor. But according to Nygren Augustine did not stop there with a pure sacrificial, altruistic *agape* in which we love others as God loves us. Augustine was not converted away from his Platonism in becoming a Christian and he still had a deep down egoistic love in which he loved God that he might be happy even here and now on earth. Also Nygren and Luther detect a self love in Augustine's celibacy which, however, was not only a Platonic ideal but also an ideal of Paul which Luther was never able to attain and which he came to criticize. So in seeking to follow scripture alone do not Luther and Nygren end up denying a lot of scripture which also sees *agape* as self-love? We are commanded to love our neighbor as we love ourselves but Nygren explains that away because it still has something of Jewish law from which the Gospel should also liberate us. So with Nygren we will explore three different models for relating *agape* and the four loves and we will see how postmodern arguments might take us beyond the modern arguments of Luther and Nygren and let us appreciate fully the mutual enhancement of *agape* and *eros*.

Part One: *Joyful Beginnings*

Gramma Goicoechea   Grampa Goicoechea

Daddy and his family at the time of his father's death

Agape and the Four Loves

His track team

His basketball team

Part One: *Joyful Beginnings*

The bounding Basque at 15

He taught us . . .

. . . to fish

Agape and the Four Loves

. . . and to hunt

Part One: Joyful Beginnings

Our log cabin

Gramma, Daddy, and me

The Lequeitio homestead

Part Two

Sorrowful Proceedings

Agape and the Four Loves

I. Father

I,4 Of starting a family in war time

I,4.1 With his first child his prayer-life grows

With the coming of his first child, Daddy's prayer-life moved
into a new phase, so that each prayer took on a new meaning.
He first began to pray when his father died, when he was five.
He identified with the mood of the mourning process and the prayers
of his mother and his sisters as they prayed for themselves
and for their father, now that they hurt so much without him.
Daddy began to pray the *Sign of the Cross*, the *Angel of God*,
the *Hail Mary* and the *Our Father* and they slowly took on for him
all the love and the devotion of his mother and his five sisters.
He fully believed in the spirit world and especially trusted that
that like his guardian angel, his father would look after him.
He said his prayers each morning and evening with his family
and the habit was established of falling asleep each night with
the name of Jesus on his lips and awakening each morning by
saying his list of prayers even before he got out of his bed.
When he was in jail for what seemed like such a long time,
his prayer went into a new phase of heart felt intensity.
Then, when he rode the rails and prayed there on the train,
he prayed that God would protect him and help him find work.
But now that his dear, sweet wife was pregnant, he slept
each night with his arm around her ever growing tummy.
He prayed that their new baby would be healthy and happy.
As he prayed: "Blessed is the fruit of they womb, Jesus," it seemed
that those words took on a new meaning, for just as he felt
his child in his wife's womb, so he now felt Jesus in Mary's.
And often, throughout the rest of his life, as he prayed those words,
that thought of her womb and its blessed fruit returned to him.
And on May 18, 1938, when he was 28, and Joneva was 20,
their baby boy was born and all his prayers were answered.
And everything that he wished he could have done with his father
he now knew that he would be able to do with his own son.

Part Two: Sorrowful Proceedings

I,4.2 He prays for a good job

Daddy had a certain taste for excellence that guided his vocation
and while he and mother shared a reverence for the holy, their
taste let them be opposites-that-attract as well as kindred spirits.
Mother loved the Mormons and their farming family values and
during that first summer of baby David's life, they lived in Carey.
Besides dealing some poker games, Daddy drove a dairy milk truck.
But, Ketchum-Sun Valley at the other end of Blaine County, only 48
miles North, up into the mountains, was a totally different world.
It was Daddy's kind of place, with its bustling night life and its
emphasis on all kinds of sport and especially its fishing and hunting.
The vast difference between the hunter-gatherer shamanic life
and the agricultural culture and Daddy's excellence in the former
made of him for mother a mix of the fascinating and the frightening
that nearly made her tremble for gambling is a dangerous play.
Daddy took a few trips to Ketchum and kept scouting it out.
Several new night clubs had just been built and Sun Valley,
the Rocky Mountain's first ski resort, opened in that year of 1938.
Earnest Hemingway was given a free suite in the Sun Valley Lodge
for the sake of publicity and he wrote there *For Whom the Bell Tolls*.
In the Fall of '38, Daddy, Mother and Baby moved up to Ketchum
and lived in a little log cabin and Daddy dealt poker as *The Alpine*
for Lou Hill and became friends with other gamblers and Basques.
However, during the Summer, Mother was very happy that Daddy
decided to work building a road over Dollarhyde Summit
which Roosevelt's after the depression back to work program initiated.
They lived in one of her father's sheepcamps and Daddy enjoyed
the hard work and exercise and in the evenings he went fly-fishing.
He got to know Warm Springs creek and Penny Lake, which he
would continue to fish for the rest of his life, with his four sons.
But with the coming of winter, Daddy did very well dealing cards
and they even had enough money to start building a brand new house.

Agape and the Four Loves

I,4.3 *His prayers are answered*

Daddy's prayers were answered and by the time he reached thirty, all seemed to be going exceedingly well with his work and family life. Joneva became pregnant again and they were living in their new home. He worked about five nights a week and would usually arise around 10:30 or 11:00 am and while he had his cup of coffee he said his prayers. He was very thankful for everything seemed to be going just his way. He had a wonderful job that he really loved, for he could hardly believe that he would be making so much money playing cards and growing in the skills of reading people, bluffing and remembering the cards. With his strong competitive spirit, he loved being a win win winner. His wife was the love of his life and he loved her more each day. His little boy was becoming his play-buddy and already wanting to go fishing with him and as he was learning to talk, he was always asking his father questions, especially about the fish he caught. Daddy had several good friends uptown and some of the older Basques, especially Paul Sagusta and Leon Bilbao sort of mentored him along. They were telling him that perhaps he should get his own club since he was so charming with people and could gamble so well. He was awfully lucky to be in such an enchanting place just as Sun Valley was beginning to flourish and to make so much money. Everyone whom he loved greatly loved him: his boss, his wife, his little boy, his many friends and their affection, friendship and *eros* were all converging to bless him and he thanked God. As Christmas neared, Daddy thought of the word "Nativity" and his wife had told him that she would like another baby for three years seemed to be a good space between children and he listened. And as he prayed: "Holy Mary, mother of God, pray for us sinners," he realized why the *Hail Mary* was his favorite prayer and his mother's mother love and his wife's mother love brought him to love Mary's mother love and he thought his father must be praying for him even to Mother Mary and that his father's prayers were answered.

Part Two: Sorrowful Proceedings

I,4.4 Bette Jo is born and the war calls him

All was going so beautifully well, but in Daddy's thirty first year,
another totally unexpected shocking surprise came out of nowhere.
America had to enter the second world war and Daddy, because of his
slightly older age, was not called to fight but to go work in the
shipyard in Bremerton Washington and he had to get there soon.
His new beautiful, baby daughter, Bette Jo, had just been born
so he would drive the 600 mile trip and take their car and
a few belongings and mother, Bette Jo, and I took the long train trip.
As Daddy drove out there, he could hardly believe it, for they sold
their house to Whitey Hirshman, a fellow gambling friend who was
older and thus could stay in Ketchum, and another dream had ended.
As Daddy drove through new country alone, he kept thinking
about his life and it seemed that a pattern was beginning to form.
As a child, all was going so well and they got their Tuttle ranch
but then his father died and that beautiful dream came to an end.
But it was transformed and he became a star athlete and was
going to college and the future looked so bright, but he was put in jail.
He went through the tough times of the depression and road the rails
and he was afraid he might even starve to death and again for a
short time, he was put in jail and he could not find steady work.
But he was a survivor and what didn't kill him made him stronger.
And down in Nevada, he began to flourish as a prizefighter until
the big black boy broke his nose and put a definite end to that.
Then slowly everything began to come together, lovely piece by
lovely piece and he was amazed at how well it went and now,
all of a sudden, for the fourth or fifth time in his short life,
he was going from riches to rags, but, as always, he still had love.
He had his lovely wife, his little boy and his beautiful daughter.
Just out off the blue, he lost his job, his house and his freedom.
Now he was forced to go work in a shipyard, but he was a
survivor and often, as he drove, he prayed to be delivered from evil.

Agape and the Four Loves

I,4.5 *Serving his country in a shipyard*

In Washington State, near Seattle, we lived in a tiny town called
Port Orchard and Daddy took the ferry to Bremerton each morning.
He did his duty there for two years and then we were able to
go back to Idaho and start life all over, but, of course, not quite.
For the war would still be on and for those in the lower 20%
of the economic spectrum, there could be no real upward mobility.
But, meanwhile, back in Port Orchard, I was a real hand-full
for my poor dad, for at the age of four, I was already telling him
crazy lies and driving him to his wits end as to how to treat me.
He would take me down to the beech with him to catch crabs
under rocks and logs, and he loved to play with me and my
new sister, but he could not let me just get in the habit of lying.
We had a little shed out back and he left the key in the door.
I took it and was playing with it and he asked me if I had
seen it and without batting an eyelid, I simply said: "No."
Then he found the key in my room and he slapped my face
and he grabbed me with one had on my crotch and the other
on my shoulder and he shook me and yelled never to lie again.
I was crying like mad and he was worried and asked me
if he hurt me and I didn't lie and I sobbed out "Yes, you did."
I knew he was sorry, especially to have grabbed me
in the crotch, but subconsciously, those things happen, maybe
to let punishment do its job by making one afraid of getting it again.
Anyway, I will recount a series of these odd events which to this day
I do not understand, but I did need to be delivered from evil.
So Daddy had loved his job, his wife, his children, his friends
and now he was called upon to change so much and love his country.
But love starts to get complicated, for he would rather not have
had to leave gambling to come here and build ships, but he could
appreciate his wife's preference for real work to gambling and I
was his son, a chip of the old block in liking to raise a little hell.

Part Two: Sorrowful Proceedings

I,4.6 *Return to Carey and his wife's parents*

By being drafted for two years into the world war II program
of building ships in Bremerton, Washington, Daddy lost his job
of dealing poker games for Lou Hill and making unbelievable money.
They were able to build and pay for a new house in just two years.
But now, all that was gone and, as he prepared to go back to Carey
and live with his wife's parents and maybe drive the dairy truck,
he felt that things could only get better and, as a gambler,
he had a hunch that as soon as the war ended, Ketchum
would be a boom town again and he could flourish once more.
So late in the summer of 1943, when he was thirty three, they
returned to Idaho to begin another stage on life's way for the four
of them back where they felt at home, even if not yet in Ketchum.
That Fall and winter, with Gramma and Grampa Coates and
Mom's sister, Aunt Mid, and her youngest brother, Uncle Elwin,
Daddy, Mother, Bette Jo and I had a wonderful time of family fun.
Aunt Mid's husband, Uncle Tony, came home on a Furlough from
Europe and Daddy took him pheasant hunting up Little Wood river
by the old Parks Ranch and they soon came home with their limit.
That was the first time I saw those beautiful ringneck roosters.
As I was admiring them, Daddy asked me if I wanted to go get more.
When we got there, I had to wait in the car while they took their
shot guns and very soon came back with two more and I never
even heard a shot and I came to see how Daddy would poach.
Daddy provided fish and game for his family throughout the year
and, according to his hunter-gatherer taste, you could break the law.
The Little Wood river canal came right by the Coates' ranch and
under a bridge and in October, they shut it off and there were
puddles here and there and as I stood on the bridge, looking at one,
I saw fish swimming in it, so Daddy and Uncle El and the Carlsons,
who were neighbors, and I raked them out by the bucket full.
And all that winter, we had rainbow trout at least once a week.

Agape and the Four Loves

I,4.7 Being a farmer and a boxing coach

In the early Spring of 1944, we moved to the old Cameron Ranch on the South West end of Carey, right next to the lava beds and Daddy got a herd of fourteen Holstein milk cows and tried his hand at farming, which he had done, but which didn't suit his taste. With two horses from Gramma and Grampa Coats, he plowed the fields, planted the alfalfa and grain, and he irrigated the crops. Uncle El came to live with us and helped with the work and he was sixteen and I was six and we road the school bus together. Daddy had played basketball on the Carey town team and they hired him at Carey High School to be the boxing coach and his team of about twelve members won all their meets and Keith Hunt got a scholarship to the University of Idaho and made their team. Uncle El had a nanny goat and Daddy talked him into killing it and using it for Coyote bait on their own small trapline. They caught a bob cat, big male coyote and several magpies. In out little farm house, Daddy said his prayers each morning as he sat by the stove and drank his coffee and I used to sit next to him and I asked him to teach me how to pray too and that is the way he taught everything, by example, so that I wanted to. I still remember how, sixty five years ago, he taught me *The Sign of the Cross* and *The Angel of God*, and how he showed me just how to use my hands for *The Sign of the Cross* and before long, after saying them together each morning, I had them memorized and he mentioned I could pray each night before sleep. I wanted to pray with him just as I wanted to fish and hunt with him, and, one day, he and one of his friends were going fishing and wouldn't take me, so I hid in the back seat of the car on the floor. After we had gone about a half mile, I arose, smiling from ear to ear to announce myself and they immediately turned around and took me home and when we walked into the house to tell mother, Daddy pulled my ear a bit and told me to be good.

Part Two: Sorrowful Proceedings

I,4.8 *The war ends and Bobby Brian is born*

Daddy's farming career was one of mixed blessings, for many
things went wrong which a true farmer's savvy could have prevented.
A kitten was killed by a rattlesnake. The nanny goat was killed.
Tony, one of the horses, broke a leg and they had to shoot him too.
The milk cows caught a disease called garget and the milking
had to come to an end, which was our only source of income.
When we got ready to move, Dad built a trailer and we took
about twenty young chickens to my grandmother and a cover
was over the top of the trailer and all the chickens were suffocating.
When we got to Gram's, Daddy got into the trailer and started
pulling off all their heads and throwing them down to me so I
could put them in piles and they were jumping all over, spurting blood.
Gramma, Grandpa, Daddy and I picked and cleaned them
and then Daddy and I went to the Carey Hot Springs, swimming
pool there at Carey Lake to get clean and a snake came
swimming into the pool and swam across as Daddy and I watched.
Finally, the war ended and Daddy started driving up to Ketchum
to look for a job and Brian Coppinger helped him find a house
and Daddy was at once offered a job dealing poker in The Tram,
which was a beautiful Saloon owned by Paul Sagusta and Leon Bilbao.
Meanwhile, back at the Ranch, Bobby Brian, Daddy's second son,
was born at the Catholic Hospital in Wendell and again
Daddy's payers were answered, and as he would drive back
and forth to Ketchum, he prayed some extra *Hail Marys*
and *Our Fathers*, asking the Holy Mother to pray for him and his,
and asking God, the Father, to "give us this day, our daily bread" and
to deliver us from evil, for there seemed to be so much bad luck.
It seemed that finally everything was going to be so good again.
And they named Bobby Brian after Brian Coppinger and Mother
especially liked the Sisters at the Catholic hospital and she loved
to see her husband teach the children to pray and she wanted to also.

Agape and the Four Loves

I,4.9 Back to Ketchum and the good life once again

Deep down, Mother really wanted to stay in Carey and live the good,
clean family farming life, for she did not trust the night life
of gambling and drinking, and the whole Night Club party scene.
She had heard a saying: "Cigarettes and whisky and wild, wild
women, they'll drive you crazy, they'll drive you insane."
And she was afraid of that for her husband and even her children.
Daddy loved her more than any other woman, especially because she
was so pure and holy and happy and she was just like his mother.
And she loved Daddy and his special kind of Catholic reverence
which she had not known before, and so, together, they were now ready
to start a new life once again up there in beautiful Ketchum Sun-Valley.
They had enough savings to buy their little old two bedroom house.
By 1946, David was in the third grade, Bette Jo in the first,
and Daddy and Whitey Hirshman had their own Rhumba Club.
Once again, everything was going like a dream come true and
there was a lovely little Catholic Church and Father Dougherty
came up from Hailey and said Mass and Mother really liked him.
And he game her instructions and she learned the catechism as
she taught her son, David, as he prepared for First Communion.
And David went to The Good Friday Service, prayed *The Way
of the Cross* with the Ketchum community and some of Dad's friends.
And Daddy felt that he had lived through Good Friday already
at least five times: when his father died, when he got put in
jail and had to leave college, when he rode the rails during
the depression, when he got his nose broken and when he
had to leave his great job and go to work in the shipyard.
He didn't even count the failed farming episode, for that was
only a step toward getting back here to Ketchum and his life.
He had known the rhythm of Good Friday and then Easter Sunday
and now he felt like he was ready for Easter forever and
he did not have Mother's premonitions that Good Friday was near.

Part Two: Sorrowful Proceedings

I,5 Of raising a family when shot

I,5.1 Daddy gets shot but it makes him stronger

In 1947, in the middle of October, on a Friday afternoon after school, Daddy drove Mother, Bette Jo, Bobby and myself down to Carey to visit Gramma Coates while he and his friend Brian went deer hunting. But on Saturday afternoon Brian came to get us and told us that he had shot my Dad and that he would take us to see him in the hospital. Daddy's ankle bone had been blown out and they stuck a handkerchief into the hole to keep him from bleeding too much and Brian helped him to get down from the mountain and to the car by nearly carrying him. Dr. Fox, who had delivered myself and Bette Jo, got as much of the shattered bone out of the wound as he could and when we got to his room he had a cast on his foot and lower leg. Whitey Hirschman would continue to run the Rhumba club and Daddy would get some money from that, but here he was again without work. Every time in his life when things were looking great some crisis came. As he lay in bed, day after day and week after week, he saw how he was dealt a very good hand and then a very bad one and a few in between and he began to see that life is like a poker game and that you have to know how to place your bets if you want to win. He had never heard of Pascal's wager, but he came to a similar insight and he began to take great pride in being a gambler so that when he wrote his memoirs for his niece, he signed it "The Gambler". As a gambler you have to know when to hold and when to fold. His secret was never to lose much so that if you have a bad hand you do not usually try to bluff, but you just lose your ante and you let the others fight it out and when your cards are good enough so that you think you can win you really go for it. Nietzsche's highest affirmation is also like Pascal's wager and had to do with Daddy's taste for himself as a win win winner who would just wait through the bad hands and not bet on them. Now, he was dealt another terrible hand but "what doesn't kill me, makes me stronger" and he wasn't dead, but only a cripple for life.

Agape and the Four Loves

I,5.2 Clifford Scott is born while Daddy is still laid up
Daddy's ankle did not heal quickly and it never healed completely.
Doctor Moritz up at Sun Valley where he set many fractured legs
for skiers, re-broke the ankle and cleaned out all the bone fragments.
For nearly two years Daddy walked on crutches and the once proud
athlete was now a limping cripple and his lifestyle changed.
In 1948, The Republicans got in with the platform that they would
outlaw gambling in The State of Idaho so the second big blow
at that same time for Daddy was that he and Whitey had to sell
the Rhumba Club and he could no longer make money by gambling.
Up until then he always dressed in good looking suits and a tie
but now his self image began to change as he realized he would
have to be a working man and he thought he would work at Sun Valley.
Most of the gamblers decided to move to Nevada where gambling was
still legal, but Joneva didn't want that and he loved Ketchum.
While he was still bed ridden, his beautiful wife conceived of their
fourth child and if he were a boy they would call him Clifford Scott.
As Daddy lay in bed for months and reviewed his life as a gambler
and pondered his hand he thought of his good friend, Clifford Toone,
who was such a good athlete back there in high school and names
for children were very important for Daddy and that was the right name.
And on January 24th, 1948, the coldest day of that year, Clifford
was born and Daddy prayed and somehow knew that Cliff
would be a great athlete and person just like himself and Clifford Toone.
So Daddy saw that he was dealing with the worst hand of his life.
He was ready to fold on this one, but he also saw that he was also
at the same time getting the cards for the best hand of his life as
his children were growing up and as he prayed for them each day.
His prayer life now took on a further dimension as he suffered
in this new way and it became the fuel of his love, for his suffering
transformed into prayer was for him what gas is for a car.
And he saw that his limping future would be more loving for all of his.

Part Two: Sorrowful Proceedings

I,5.3 *Daddy begins his new life as a day laborer*

A most important part of Daddy's self image was to be a good
provider and as soon as he could he began to work for Sun Valley
as a ski-lift operator on Bald Mountain and his ankle could stand that.
Then in the Summer he worked on The Ground Crew and helped keep
Sun Valley well groomed and for the first time since Bremerton
he had to sleep at night in order that he might work all day.
On his weekends off he would go uptown and socialize and drink
through the night and they saw themselves as the town fathers.
Some of them began to play pinocle for money and Ted Weary
at the casino felt that that was safe even if a law officer came in.
Daddy would never go to communion if he had been drunk unless
he had gone to confession and so each Sunday until Christmas
or Easter he would not go up for communion with most of the others.
And in those days quite a few would not receive if they had sinned.
Father Heeren, a young priest from Ireland, replaced Father Dougherty
and he was always very kind and good humoured with Daddy, but
most of all, Mother greatly appreciated his spiritual advice and
Holy Mother Church began to help our family in many important ways.
Daddy's highest priority was that his children do well in school
and all get through college and get good jobs as he had wanted to do.
When I was in the third grade I brought home a report card with
very bad grades and Daddy studied with me several evenings a week.
I got straight A's but then the next time the grades were bad again.
So again as the good coach that he was and with his own discipline he
was able to be a teacher for me and from then on I got good grades.
Father Heeren taught us Catechism once a week in the little church
right next to our school and I learned the art of memorization from
the Baltimore Catechism so the school, the church and the home
were our three sources of education and they worked well together.
Daddy's new life style had begun and he was providing for and
caring for his family, but he did not like working for Sun Valley.

Agape and the Four Loves

I,5.4 *Daddy's fourth son, Tommy Joe, is born*

On April 23, 1950, Thomas Joseph was born and Mother named him
after her two favorite men at the time, her husband and Father
Thomas Heeren, and for Mother and Father, names were very important.
And Daddy was so happy to have his wonderful daughter and
his four sons who could carry on the name Goicoechea and he was
the only boy in the family and he sometimes expressed his pride
in making sure that the name would live on in many Goicoecheas.
And Bette Jo and Tommy Joe both had his name and years later, when
his first grandchild was about to be born, he asked: "What are you
going to name that little boy?" and his name became Joseph Robert,
after his grandfather and my brother, Bobby, his godfather.
And the little old Ketchum house was pretty well filled now with
double bunks for four boys in one bedroom, Mother and Daddy in the
other bedroom and Bette Jo slept on a couch in the front room.
I was twelve years old now and Daddy bought me a fly-rod when
I was eleven, so I went fishing with him in the evening at least
twice a week and we fished our favorite spots on Sliver Creek,
Trail Creek, Warm Springs, Big Wood River and various beaver ponds.
His ankle was now strong enough to walk the streams with waders
and we became great friends as we ate our peck of salt together.
And still sometimes I would do the oddest things such as once I had
a sore on my tongue and when Mother asked what happened, I said
that a neighbor boy who was three years older than myself had
pinched my tongue with a pair of pliers and she told my Dad.
So he asked the boy's mother and when she asked the boy he swore
on his scout's honor that he never did such a thing and when she
told this to my Dad he confronted me and I could really say nothing.
So he slapped me a few times and told me never to tell lies again.
By now I was already serving Mass on Tuesday, Friday and
Sunday mornings, and Father Heeren mentioned to me the seminary
where he had gone and I began to think about being a priest.

Part Two: Sorrowful Proceedings

I,5.5 *Daddy was not suited to work for others*

Daddy grew more and more unhappy working for Sun Valley on The
Chair Lift and on The Ground Crew and he often talked with Joneva
about having to find some kind of work where he could be his own boss.
He talked with his friends uptown and she talked with Father Heeren.
It was suggested to him that many of the places in town really needed
a reliable garbage man, and Mother thought that would be a good idea.
So Daddy bought an old truck and started cleaning up the town and
many families signed up and he would pick up their trash once a week.
In three days of good, hard work, he could take care of his route.
So far the next thirteen years, he was his own boss and he and his
sons who helped him kept people happy and the town clean.
Daddy felt that he was playing a good hand for he had a way of life
that he thought was good for his family given the circumstances.
His passion was to be the best Dad possible and that total passion
let him evaluate how to choose one thing rather than another and it
motivated him to work hard and faithfully for his family values.
He became more and more of an alcoholic as he went uptown and
drank with his friends about five times a week, but as his
children grew so did his love for them and he prayed for them daily.
He was no longer the proud, well-dressed gambler who made lots
of easy money, and even with a certain shame in his old clothes
and with his stinking old garbage truck and even feeling a certain
shame for his children he was becoming a prouder and prouder Dad.
In my Baby Book, under a section called "Recognition of Father," Mother
wrote "David thinks his Dad is a play-fellow" and he was that
for with his children he was like a playful, joyful child
and each one of us was a favorite of his in our own special way.
And we always loved each other just as he and Mother loved each other
and just as he and his mother and sisters loved each other and
especially sacrificed themselves that he might get his special education
and his passion was born of his family's passion and his wife's passion.

Agape and the Four Loves

I,5.6 We can live like kings

Daddy had a certain kind of Basque poetry about him and just as I
was graduating from the eighth grade he said to me that if I wanted
we could each morning clean out Louie Accaturri's Sawtooth Club
and I could help him with the trash route and we could live like Kings.
There is a saying that "Every Basque is a King" and even though we
would be the lowliest of janitors and garbage haulers Daddy truly
felt that and in some way it was true for as a fourteen-year-old, I
made more money that summer than the other kids and I needed it,
because that Fall I would be going away to study to be a priest.
So, each morning, Daddy and I would get to the Sawtooth at about nine
in the morning and clean the floors and stock the beer into the cooler.
Even though Gambling had gone out in '48, Slot Machines were still
legal and a couple of times a woman was still there playing the nickel
and dime machine when we got to work in the morning and I played
the machines a bit during our break and Daddy told me about them.
They were set to pay out so much and you should play when they paid.
That summer I got to know much better some of the people in our town
as we stopped at their homes and got their trash and we did work hard,
and very often we went trout fishing in the evening and we caught some
big Bass that Summer down at Carey Lake, and I could fish for them
with Streamer Flies and Chest Waders just as well Dad's friends.
And that Summer, my mother had a miscarriage and an hysterectomy
and I went up to the hospital to see mother with my Dad and he took her
Rosary and he kissed it when he put it in his pocket and our second
little sister, who died was named Mary Teresa, and Daddy and I dug
her grave at the Ketchum cemetery and we ate our peck of salt together.
And very early that September after our Summer of living like Kings,
Father Heeren came to our house for dinner and then we picked up
David LaPrise, my friend, and we began our drive to Mount Angel.
We said the Rosary together and slept in a motel and Daddy's dream
began to become true as his first child went away to begin his schooling.

Part Two: Sorrowful Proceedings

I,5.7 For Basques church and family went together

In my Baby Book, in the section entitled "Attitude toward other children"
Mother wrote: "David liked little children and was very affectionate
towards them." I learned this by identifying with both mother
and father for their *agape* let their affection flourish.
The death of Daddy's father increased their family affection
and their hard times and suffering fueled their love.
Their daily prayers together was their agapeic love that schooled them
in praise, love, worship and adoration; in asking for forgiveness,
healing, deliverance and salvation; in being thankful for their blessings,
gifts, graces, and moments of inspiration and in begging for the grace,
inspiration, love and mercy that they needed to have wonderful lives.
Daddy's affection and *agape* went hand in hand helping each other grow.
Daddy, with his happy-go-lucky joy and laughter was always friendly
and he always had his inner circle of terrific friends which went
back to his high school days when as athletes they truly were the other
half of each other's soul and that always continued through his life.
Brian Coppinger after whom he named Bobby Brian and who shot him
became even a closer friend as they lived through the accident together.
Art Winters used to come get him not too long after he was shot to take
him downtown for a bit of card playing and Art was one of the first
to lead the way to the Bass fishing at Carey Lake and to teach us how to
clean the bass and how to cook them and how to really enjoy them.
And Daddy loved wing shooting, especially with Ted Tittenger and
he was good friends with the Basque Gamblers who moved to Nevada.
And in Daddy's friendship there was an affection and an *agape* as
can be seen in his naming of two of his children Brian and Clifford.
And, of course, the erotic love of Daddy's life was Mother, and he was
so glad to see her become such a holy Catholic and his two sisters
Claudia and Dorothy, helped her to better understand the Rosary.
And Daddy's prayer life was very simple, with just a few prayers
but their praise, repentance, thanksgiving and petition filled his life.

Agape and the Four Loves

I,5.8 *The worst of times were the best of times*

Even though Daddy was the town drunk and would often come staggering home Mother and we children and his friends could see through his faults and know and love his loving heart and mind. Love is not blind and can see all kinds of good in the loved one. As he talked with his friends about life and looked back over his life he saw that out of the worst could come the best and that all started when the death of his father brought such an intensity of love into his family and he saw that the worst suffering brings out the best love. Daddy came to know intimately and even to reflect upon that saying: "Blessed are the poor, for they shall inherit the Kingdom of God." He saw how being poor brought his Mother and sisters to rely more on Holy Mother Mary and on Holy Mother Church and to really live in that special kingdom of love in which his family was now living. His daughter Bette Jo was such a good student that he never had to work with her on her homework and now Bobby was also becoming an Altar Boy and first Cliff and then Tom loved to wrestle and play with him and he began to take them fishing and hunting. And the great thing about the trash route was that as they grew up they could each help him and save money for college and live like Kings. He came to think that it wasn't so terrible after all that gambling was outlawed and that he got shot and even had to be a garbage man. He also saw that it was good to be humble and he even took pride in being humble and poor and lowly because he saw that that could motivate his children to want to be the best just as he had always wanted. The relation between sorrow and joy, or, as he would put it, between suffering and being happy-go-lucky, dawned on him more and more. You could be more happy-go-lucky if you had had a lot of bad luck which could help you appreciate the good luck and which could deepen your passion in loving your family than if there were no suffering. Of course, everybody suffers and everyone has their cross to bear and Daddy clearly saw that the worst of times are the best of times.

I,5.9 Lives in the spirit

By 1955, when Daddy was forty five, suffering continued to come his way and as he put it he had to have all his teeth yanked out. He didn't like false teeth so he was now a limping old gummer and one of Betty Jo's friends asked her: "Who is that old man that drives that dirty old truck? Is he your father or your grandfather?" Bette Jo was a bit embarrassed but she only loved her Dad the more. For Daddy and his family lived in the realm of the spirit and that world of *Agape*, which he began to know when he was five now came to have five noticeable dimensions for them. When he prayed *The Our Father*, God, the Father became more and more real for him and in some Basque way, he identified with the Father God when he prayed:

> Glory be to the Father, and to the Son
> and to the Holy Spirit,
> as it was in the beginning, is now,
> and ever shall be, world without end. Amen.

He became more and more aware of the three persons of the Trinity and of the God who is love, but, whereas his mother, sisters, and wife would be especially fond of the Sweet Jesus that was not quite his taste, even though he did appreciate their feminine taste. And as he said *The Hail Mary* each morning and night, he really did ask her to pray for him and his family and his loved ones. And as he said *The Angel of God*, he was aware of that third dimension and he taught *The Angel of God* first to all his children. And besides the dimension of God, of Mary and of The Angels, there was the communion of Saints and his father was there, needing his prayer and praying for them and more and more he kept loving the realm of the blessed dead and then finally there are all of us here and he and his lived in this world. And Daddy knew that all the Basques lived in this world as spirit and he was so happy that his wife had converted to it with him.

Agape and the Four Loves

I,6 Of being an alcoholic garbage man

I,6.1 Daddy's mid-life crisis

From his mid-forties to his mid-fifties Daddy's loved ones
and his faith, hope, love and prayer graced him through
his mid-life crisis as his tormenting addictions increased.
By 1956, when he was 46 years old his garbage route was
flourishing as he worked very hard cleaning up the town.
Most of all at the very center of his life his wife and children
were the dear ones of his affection and he was deep-down happy
to be able to work for them and to provide for them as he saw
each of them doing so well and moving toward fulfilling his dreams.
His wife like his mother and sisters was in his eyes the picture
of perfection as she in her sweet, lovely, happy, saintly way
cared for him, their children and all with intelligence and industry.
At Mt. Angel with the Benedictines I had finished High School
and Daddy was pleased with my grades and so happy that
Holy Mother Church was raising me in the best way possible.
Bette Jo was the top student in her second year of High School
and Bobby, Cliff and Tom were each doing very well in Grade School
and Bobby who was now twelve was beginning to help him
with the trash route to save money to go away to university.
Daddy had a few good friends downtown in the different clubs
and he had more fun each year fishing and hunting
especially with each of his sons as they became his partners.
His wife was deeply bonded with him not only in affection and
in friendship but Father Denardis, who was now her spiritual adviser,
told her that each time she and her husband made love it was a
further Consummation of the sacrament of their holy matrimony.
Her husband had always been such a wonderful lover and she
knew that he felt that their love making was growing in loveliness.
Her *agape* joined with his and brought new opening dimensions
to their affection, friendship, *eros* and to his friendship with all.
And yet with all of this his addictive afflictions were also growing.

Part Two: Sorrowful Proceedings

I,6.2 With cigarettes, whiskey and gambling

The *agape* of Daddy's Basque culture had a permissive attitude
quite unlike that of the Mormons, for it almost seemed to encourage
smoking, drinking and gambling not to mention coffee and sweets.
As a youth at the Boarding House he began to develop his skill
at gambling and up at the sheep camp with Uncle Pete he watched
him say his morning prayers as he had his cup of coffee
and then roll his cigarette after they finished their breakfast.
Even his mother would sometimes have a glass of red wine
and Daddy got a bit even as a kid and by his early twenties
he was drinking beer and hard stuff with his friends with gusto.
Mother had mentioned through the years without ever nagging
that all these habits would catch up with him and now he was
beginning to see the results that could come to addicted ones.
He had already lost his teeth and his doctor told him that the rash
on his face could develop into skin cancer and he advised him
to stop both his smoking and his drinking that was dangerous.
But the affliction of his addiction meant first of all that he
really needed to smoke and drink or he would be very miserable.
As he came into his mid-life crisis all was going well
for all his loved ones but not so well for his own poor body.
Even though gambling was outlawed he was gambling more
and more and he was beginning to run a poker game for
Ted Weary at the Casino and they started splitting the profits.
He worked hard hauling garbage during the week and on Friday
evening he would start a poker game that might last all night.
He loved to clown around and perhaps play the drunken fool
to sucker the rich Sun Valley guests into a game where they thought
they could easily beat this old gummer with his slurred speech.
So Daddy's addictions were a mixed bag in which he was
threatening his health and yet beginning to save thousands
of dollars in coffee cans in the basement from his poker winnings.

Agape and the Four Loves

I,6.3 Bette Jo is accepted at Portland University

As Daddy underwent more and more the affliction of his addiction
he primarily prayed each morning and evening for his children.
He did not yet really pray for himself and for his own healing
and his prayers were being answered for Bette Jo was accepted
at Portland University with a scholarship which was run by
the Holy Cross Fathers who also ran Notre Dame in Indiana.
Daddy was a gregarious extrovert who loved talking with his
friends and many acquaintances and even strangers around the bar.
If any man fooled around with women Daddy thought of him
as a punk kid and against almost any local in town he upheld
the values of a university education or as he put it "going to college".
So he told many about David's studying Latin and Greek in the
seminary and now he could brag about Bette Jo at Portland U.
He even became known by the young students working at Sun Valley
as a sort of strange phenomenon to behold for here he was
a totally dilapidated old, alcoholic garbage man almost preaching
from his pulpit with a bottle of beer in his hand on the values
of a good education and even the values of faith and loving prayer.
He looked like a contradiction in terms or even a hypocrite.
And yet he got much more exercise than most of his age
with all the work he did of lifting heavy cans of garbage and
shoveling crap out of his truck at the dump and eventually
he got a dump truck hoist so he could just have it dumped.
And he did go to Mass faithfully each Sunday and he did get
out fly fishing a couple evenings each week so underneath
it all he was a very genuine though paradoxical character.
By now I had finished my six years at Mt. Angel Minor Seminary
and was ready to go to the Major Seminary in Seattle, Washington.
After three years of Summer work in the Inn Kitchen and then three
more Summers as a night janitor I was now working on the
Trail crew up on Baldy and Daddy and I started salmon fishing.

Part Two: Sorrowful Proceedings

I,6.4 *Bobby goes to Mt. Angel*

Daddy's prayers continued to be answered for as soon as
his son, David, left Mt. Angel his son, Bobby, after a year
at the local high school, decided to go to Mt. Angel Seminary.
Bobby was an artist by nature and was the first to try
seriously hunting with a bow and arrow for mule Deer.
Bow season opened early and Daddy took us up Wood River
and Bobby got a shot with his long bow but missed.
Tom would go on following Bobby's example to become
a great bow hunter and he and his sons would be the best.
But in the Summer of 1960, the big thing was the salmon fishing.
Up until then we had used store bought salmon eggs with very
little success, but Daddy started curing his own fresh cluster eggs
and right away we had a terrific summer as he caught sixteen
and I caught ten and we went nearly every Friday afternoon
from around the 4th of July until nearly the middle of August.
He had his little list and would make sure he got everything
for Friday evening dinner and Saturday breakfast and lunch.
Our two sleeping bags were on a mattress in his Plymouth suburban
and soon after going over Galena Summit on the new paved road
we dropped down into the headwaters of the River of No Return.
He had plenty of ever new stories especially about salmon fishing
to tell me on the way and we would talk about baseball and sports.
I had actually gone salmon fishing with him for the first time
when I was about eight years old on the East Fork of the Salmon.
But this year we first started having luck at the Sheep Bridge Hole
just a few miles before crossing the water coming from Red Fish Lake.
After our dinner with sheepherder spuds and some evening fishing
and a good night's sleep we arose at daybreak and Daddy lit
his premade campfire upon which was his coffee pot and I began
to fish the head of the hole and he the middle and at about sunup
he got about a twenty pounder and I got a sixteen pound Chinook.

Agape and the Four Loves

I,6.5 *Donny dies and I leave the seminary*

Throughout the Summer of 1961, Daddy and the rest of the family were each wondering what was going on with me for I would often go up to the Valley in the evening and not get home 'till 10:30. That Summer when I was twenty-three I met Jane Sheldon who was nineteen and I fell in love with here and thus my late nights. One evening she told me that she met this old man down in Ketchum at a bar and she heard he was my father and she wanted to talk with me about him but I didn't want to go there. I had a certain shame and I didn't want her associating me with him and I didn't want to explain the man behind the appearance. As we will see as we go along it is almost as if he tried to do certain things that would shame us as if maybe to motivate us. Just as he when young had a passion for excellence to show that his dear father had not come here and died for nothing so maybe he unconsciously felt that we would strive for excellence to show that this crazy old man was really the greatest after all. He had now come to his fiftieth year and what would turn out to be his skin cancer was getting worse and he was gambling more and more. That August his nephew, Donny, died who was the helpless child of his dear sister, Claudia, and his dear mentor, Uncle Pete. We drove down for the funeral and seeing all his family and feeling once again the power of death that can fuel our passion, just as gas fuels a car, he began to think of giving something to his children even before he died if that could possibly be. He decided to save five big red coffee cans and he would put ten thousand dollars in each of them to give to his five children when Tommy the last of them would graduate finally from college. And he had a hunch that I might leave the seminary because he had heard about my girl friend and he told me to tell him first so that he could gently break the news to my mother. And after nine years I did come home from the seminary that Fall.

Part Two: Sorrowful Proceedings

I,6.6 Gramma Goicoechea dies

After the death of Donny it seemed that death after death kept
coming his way and when he was fifty two his mother dearest
passed away to be with her first husband and his father once again.
Now he prayed for both his father and his mother and asked them
each day to pray for him and all of his and now he felt closer
to his mother than he had ever since he was separated from her.
Before she had been many miles away and now she was just
a prayer away and he knew that she could mother him again.
And perhaps under her influence when he went to confession
at Christmas time he did begin to think about stopping his drinking
and even his smoking but the gambling was going better than ever.
Because his wife did not like his gambling he did not even tell her
about the coffee cans he had hidden in the basement and he knew
that his mother with her Basque instead of Mormon *agape* was
not opposed to playing cards and winning a few dollars.
Of course, he wouldn't want his own children smoking, drinking
or even gambling especially if they didn't savvy the game.
That same year that Gramma Goicoechea died I went to Loyola
of Chicago to start working on a Ph.D. in philosophy and Daddy
was glad that I got a fellowship and did not need money.
In the meanwhile Bette Jo had transferred to Gonzaga University,
another Jesuit University in Spokane, Washington, and again Daddy
was proud that two of his children were studying at universities
that were run by the Jesuits since that order was founded by a Basque.
Daddy always wore his emotions on his sleeve and he was very
black and white either for something or against it and he could
often get very angry very quickly and he confessed that too.
And even though at his bi-annual confessions he prayed
that he firmly resolved to amend his life it seemed that it
just couldn't happen for his anger and his using the name
of the Lord his God in vain were as habitual as his smoking.

Agape and the Four Loves

I,6.7 *Daddy's anger and his swearing*

And perhaps deep down his anger and his swearing were
a more deeply rooted part of his mid-life crisis than even
his smoking and his drinking which could relax his frustration.
One time Zygmunt Adamczweski an older philosopher and mentor
with whom I taught and from whom I learned a great deal said
to me: "You must have had a very good father." and I don't know
exactly what he meant, but perhaps he felt I related to him
as I would relate to my father with respect and no messing around.
That is the way it was with me and Daddy for he got angry
at me and really knocked the hell out of me about five times.
That really did get rid of the hell in me at least around him and
and I came to know anything that would anger him and I knew
how to avoid it and be on my best behaviour simply out of fear.
And in his shamanic Basque culture where the braves followed
the chief with no ifs, ands or buts I knew the fear of the Lord.
I knew of a deep down everlasting love and mercy but I also
knew of the rods of men and how to behave around authorities.
None of his children became addicted to smoking or to drinking
and perhaps I am the only one with the habit of anger and swearing.
While I would smile at everything and never get angry around him
I too confess my anger and swearing all the time without improvement.
No doubt he would have preferred to have finished college and
to have been a math teacher and athletic coach in High School and
failing that he did take pride in being a dealer in a nice Casino
and dressing sharply in suit and tie and being the hero he had been.
But the game of life dealt him this most humble life of being
a garbage man and maybe he did feel some shame and frustration.
But being the poetic story teller that he was he lived like a king
and if anyone didn't treat him like a king he let them know it.
He knew he had the loveliest, most wonderful wife he could imagine
and with her he was raising children of whom he could be proud.

Part Two: Sorrowful Proceedings

I,6.8 A year of graduations

By 1963, Ketchum was growing and so was the garbage route.
Bobby helped him during the summer vocation and Cliff who
was now in the 8th grade helped him during the school year.
A neighbor by the name of Joe Clements began to help him
and even started learning how to be a good salmon fisherman.
That Spring there were three graduations in the family and
Daddy felt that that College education for each of his children
was now a sure bet, and he knew that his wife was a big part
of that success story for she too lived the intellectual life.
Cliff graduated from the 8th grade and was an excellent athlete.
Bette Jo got her bachelor of arts degree from Gonzaga and
right away got a job as a parole officer for delinquent girls.
David got his Master's degree in philosophy at Loyola and
on August 5th, on the feast day of Our Lady of the Snows who is
the Patron of the Parish of Ketchum-Sun Valley, he married
a wonderful lady Wilhelmina van Wersch in the Chicago cathedral.
She was a nurse from Limburg in Southern Holland, and when
Daddy and Mother met her the winter before they were so happy
that their son was marrying such a holy, caring person.
Daddy began talking with some of his friends about selling
the trash route which was now getting to be quite valuable.
He was proud to own the Franchise and with many new
homes being built it was really getting to be almost too much.
And besides, his poker game down at the casino was also
doing so well that he thought he would rather play more
cards and retire from the hard work of all that heavy lifting.
Cliff and Tom could probably still earn great money helping
whomever would buy it for Cliff already knew the route well.
As he thought of selling it Daddy began to think that in some ways
it had been the best of jobs because it was so good for his sons.

Agape and the Four Loves

I,6.9 *A new daughter-in-law*

By the time Daddy was 55 a new phase of life was beginning.
He had lived through his mid-life crisis and even though he was
still smoking, drinking, gambling, getting angry, and swearing,
the success of his family life was now obviously flourishing.
Bobby in that graduation year of 1963, also graduated from Mt. Angel
Seminary High School and he decided not to be a Benedictine Monk
but to go out to Loyola of Chicago and to study to become a poet.
I had been living with Mr. Kelling until I married and now
Bobby moved in with him to care for him for free room and board.
Wilhelmina and I went out to Ketchum that summer and Mother
called her Willie and she was a forerunner of the other dearest
daughters-in-law to come and in their Catholicism those
Limburgers from Southern Holland were as devout as Basques.
At Sunday Mass Mother and Daddy and Wilhelmina and I knelt
side by side and prayed for each other and the rest of the family.
Tom and Cliff served Mass and Bette Jo made her European trip
and visited family in the Basque Land and some of Wilhelmina's family.
Wilhelmina and I went to Carey and stayed with Gramma Coates.
We met Aunt Mid and Uncle Larry and their children, Wes and Leila.
We took brother Tom and Cousin Wes on a fishing trip over
Trail Creek Summit and then back over Fish Creek summit.
We all stayed in our tent and caught oodles of trout and
feasted on sheepherder spuds and visited the very ponds
where Uncle Pete's sheep camp used to be and where Daddy first
started fly fishing and ate sheepherder spuds with Uncle Pete.
When Wilhelmina told Daddy about all this he had a great time
telling her stories about growing up high on the wild, fishing,
hunting and even trying to catch a wild horse which never happened.
As Daddy had such a good time with his new daughter-in-law
it almost seemed as if his mid-life crisis was fading away
and though he still suffered afflictions of addiction he was happy.

II. Nietzsche

II,4 Reconciling Plato with Jesus' kingdom of love

II,4.1 From the camel's virtue to the child's sacred yes

The original Zarathustra of Persia was the first to clearly establish
a physiology of the opposites with his journey from night to light.
Nietzsche's drama of Zarathustra unfolds the history of that heritage
by tracing it from the camel of Christian Platonism, to the lion of the
Enlightenment, to the lioness of the Romanticism, to the child of his
own post-modernity, which is the image he uses for Jesus and himself.

> What is heavy? asks the weight-bearing spirit,
> thus it kneels down like the camel
> and wants to be well-laden.

Plato and the Platonists climb up out of the cave on the ladder of love,
and, with their virtues of self-control, courage, wisdom and justice, they
become heroes of a weighty gravitas, with their hierarchy of virtue.
By practicing their physical, vital, intellectual and spiritual exercises,
they are able to appropriate beauty, goodness, truth and holiness.
They kneel in reverence before the form of forms, like the camel
and work with great effort to educate themselves with the literature
that goes beyond everyday myth, to science and mathematics, and
finally to philosophy, with its dialectical establishing of first principles.
Plato thinks that our souls have fallen from the world soul because
of a double burden of forgetfulness and wrongdoing, and thus we
can redeem ourselves with recollection, and that virtue that allows
our souls to become free from the body, to be one with the world soul.
In the first chapter of Book one *Of The Three Metamorphoses*,
Zarathustra says that:

> The child is innocence and forgetfulness
> a new beginning, a sport, a self-
> propelling wheel, a first motion, a sacred *Yes*.

Whereas Plato is guilty because of a forgetfulness that can
be redeemed by remembrance, the child is innocent in forgiving
and forgetting with a sacred *Yes* for every existing thing.
The child playfully loves the earth while Plato seriously flees it.

Agape and the Four Loves

II,4.2 *From body-despising after worldsmen to creativity*

For Plato, we are here in the bottom of this cave of illusion because
our soul has fallen into our body and will through rebirths arise
until finally it is purified through a recollection or remembrance
of the form of the one, true, beautiful Good, which it previously knew.
Plato's mystical way up the ladder of love out of the cave is thus
a great Gnostic way of salvation through proper knowledge of the form.
Plato's is a great spiritual philosophy, with its two ultimate principles
of the immaterial soul knowing the immaterial form as it was
in the beginning, should be now, and ever shall be, world without end.
An original evil within the world Soul brought bits of it to fall
into bodies here so that we can return through virtuous knowledge.
Our souls were not created in an original goodness, but evil was
there in the beginning, bringing us to birth because of ignorance.
So we are here now in the bottom of this cave, believing in shadows.
Thus, Platonists are Afterworldsmen, not believing in this world's
worth, but working hard to get beyond it to the one, true world.
These Platonists are despisers of the body, believing that the soul
should not be trapped in this body, but should rather free itself
from it, with the true love and knowledge of the true God beyond.
Serious men of gravitas will no longer be fooled into believing
that the body and material world are things of beauty and worth
but rather, in their wisdom, they will despise the world and the flesh.
From the child's point of view, which Nietzsche shares with Jesus,
nothing really new and good can be created in this Platonic world
and thus individuals can have no eternally recurring worth.
For Plato, all things come from an original evil and will be
individuals as long as that evil ignorance and vice persist.
The creative child must expose and say "*No*" to all this *No*-saying.
For only where there is creativity can there be an original good
for each and every individual in his or her eternal recurrence.
Jesus' *Yes*-saying-love lets Zarathustra see through Platonism.

II,4.3 Joyfully loving pale criminals

The love of Jesus and Zarathustra for all persons clarifies itself
by showing how it loves the good, even in the most wicked criminals.
Perhaps, he is a murderer and must pay the penalty of death.
As Zarathustra loves him and his condemning judge, he says:

> The thought is one thing, the deed is another
> and another yet is the image of the deed.
> The wheel of causality does not roll between them.
> An image made this pale man pale.
> He was equal to his deed when he did it:
> but he could not endure its image after it was done.

So the criminal had a good intention before he performed his crime.
But then, after the deed, he got another image that shocked him.
He bowed his head in guilt, and the judge could have a good image
of his condemning him, for he convinced the criminal to change images.
The judge is caught up in a sorrowful passion because he has to
condemn the criminal, but he can learn to joyfully suffer his passion.
Thus, Zarathustra loved the judge by saying to him:

> It is not sufficient that you should
> be reconciled with him you kill.
> May your sorrow be love for the Superman:
> thus will you justify your continuing to live.

Jesus is the Superman, whose joy overcomes sorrow by giving
meaning to the earth, the flesh and our life in the here and now.
It is exactly this criminal and this judge that will return again
and again throughout deep, deep, eternity because they are loved.
Zarathustra loves the criminal by teaching him that, even if
he comes from the race of the hot-tempered, or of the lustful,
or of the fanatical, or of the vindictive, his passions can become
virtues and joys, and all of his devils can become angels.
He need not have a Platonic image of his passions as vices,
for if he can but joyfully suffer them, they can be his virtues.

II,4.4 A dancing god gives his sermons on the mount

One evening, Zarathustra climbed a high mountain, and seeing a young man sitting sadly beside a gigantic lone tree, he said to him:

> This tree stands here alone on the mountain side;
> it has grown up high above man and animal . . .
> Now it waits and waits— yet what is it waiting for?
> It is waiting, perhaps, for the first lightening?

And the young man responded:

> Yes, Zarathustra, you speak true.
> I desired my destruction
> when I wanted to ascend into the heights.
> You are the lightening for which I have been waiting!
> It is my *envy* of you which has destroyed me.
> Thus spoke the young man and he wept bitterly.
> But Zarathustra laid his arm about him
> and drew him along with him.

A young man might Platonically seek to rise above the world, the flesh and the devil, but his passions increase as he denies them. But with lessons about *Reading and Writing*, Zarathustra says:

> untroubled, scornful, outrageous—
> that is how wisdom wants us to be:
> she is a woman
> and never loves anyone but a warrior.

That is the secret Jesus, the child of Lady Wisdom, knew as he spoke with cynical aphorisms and gave his sermon on the Mount. Zarathustra said:

> I should believe only in a God
> who understands how to dance.

And he said to the young man:

> By my love and hope, I entreat you . . .
> Keep holy your highest hope.

II,4.5 Saying no to ascetics and yes to warriors

Platonists are not only like Hindus but also like Buddhists, for as afterworldlings who despise the body, they are preachers of death.

> Yellow men or black men:
> that is what the preachers of death are called.

Like yellow robed Buddhists and black robed priests, they say:

> Lust is sin— let us go aside
> and beget no children.

Zarathustra points out that when:

> They encounter an invalid or an old man
> or a corpse, straightway they say:
> 'Life is refuted!'
> But only they are refuted,
> they and their eye
> that see only one aspect of existence.

From his many perspectives, Zarathustra sees good in all life.
And to Plato and yellow-robed and black-robed monks, he says:

> We do not wish to be spared by our best enemies,
> nor by those whom we love from the very heart.
> So let me tell you the truth.
> My brothers in war, I love you from the very heart.
> I am and have always been of your kind.
> And I am also your best enemy.

Plato, the Buddhists and the Priests are Zarathustra's best friends, for they are always seeking to overcome themselves and become greater. Even as heavily-laden camels, they are striving to be supermen. But he is also their best enemy by saying "*No*" to their *No*-saying. For they do say "No" to the body, the earth and even to this dear life.

> War and courage have done
> more great things than charity.
> not your pity but your bravery
> has saved the unfortunate up to now.

II,4.6 Plato's *Republic* and Luther's Nation State

In this chapter, "On The New Idol," Zarathustra begins to show how Plato and Luther belong together as the camels of Christian Platonism. The Lutherans had their famous formula: "*cuius regio, eius religio.*" "Whoever state it is, its his religion" and with the coming of modernity, there was no longer a Christian Europe of many peoples. These peoples were collected into a few warring Nation States. So it was in the vision of Plato's *Republic*, for the Greeks were three peoples with three cultures: Highlanders, Lowlanders, Islanders. If they could all unite under one Philosopher King, Highlanders could be warrior-guardians, Lowlanders farmers and Islanders traders. Such a division of labour would be efficient and make for power, prosperity, security and the leisure needed for the love of wisdom. But, this New Idol has all the shortcomings of the camel attitude.

> There are still peoples and herds somewhere
> but not with us, my brothers:
> here there are states . . .
> The state is the coldest of all cold monsters.

The state easily degenerates into secularity, with its values of power, prosperity and peace at any price, for

> It was creators who created peoples
> and hung a faith and love over them:
> thus they served life.

But this cold monster, the state, treats persons as superfluous and the leaders, who are preachers of death, only use them;

> Just look at these superfluous people!
> They acquire wealth and make themselves poorer with it.
> They desire power and especially the lever of power,
> plenty of money—these impotent people.

The Camel takes on the heavy burden of a virtue that can be used for power, prosperity and a peace that makes for constant war. Childlike peoples can more easily have a creative love and faith.

II,4.7 Why flies in attack Jesus and Zarathustra

Even though Zarathustra loves every single individual, he finds
that in the nation state of Plato, Luther and the Jews of Jesus' time,
the people who are but means to an end become bits of a mass society.
They are like flies in the market place who want to bite and suck
the blood out of creators like Jesus and Zarathustra, and poison them.

> They punish you for all your virtues.
> Fundamentally they forgive you only—your mistakes.
> Because you are gentle and just minded, you say:
> 'They are not to be blamed for their little existence.'
> But their little souls think:
> 'All great existence is blameworthy.'

Zarathustra learns that he should go into his solitude and be creative.
For the people have little idea of greatness, that is to say, creativeness.
As Zarathustra does his phenomenology of the camel attitude,
he sees that the masses who are treated only as means to an end
have a logic of exclusive opposites and demand that of him:

> But the hour presses them: so they press you.
> And from you too they require a Yes or a No.
> And woe to you if you want to set
> your chair between For and Against.

With his logic of mixed opposites, Zarathustra says *Yes* and *No*.
He says "*No*" to the *No*-saying of Platonic and Lutheran camels,
but he has a heartfelt loving *Yes* and *Amen* for every person
and especially for all the little people, just as did Jesus.
His perspectivism gives him his flexible *Yes* and *No*:

> Do not be jealous, lover of truth,
> because of these inflexible and oppressive men!
> Truth has never clung to the arm of an inflexible man.

Thus his inner voice commands him:

> Return to your security because of these abrupt men:
> only in the market-place
> is one assailed with Yes? or No?

II,4.8 Why Plato should be celibate but not Luther

As Zarathustra does his phenomenology of chastity, he lays out four different types, that of: the masses, Luther, Plato and himself and Jesus. He begins by saying:

> I love the forest. It is bad to live in towns:
> too many of the lustful live there . . .
> Is it not better to fall into the hands of a murderer
> than into the dreams of a lustful woman?
> And just look at these men: their eyes reveal it—
> they know of nothing better on earth than to lie with a woman.

The sexuality of the masses is not innocent as it is with the animals. Then he describes the likes of Luther:

> Those to whom chastity is difficult
> should be dissuaded from it
> lest it become the way to Hell—
> that is, to filth and lust of soul.

The great Plato discovered the art of sexual sublimation which he clarifies in his *Phaedrus* 245c, which produces a creative inspiration of Enthusiasm and Divine Madness, such as Nietzsche's. Kierkegaard and Nietzsche ushered in Post-modernity as it began in May, 1838 and August 1881 with Platonic sublimation. Thus Zarathustra makes distinctions:

> Do I exhort you to chastity?
> With some, chastity is a virtue,
> but with many it is almost a vice.

For Plato, Kierkegaard, Nietzsche and Dante, it was a virtue. But then, there is the fourth type, like Jesus and Zarathustra:

> Truly, there are those who are chaste from the very heart:
> they are more gentle of heart and they laugh
> more often and more heartily than you.
> They laugh at chastity too, and ask: "What is chastity?"

II,4.9 He is friend and best enemy of Plato and Luther

Zarathustra, the child, says "*No*" to the camel's *No*-saying, and yet good Platonists and good Lutherans are also his best friends for, as a hermit, he needs the third to take him from his depths to his heights:

> I and me are always too earnestly
> in conversation with one another:
> how could it be endured,
> if there were not a friend?
> For the hermit, the friend is always the third person:
> the third person is the cork that prevents the conversation
> of the other two from sinking to the depths.
> Alas, for all hermits, there are too many depths.
> That is why they long so much
> for a friend and for his heights.

With Plato, he shares that wonderful miracle worker-sublimation. There were many Lutheran pastors on both sides of his family and his father's spirit was a good shepherd for him, just like Jesus. However, Plato, with his one-sided spiritualism, denied the body and the earth, and, as an afterworldsman, was a preacher of death who proposed a Republic which used persons as superfluous things. As Plato despised the body and the earth for the sake of his soul and so Luther went to extremes with his exclusive logic of *Sola Scriptura* and *Sola Fidei*, for with scripture alone, he got rid of Plato and philosophy, and fifteen hundred years of tradition. With his faith alone, he got rid of good works and the prayer and work of the Benedictines and of Augustine's motto: Pray as if God does all and work as if you do all.
So Zarathustra says:

> In your friend, you should posses your best enemy.
> Your heart should feel closest to him
> when you oppose him.

Plato, Luther and Nietzsche can push each other to new heights.

Agape and the Four Loves

II,5 Reconciling Luther with Jesus' "resist not evil"

II,5.1 Beyond Luther to one humanity

In this chapter on a thousand and one goals, Zarathustra further describes the Camel mentality by showing how a thousand peoples have made themselves distinctive with different values. They each live according to their own good and their own evil, in accord with their geography, and as different from their neighbors.

> A table of values hangs over every people.
> Behold, it is the table of its overcomings;
> behold, it is voice of its will to power.

So here we first meet Zarathustra's leading concept of the will to power, in terms of which humans seek not only to survive, but to prevail with the best possible way of life:

> Zarathustra has seen many lands and many peoples:
> thus he has discovered the good and evil of many peoples.
> Zarathustra has found no greater power on earth
> than good and evil.

Luther, as the great protestor, set up a new table of values. He saw the Renaissance as evil, the pope as evil, the seven Holy Orders as evil, the seven sacraments as evil, Mariolatry as evil, monasticism, with its poverty, celibacy and obedience as evil, any religion except that of his scripture as evil and anyone trying to perform good works without faith as evil. But Zarathustra rises beyond good and evil and sees and loves the good in all as did Jesus, who did not resist evil and thus Zarathustra says:

> Yet tell me, my brothers:
> if a goal for humanity is still lacking,
> is there not still lacking—humanity itself?

Zarathustra, like Jesus, sees all humanity as brothers and sisters, whereas Luther ushered in modernity by standing alone before God. In meditating on Luther, who most of all denied the Pope, we might consider Book four and the chapter "Retired From Service".

II,5.2 Love not the nearest but the most distant

Agape's second commandment is "Love your neighbor as yourself."
But neighbor can mean only the one who is near, and that is
what it meant for Luther, who saw most humans as unsaved.
With the belief that faith alone can save, most are not to be loved.
As Luther stood alone before God with scripture alone, he got
rid of all that scripture which had to do with Jesus founding
his church upon Peter and which saw all as members of Christ's body.
So Zarathustra, with Jesus, says:

> I exhort you rather to flight from your neighbor
> and to love of the most distant . . .
> Higher than love of one's neighbor
> stands love of the most distant man . . .
> Your bad love of yourselves
> makes solitude a prison to you.

To bring a limited preferential love of one's own to an unlimited
universal love, Jesus said: You must hate your mother and
father and those closest to you, just as Zarathustra here says
take flight from the neighbor as the one closest to you that
you might love all humans who are most distant from you.
The second great commandment said to love your neighbor
as you love yourself, but Zarathustra talks about the camel's
and Luther's bad love of themselves as a solitude or a Prison.
As Luther stood alone before God, as the modern isolated man,
Zarathustra says he is in prison without that third who
can let him rise to the heights by breaking the monadic dyad.
Zarathustra says:

> I do not teach you the neighbor, but the friend.
> May the friend be to you a festival
> and a foretaste of the Superman.

And that is what happens when the old Pope comes up to visit
Zarathustra in Book Four, for since God is dead, he is retired from
service, and at first, Zarathustra dislikes him, but they become friends.

Agape and the Four Loves

II,5.3 *The solitary Luther and the way of the creator*

Nietzsche and his Zarathustra were both solitary men, even though they wanted to be affectionate, friendly and gregarious, for, as we saw with Nietzsche in relation to women:

> The solitary extends his hand too quickly to anyone he meets.

But the childlike Jesus and Zarathustra are creators and their way is that of the solitary that lets them become *free from* their affliction, in such a way that they become free for creativity. Their Joyful Wisdom transforms their affliction into universal love. Zarathustra warns the solitary creator:

> Be on your guard against the good and the just.
> They would like to crucify those
> who devise their own virtue—
> They hate the solitary.

At first, Luther wanted to be a solitary creator and he became an Augustinian monk, but he could not be celibate.

> Solitary man, you are going the way of the creator:
> You want to create yourself a god
> from your own seven devils.

But Luther saw the failure of good works as he could not get the sublimation process to work, so he became a happily married man, and as good and just, he attacked those relying on good works. With his *sola scriptura* and his *sola fidei*, Luther did stand as a *solitary* before God, but when the solitary becomes a child and a creator, he comes to love even his enemies from his heart:

> Solitary man, you are going the way of the lover:
> you love yourself and for that reason
> you despise yourself as only lovers can despise.

Jesus and Zarathustra come to bring the sword and not peace against self love, and thus their followers must always make love of all others their highest priority, and with good works, transform their seven devils into God who is love.

II,5.4 Lutheran pastor's daughters

As Nietzsche knew from his Lutheran tradition, the father-son relation took on a new significance as the sons of Pastors became pastors. But what was there for daughters who could never follow in their beloved father's vocation and if a pastor had only daughters, would he and they not feel left out, as other pastors built up their sons? So the little old woman asked Zarathustra:

> 'Speak to me too of woman.
> I am old enough soon to forget it.'

Zarathustra obliged her and said:

> Everything about woman is a riddle
> and everything about woman has one solution:
> it is called pregnancy.
> For the woman, the man is only a means:
> the end is always the child.

In this camel world of Christian Platonism, the woman, too, will kneel and reverently take upon herself the heavy burden of the loving mother. But Zarathustra has more than camel goals for her:

> Let the flash of a star glitter in your love!
> Let your hope be; 'May I bear the Superman!'

But, in this drama of Zarathustra, she ends by telling him:

> Are you visiting women? Do not forget your whip!

We must see how this drama of the woman will unfold as we watch her next with the lion, and then the lioness, and then the child. Meanwhile, back with the retired Pope, Zarathustra learns from him how God died because he was there to watch it and the old Pope said that this God of Christian Platonism died because he failed to put all the emphasis on universal love, as do Jesus and Zarathustra:

> Whoever honors him as a God of love
> does not think highly enough of love itself.
> Did this God not also want to be a judge?

Agape and the Four Loves

II,5.5 *The adder's bite and justice without noble love*

One day while sleeping, Zarathustra is bitten by an adder in the neck. As he awakens, the serpent starts to slither away, but Zarathustra tells him to come back, for he wants to thank him for awakening him. The snake returns, and he tells him to suck the poison from his neck. Zarathustra's disciples ask what the moral of the story is, and he tells them the justice of noble love:

> When you have an enemy, do not requite him
> good for evil: for that would make him ashamed.
> But prove that he has done something good to you.

Thus, a noble universal love thanks any enemy for his goodness and returns some little injustices in revenge.

> A little revenge is more human than no revenge at all . . .
> It is more noble to declare yourself wrong
> than to maintain you are right,
> especially when you are right.

As always, Zarathustra speaks aphoristically with a cynical wisdom, as did the historical Jesus, and as always, love is first and then there needs to be a secondary justice in service of love. When Luther started modernity, he switched things around and did away with universal love for the sake of atonement justice. With faith alone, the works of love no longer were possible and thus Luther could not maintain that his enemies could be right. He never could thank the Pope and the great Catholic tradition, for he saw them as only unjust and against *sola scriptura* and *fidei*. Thus, according to the old Pope, this God had to die, for

> 'When he was young, this God from the orient,
> was hard and vengeful and built
> himself a hell for the delight of his favorites.'

In the postmodern age of our Global Village, when we can see humankind's highest affirmation, this old God of Hell and vengeance is dead and protesting modernity is dying.

II,5.6 The bitter cup of marriage can teach true love

The whole of *Zarathustra* is about true love and how to better love. Thus, affection, *eros*, and friendship within marriage and family life will suffer until finally there is the right order of love and so marriage is for the sake of the Superman, that we might overcome ourselves until finally we get the *amor fati* of *agape* for everyone. Zarathustra beholds the marriages of the superfluous in our modern secular world, and says:

> Do not laugh at such marriages!
> What child has not had reason to weep
> over its parents?

As a remedy to this Christian Platonic love, in which women are not seen as equal to men, Zarathustra says:

> One day you shall love beyond yourselves!
> So first learn to love.
> For that you have had to drink
> the bitter cup of your love.
> There is bitterness in the cup
> of even the best love:
> thus it arouses longing for the Superman.

Zarathustra speaks against the good-sacred and the evil-profane, but he is all for the holy, and thus he says:

> A creator's thirst, arrow,
> and longing for the Superman:
> is this your will to marriage?
> I call holy such a will and such a marriage.

Grandmothers can be wise shamanic guides, but as the old Pope described for Zarathustra the death of the protesting God, he said:

> But at length he grew old and soft
> and mellow and compassionate,
> more like a grandfather than a father,
> most like a tottery old grandmother.

Agape and the Four Loves

II,5.7 *Love lets anytime be the right time to die*

Nietzsche thought much about the untimely, and because his father died when he was so young his *Untimely Meditation* let him meditate on how to make his father's death timely through his own creativity for him and for all of his readers.

> And when shall I wish it?
> He who has a goal and an heir
> wants death at the most favourable time
> to his goal and his heir.

Zarathustra teaches that we should freely die at the right time.

> In your death, your spirit and your virtue
> should still glow like a sunset glow
> around the earth:
> otherwise yours is a bad death.

And Zarathustra, here in the early part of this drama, even thinks that Jesus died when he was too young:

> He died too early;
> he himself would have recanted his teaching
> had he lived to my age!
> He was noble enough to recant.

What teaching might he have recanted, since Nietzsche, in the *Antichrist*, seems to love Jesus and all of his teachings?
Is it that Jesus always loved his Father God?
At the end of the section with the retired Pope, Zarathustra says: "Better no god, better to produce destiny on one's own account."
But then, the Old Pope says:

> O Zarathustra, you are more pious than you believe,
> with such an unbelief!
> Some god in you has converted you to your godlessness.

And that God must be Jesus, with his unconditional love
for every page of *Zarathustra* is about that love which
Nietzsche first learned when his father died and which grew and grew.

II,5.8 Bestowing love is the highest virtue

As Zarathustra prepares to leave the town in which he has
exposed the atonement justice theology of Christian Platonism,
his beloved disciples give him the gift of a walking stick,
which has a gold orb on top with a serpent wrapped around it.
He thanks them for the perfect gift, because gold is the symbol
of pure giving, and the serpent is the wisest of his animals.

> The highest virtue is uncommon and useless,
> it is shining and mellow in luster:
> the highest virtue is a bestowing virtue.

There are faith, hope and love and the greatest is love.
Though love which bestows itself upon others is rare, it is
a star that can guide persons to the Superman or loving child.
Since Luther argues that faith alone in the Redeemer redeems us
and not the works of love, Zarathustra reminds us that we
need to be redeemed from Luther's redeemer through bestowing.
Thus, after learning from the Pope why and how Luther's God
is dying in our postmodern age, Zarathustra says:

> But very well! One way or the other,
> he is gone!
> He offended the taste of my ears and eyes,
> I will say no worse of him.

Luther no longer wanted the authority of the Pope, because those
Renaissance Popes wanted to trade indulgences for German money,
that they might build St. Peter's Cathedral and the Sistine Chapel.
Nietzsche knew the German Lutherans well, and at first Zarathustra
did not like the Pope either, but after bestowing love upon him,
he began to learn from him about the death of God and then
he began to accept the Pope's authority, as the Pope began
to teach him about himself, and how he was more pious than he knew.
As Zarathustra's disciples in the town of the Pied Cow learned of the
greatest of virtues from him, so Zarathustra learned from the Pope.

II,5.9 Bestowing love lets there be God's kingdom

Part Two of *Zarathustra* begins with a motto from *Of the Bestowing Virtue*.

> '-and only when you have all denied me
> will I return to you.
> 'Truly, with other eyes, my brothers, I
> shall then seek my lost ones; with another
> love I shall then love you.'

Zarathustra, who is another Jesus, has the same experiences as Jesus. The Jesus of Q[1], who is Nietzsche's Jesus, left the beloved Q community, and immediately they interpreted him as the rewarder-punisher Christ. Jesus' unconditional love reveals the God of love, who is beyond good and evil, and the primacy of atonement justice, but time after time through history, the God of love is loved and then quickly denied. If you look at Luther's 97 theses, there are as many against the Franciscans as there are against indulgences and Rome's Pope. St. Francis truly knew the love of Jesus and practiced a spirituality that could bestow love upon the poor coming into the cities to work. But as soon as Portugal, Spain, England and Holland started to emerge as powerful nation states, Luther devined that the Germans wanted that too, so the kingdom of love was denied and the new kingdom of the state came forth as the cold monster. Zarathustra, as the love child, has exposed all the non-love of the camel's Christian Platonism, and many beloved disciples follow him, as Jesus' first disciples all wanted to follow him. So as Zarathustra departs, he tells them that he will return once they have denied him and that denial is one of mixed opposites. The disciple needs to mature by going beyond the disciple stage, and that happens when he find his own unique way of loving. However, the denial can also be a denial of the primacy of love. So Zarathustra's coming to them and speaking to them was a gift of bestowing love and now his departure is another gift. How will love change as Zarathustra moves from camel to lion?

II,6. Reconciling Kant with the Jesus of retarded puberty

II,6.1 How the enlightenment lions become free

The drama of Zarathustra develops through the five acts
of spirit-camel-lion-lioness-child and spirit is
the interplay of the forces of will to power that can act
foolishly or wisely and even with the child's wise-folly.
The camel of Christian Platonism loves God and neighbor
for the afterlife and thus with ressentiment against this life.
We have seen how Christian Platonism and Luther did that.
The lion of Enlightenment Humanism loves God and neighbor
for a better future but with ressentiment against the present.
In the poetry of *Zarathustra* we can see how Nietzsche
treats Kant and the Buddha as the lions of the Enlightenment.
In Part one, chapter one on *The Three Metamorphoses*, Nietzsche
introduces this lion of the Enlightenment by saying:

> In the loneliest desert, the second metamorphosis occurs:
> the spirit here becomes lion;
> it wants to capture freedom
> and be lord in its own desert.
> It seeks here its ultimate lord:
> it will be an enemy to him
> and to its ultimate God,
> it will struggle for victory with the great dragon.

Kant takes Lutheranism to a second stage of secularity.
His great formula is "Religion within the limits of reason alone."
Luther had faith alone in scripture alone with its "Thou shalt."
Kant is an enemy of any "Thou shalt" that is imposed from
the outside for he wants to be the lord in his own desert
and to capture freedom so that he is the source of all truth.
In Part Two of *Zarathustra* the Enlightenment lions are criticized.
They attain freedom from external laws and they get the freedom
for creativity but they do not yet become the creative child.
We can now ponder Nietzsche's treatment of Kant and his influence.

Agape and the Four Loves

II,6.2 A Twilight of the Idols summary of Zarathustra

In *Twilight of the Idols* in the section on *How the "Real world" Finally Became a Fable, History of an Error*, Nietzsche gives a one page summary of the drama of *Zarathustra*:

1. The real world attainable for the wise man, the pious man, the virtuous man, *he is* it.
   (Most ancient form of the idea, relatively clever, simple, convincing. Paraphrase of the proposition: I, Plato, *am* the truth.)
2. The real world unattainable for now, but promised to the wise man, the pious man, the virtuous man ('to the sinner who repents').
   (Progress of the idea: it becomes more cunning, more insidious, more incomprehensible— *it becomes a woman*, it becomes a Christian ...)
3. The real world unattainable, unprovable, unpromisable, but the mere thought of it a consolation, an obligation, an imperative.
   (The old sun in the background, but seen through mist and skepticism; the idea became sublime, pale, Nordic, Könsigsbergian)
4. The real world— unattainable? at any rate unattained. and since unattained also *unknown*. Hence no consolation, redemption, obligation either; what could the unknown oblige us to do? (... First yawn of reason. Cock crow of positivism.)
5. The 'real world'— an idea become useless, superfluous, *therefore* a refuted idea: let us do away with it!
   (Broad daylight; breakfast; return of *bon sense* and cheerfulness; Plato's shameful blush; all free spirits run riot.)
6. The real world— we have done away with it; what world was left? the apparent one, perhaps? ... But no! with the real world we have also done away with the apparent one!
   (Noon; moment of the shortest shadow; end of the longest error, pinnacle of humanity; INCIPIT ZARATHUSTRA.)

We have already examined points one and two with Plato and Christianity up until Luther so now we must examine point three.

II,6.3 The old God is dead for the enlightenment men

After being with those of the camel attitude through Part One
now at the beginning of Part Two we meet Zarathustra
once again living high up in his mountain peaks in solitude.
He is eager again with love to go down to the people below.

> I can go down to my friends again
> and to my enemies too!
> Zarathustra can speak and give again,
> and again show love to those he loves.
> My impatient love overflows in torrents
> down towards morning and evening.

In the first chapter of Part Two, *The Child with the Mirror*
Zarathustra awakens from a dream in which a child
has held a mirror before him and he saw the sneering
face of the devil looking out at him and he knew that
his enemies had distorted the meaning of his doctrine of love.
His teaching had always been the *amor fati* of the child Jesus.
So in a dream this child has come to him to remind him of this.
For now the enlightenment lions have come to his disciples
with their doctrine that the "real world" is unattainable,
unprovable, unpromisable but the mere thought of it
is a consolation, an obligation and an imperative for all.
Now Zarathustra must come down and love his enemies,
the enlightenment lions and teach them of the eternal return
and its *amor fati* for this world and all flesh here and now.
In chapter two of Part Two he sails to the Blissful Islands
of his friends and disciples and his wild lionine wisdom
speaks out to the enlightenment men:

> Ah, if only my lioness wisdom
> had learned to roar fondly.

He must teach the lion to roar out fondly against
even the camel and the camel's dead rewarder punisher God.

Agape and the Four Loves

II,6.4 And as unprovable is to be replaced by the overman

Zarathustra's main message for the enlightened men is that they should always be overcoming themselves and thus be the overman or self-overcoming man who is becoming childlike. Thus he begins chapter Two on the Blissful Islands by saying:

> Once you said 'God' when you gazed upon distant seas; but now I have taught you to say "Superman".

This tradition into "Superman" can be confusing and often leads people to think of the opposite of the simple child. The enlightenment men might think of themselves as supermen. But Zarathustra wants them to overcome themselves and be overmen in the sense of overcoming themselves to be childlike. The thought of the "overman" came to Zarathustra and implied that: (1) since God is not conceivable and is thus a supposition, he is dead; (2) since as one, perfect, unmoved, sufficient and intransitory his perfection belittles the perfection of the earth, he is dead; (3) if there were gods, how could I endure not to be a god! *Therefore*, there are no gods. (4) Since man cannot create a god— he should be silent about all gods! But you could surely create the Superman. Zarathustra and the enlightenment men are in agreement about all of this for St. Thomas would have his five arguments for the existence of God, but these five refute his famous five. Zarathustra says to Kant and the enlightened lions:

> you yourselves should create what you
> have hitherto called the world:
> the world should be formed in your image
> by your reason, your will, and your love.
> Truly it will be to your happiness you enlightened men.
> How should you endure life without this hope,
> you enlightened men?

II,6.5 Zarathustra has a spear for his beloved enemies

As Zarathustra goes down to the enlightened men who have led his disciples astray he goes with love for them and yet a spear. In chapter one, *The Child with the Mirror*, he says:

> I want to sail across broad seas
> like a cry and a shout of joy,
> until I find the Blissful Islands
> where my friends are waiting—
> and my enemies with them!
> How I now love anyone
> to whom I can simply speak!
> My enemies are part of my happiness.
> And when I want to mount my wildest horse,
> it is my spear that best helps me on to it . . .
> The spear which I throw at my enemies!
> How I thank my enemies
> that at last I can throw it.

Kant is the prototype of the enlightened man and Zarathustra begins to throw his spear of criticism at him in Chapter Three *On The Compassionate* in which he says:

> The enlightened man goes among men
> as among animals.
> The enlightened man calls man himself;
> the animal with red cheeks.
> How did this happen to man?
> Is it not because he has had
> to be ashamed too often?
> Thus speaks the enlightened man:
> 'Shame, shame, shame—
> that is the history of man.'

So Kant will notice the shame of man and have compassion on him but this compassion is a pity that also can shame.

II,6.6 Kant's critique of pure reasoning is enlightening

There are four great theories about the "Real World" and they are: (1) the ultra realism of Plato, (2) the moderate realism of Aristotle, (3) the conceptualism of Kant and (4) the nominalism of Ockham, Nietzche and all of the postmodern philosophers. For Plato the transcendent form of the Good in which all things here participate is the "Real world" and this world is but its shadow. For Aristotle things here are real and to know them we abstract the common form of things and that form lets them be real. Kant in going beyond the Platonists and the Aristotelian Christians argues that there is not a correspondence truth in which our minds conform to the form of things but there is only a coherence truth in which there is consistency in our concepts. The forms in our mind make experience possible but we do not know things in themselves as belonging to a formal class. The ultimate forms of things such as their quantity, quality, relation and modality are categories of our minds and allow us to experience things so that we are lords in our own desert. The enlightened man believes that all we can know is what we experience for we cannot know the thing in itself which beyond our experience and thus the "Real world" is unattainable, unprovable and unpromisable as we are told in *Twilight*. The next step after this is positivism and pessimism in which there is no consolation, redemption or obligation either. For in this negative skepticism how can the unknown oblige us? At this point we can become nominalists like Zarathustra and know that each individual is so unique that in can never be reduced to a general form but this can allow us to make joy's leap of faith in the eternal return of each. Insofar as the God of Christian Platonism is not knowable Kant can become the lion in his own desert and capture freedom, the freedom of the moral law within that is the categorical imperative.

II,6.7 His critique of practical reason is compassionate

Toward the end of the chapter *On The Compassionate* Zarathustra says:

> Thus speaks all great love:
> it overcomes even forgiveness and pity...
> Alas, where in the world have there been
> greater follies that with the compassionate?
> What in the world has caused more suffering
> than the follies of the compassionate?...
> All great love is above pity:
> for it wants— to create what is loved.

Zarathustra thinks that ultimately the moral law for the enlightened is one of compassion that is not founded on utility or pleasure or the virtues that lead to self realization. The moral law within is our conscience which commands us to act according to that maxim which is universalizable. I should not do to others what I would not want them to do to me so I should not lie since I would not want to be lied to. Nothing according to Kant is good without qualification except a good will which will never treat another person as a thing. This moral truth which reason could never find is the basis for the will's freedom, God's existence and the soul's immortality. But while Zarathustra in his chapter on The Virtuous gives twelve reasons why we should not trust a virtue ethic he does not go from there with Kant to the categorical imperative. It is ultimately based on compassion for others and that can be an ethics of pity toward them rather than true love. Zarathustra tells us that the devil said to him:

> Even god has his hell,
> it is his love for man
> and lately I heard him say
> God is dead;
> God has died of his pity for man.

Agape and the Four Loves

II,6.8 His critique of judgment reveals the sublime

In his chapter *On The Virtuous* Zarathustra's tenth critique of the virtuous says:

> And many a one who cannot see
> the sublime in man
> calls it virtue that he can see
> his baseness all-too-clearly:
> thus he calls his evil eye virtue.

In the camel world of virtue ethics the sublime in everyone was not noticed as Aristotle and other Platonists concentrated on man's vices and misery to overcome them by being virtuous. Kant the enlightened man who went beyond virtue ethics which saw the virtues as means to the end of my happiness was able to appreciate Rousseau's sublime moral law within and the science of Newton's starry sky in its sublimity above. By developing a sense for this aesthetic sublimity he showed how the great men of the enlightenment: Voltaire, Newton, Rousseau and those of the French Enlightenment tried to get beyond the caste system of the virtuous clergy and nobility which brought some to the rabble of the working lower class. Kant, however, with his compassion sees the sublime moral law to be within every person and prepares the way for the freedom, equality and brotherhood of all humans with a true enlightenment. But in his chapter *On The Rabble* Zarathustra completes his list of the four great afflictions which the child will overcome. Besides shame and pity he now speaks of weariness and disgust. Zarathustra says:

> Not my hate but my disgust
> hungrily devoured my life!
> Alas, I often grew weary of the spirit
> when I found the rabble, too,
> had been gifted with spirit.

II,6.9 The child loves everyone as a gift

At the end of the chapter *On The Compassionate* Zarathustra
clearly states his message which runs all through his book:

> Thus speaks all great love:
> it overcomes even forgiveness and pity . . .
> All great love is above pity:
> for it wants— to create what is loved!
> 'I offer myself to my love,
> *and my neighbor as myself.*'

The camels of Christian Platonism saw everyone as a problem.
Plato sees the soul as fallen into a body because of forgetfulness
and wrongdoing and virtue can rejoin our soul to the world-soul.
For Christians especially Lutherans and Calvinists we are fallen
and totally depraved simply by inheriting Adam's original sin.
It is shameful to be an ordinary human for we are not lovable.
The lions of the enlightenment also see everyone as a problem.
For man is a wolf to man in our society and if we are to follow
the moral law within we need a revolution to right the caste system.
In his compassion for the rabble the enlightened man takes pity
and that pity sees everyone as a problem rather than a gift.
The great love of Zarathustra's postmodern child that gets
beyond modernity and the enlightenment is creative in seeing
the beautiful good of every creature with a Yes and Amen prayer.
The childlike Jesus of Nietzsche and Q[1] is not a great lion
of the enlightenment for his great love is beyond shame and pity.
Rather this childlike adult has something of a retarded puberty
and as Dostoyevsky would argue is even something of an idiot.
But, in *The Anti-Christ* in section eleven Nietzsche turns
the tables on Kant and argues that he has become an idiot.
He did not see that an action compelled by the instinct of life
has in the joy of performing it the proof that it is a right
action and thus his abstract imperative missed joyful love.

Agape and the Four Loves

III. Q² and Q³

III,4 The Q³ sayings

III,4.1 Mack's 8 groups of Q³ sayings

On page 173, Mack lists the 8 Q³ sayings and the three new themes of Q³:

> The story of the temptations of Jesus
> introduces three new themes
> characteristic of Q³. They are:
> (1) the mythology of Jesus as the son of God,
> (2) the relationship of Jesus as the son of God
>   to the temple of Jerusalem, and
> (3) the authority of the scriptures.

The eight key sayings of Q³ are:

1. QS 6   The Temptation Stories
2. QS 24   Secret Revelation to Little Children
3. QS 31   Those who Listen to God's Teaching
4. QS 34   Qualifications about Charges against Pharisees
5. QS 36   Sayings about Hellfire
6. QS 49   Lament over Jerusalem
7. QS 56   Sayings on the Law
8. QS 62   His Followers Will Be Judges

The Roman-Jewish war lasted for about ten years from about 66 C.E. to about 76 C.E. and Mack tells us how the Q³ writings provide us with a bit of a peek into those most troublesome times for all the groups of the Jewish people, who fought against each other and for the various groups of Jesus followers and Christians in their beginning.

III,4.2 Jesus tempted by the accuser

Now for the first time in the Q text Jesus is called the son of God.

> The accuser said, "If you are the son of God,
> tell this stone to become bread."

Paul had been referring to Christ Jesus already for twenty years
as the son of God but the Jesus people of Q^1 saw him as
the child of wisdom and the Jesus people of Q^2 saw him as
the son of man and now they begin to see him as the son of God.
The next temptation has to do with the temple which, by the way,
has by this time been destroyed:

> Then the accuser took him to Jerusalem
> and placed him at the highest point
> of the temple and said to him:
> "If you are the son of God,
> throw yourself down, for it is written,
> 'He will command his angels to protect you.'"

Jesus answered him:

> "You shall not put the lord,
> your God to the test."

So now in Q^3 Jesus is recognized as the son of God and he
speaks of himself as "the Lord and your God." This is new
in Q^3 and is the main clue for determining Q^3 texts.
Then the accuser says he will give Jesus all the kingdoms
of the world if he will bow down and worship him but Jesus
responds:

> It is written, "You shall reverence
> the lord your God and serve him alone."

So here in QS 6 we meet the son of God and we see him as
recognized by the devil as being the lord God and in this last
of the three exchanges the son of God even quotes scripture
against the devil so that as Mack says we see the son of God
in relation to the temple and to scripture as having authority over both.

Agape and the Four Loves

III,4.3 Secret revelation to little children

The next Q³ text brings out the theme of the child for:

> Unless you become like little children
> you cannot be my disciple.

In the context of a loving prayer to his father the son of God says:

> I am grateful to you, father,
> Master of heaven and earth
> because you have kept these things
> hidden from the wise and understanding
> and revealed them to babies.
> Truly I am grateful, father,
> for that was your gracious will.

Right away this Q³ Jesus as the son of God seems much more loving and less judgmental than the apocalyptic son of man of Q². This image and symbol of becoming like the child is of central importance for Nietzsche as he distinguishes Jesus from Paul's Christ. To become childlike is the fulfillment of the drama of *Zarathustra*. This Q³, 24, saying goes on to develop the theme of the son of God. The Jesus of Q³ continues:

> Authority over all the world
> has been given to me by my father.
> No one recognizes the son
> except the father;
> and no one knows who the father is
> except the son and the one to whom
> the son chooses to reveal him.

This third stage of the Q community is now receiving a new and fuller revelation about Jesus who first taught them in Galilee. As the child of wisdom he revealed to them a childlike love for all, especially enemies, that did not resist any evil. Then after his death the persecuted community was inspired to understand him as a judge and now he is the child of God.

Part Two: Sorrowful Proceedings

III,4.4 Hearing and keeping the teaching of God

Following the saying about the son of God revealing his father to those who are childlike we are now led to ponder how important it is to hear the word of God and observe it:

> As he was saying these things
> a woman from the crowd
> spoke up and said to him,
> "How fortunate is the womb that bore you,
> and the breasts that you sucked!"
> But he said, "How fortunate, rather,
> are those who listen to God's teaching
> and observe it!"

We are starting here to see the need for the infancy narratives that Matthew and Luke will give us and the beginnings of a devotion to Mary are here, but Jesus emphasizes Revelation. The themes that Burton Mack picked out of the son of God and the emphasis on the word of God in revelation continues to be developed step by step throughout the Q^3 sayings. The son of God was sent to reveal the will of the father and the son alone knows the father.
These Q^3 sayings continue to echo the Q^1 sayings with the form of the beatitudes with their "how fortunate" or "how blessed" one is. The son of God stresses:

> "How fortunate are those who listen
> to God's teaching and observe it."

The son of God reveals that authority over all the world has been given to him by his father and the devil recognized this when he was tempting Jesus and talked about giving him the world if only the son of God would worship the devil whose world it is. The son of God has come to save all flesh from the world and the flesh insofar as they are under the power of the devil. All those will be blessed or saved if they hear the word of God's love.

Agape and the Four Loves

III,4.5 *Qualifying the charges against the pharisees*

The Q³ saying in QS 34 is only one sentence:

> These things you ought to have done,
> without neglecting the others.

Just before this the son of man had said:

> Shame on you Pharisees for you are
> scrupulous about giving a tenth
> of mint and dill and cumin
> to the priests, but you neglect
> justice and the love of God.

The son of man wanted a balance of true love and true justice and he could have implied that scrupulosity about tithing was worthless, but now the son of God makes further distinctions. Being scrupulous is good and so is tithing and as was said by the son of man full love and full justice should not be neglected. The son of God agrees but he is more loving toward the Pharisees. Now that Judaism is in dire straits after the Roman war the Pharisees are no longer a great threat and the Jesus people at the time of Q³ can go out in love to all their Jewish brethren. As Burton Mack argues on page 176:

> The debate with the Pharisees
> was no longer wrenching.
> The Jewish scriptures could now
> be used as ethical guidelines.
> There was a move toward an
> accommodation of Jewish sensibility
> even to the extent that Jewish-Christianity
> became a very popular and long-lived
> legacy for the Jesus people.

So the move from Q² when the Jesus people were persecuted by the Pharisees to the new context of Q³ when there is no longer any Jewish persecution has great implication concerning scripture.

III,4.6 The threat of hell fire

The Q³ saying in Q 36 is again only one sentence:

> Rather fear the one who is able to destroy
> both body and soul in Gehenna (hell fire).

So while the son of God may not be an apocalyptic Judge
Jewish eschatology is taken over here by the Jesus people.
This Gehenna or hell fire for both the body and the soul is
a Jewish understanding of life after death and not at all Hellenic.
Plato and Aristotle developed proofs for the immortality of
the extracted soul and Neither Hindus nor Greeks believed in
bodily resurrection which became central with the resurrected Jesus.
While they no longer need to fear the Pharisees they should
know that: "The fear of the Lord is the beginning of wisdom."
Again: "the fear of God" is a Jewish idea that the Jesus people
can now feel at home with for it sets up their new priorities.
If the love of God and neighbor is all important and will
keep one out of hell then this negative motivation is helpful.
One can be motivated by the sheer self-evidence of love's value.
The very personality of Jesus as child of wisdom, as son of man
or as son of God could have positively motivated his disciples.
But this notion of self destruction is also a very strong motivator.
It is easy to see how many become addicted to bad habits
and suffer a hell upon earth and it is natural to think that
that can only continue after death until purgation is accomplished.
From the beginning of Q² the son of man threatened with hell fire:

> Every tree that does not bear good fruit
> is cut down and thrown into the fire.

But in the Q¹ sayings the child of wisdom says:

> Be merciful even as your Father is merciful.
> Don't judge and you won't be judged.

So one might think that hell fire will not be everlasting pain.
The father is merciful according to the Jesus of unlimited *agape*.

Agape and the Four Loves

III,4.7 Lament over Jerusalem

This lament over Jerusalem by the son of God reveals a beautiful kind of near motherly love as he compares himself to a mother hen and her chicks whom he would like to protect under his wings but they would not and the rebellious Zionists got Jerusalem destroyed. Jesus says in QS 3, 49,

> O Jerusalem, Jerusalem, killing the prophets
> and stoning those who are sent to you!
> How often would I have gathered
> your children together as a hen gathers
> her brood under her wings,
> and you refused.

For the first forty years off the life of the Q community the Jesus people were persecuted in Jerusalem and their prophet, Jesus, was killed there and Stephen and other disciples were stoned there. Jesus tried to love all the Jesus people and gather them under his wings like sweet, little, yellow chicks but they would rather run about and be devoured by a serpent and thus it happened. Jesus goes on to say in QS 49:

> Look, your house is left desolate.
> Now, I tell you, you will not see me
> until you say, 'Blessed is the one
> who comes in the name of the Lord.'

The Temple was razed for a second time and many Jewish people were killed or frightened away into the diaspora. The son of God now tells the Jewish people that they will not see him until they bless those who come to them in his name. On page 175, Burton Mack tells of Josephus' account of how terrible the war was with all the bloodshed in the temple precincts. The son of God does not try to say; "I told you so!" but out of love does truly lament and does give hope that some day all the chicks of the world, both Jewish and gentile, will come to him.

III,4.8 The kingdom and the law

Burton Mack tells us of the three new themes in Q³:

> (1) the mythology of Jesus as the son of God,
> (2) the relationship of Jesus as the son of God
>   to the temple of Jerusalem, and
> (3) the authority of the scriptures.

Now with QS 56 we come fully to the third theme:

> The law of Moses and the prophets
> were authorities until John.
> Since then the kingdom of God
> has been overpowered by violent men.

As Jesus established the Q community as the kingdom of love
Moses and the prophets were authorities that lasted until John.
With the persecution of the Jesus people beginning when Jesus was
put to death that authority of Moses and the prophets was read anew.
The Q community in its second phase saw Jesus as the son of man
using Moses and the prophets against their persecutors and primarily
as a description of their persecution which was like that of the prophets.
But now after the fall of Jerusalem a new third relation between
the law of Moses and the kingdom of love is being worked out:

> It is easier for the heavens and the earth
> to pass away than for one stroke
> of the law to lose its force.

If the Jesus people really live according to the law of love they will
also live according to the important laws of Moses and the prophets.
In fact the son of God goes on to say:

> Everyone who divorces his wife commits adultery,
> and the one who marries a divorced woman
> also commits adultery.

So in the Kingdom of love the Jesus people must be very serious
about the right ethical life and living according to all the
   commandments.
Adultery is very serious and will be punished by the rods of men.

Agape and the Four Loves

III,4.9 *Judging Israel*

How and when judgment will happen in the afterlife is a mystery.
In the New Testament and quite in accord with Jewish eschatology
there is a variety of views about judgment and even in the Book of Q
there is a lot about the apocalyptic son of man as judge and now we
are told about this new possibility by the son of God:

> And you who have followed me
> will sit on thrones,
> judging the twelve tribes of Israel.

This Qs 62 is the last of the Q sayings and end the Q document.
So what might it mean to say that the followers of Jesus
who belong to the Kingdom of love will sit on thrones as judges?
In this Kingdom each lover who really loved all of existence
and forgives his or her enemy is already a judge like Jesus.
For when they sincerely pray and live out the Lord's prayer
they are already judges like their merciful father as they pray:

> Forgive us our trespasses
> as we forgive thwho trespass against us.

There will be hell fire and the followers of Jesus will judge
the twelve tribes of Israel and all peoples by praying for them
and asking the Father to be merciful to them as Jesus taught them.
All will be judges in the afterlife and once everyone is finally
a follower of Jesus and they all forgive each other then the hell fire
of purgatory will come to an end and all flesh will be saved by that
love which Jesus taught when he said:

> Don't judge and you won't be judged.
> For the standard you use will be
> the standard used against you. QS 10

The followers of Jesus are judges because they are merciful
even as the heavenly Father is merciful and they will see
and love all the good and the love in the twelve tribes of Israel.

III,5 Three stages of agape in the Book of Q

III,5.1 The unconditional love of Q^1

On pages 73 to 80 of his book Burton Mack gives a separate list of all the original Q^1 sayings and in this first stage of the Q text if you focus on *agape* you can already see three stages of love. The first third of the sayings stress a totally unconditional love. Jesus clearly tells his people:

> I am telling you, love your enemies,
> bless those who curse you,
> pray for those who mistreat you.

If they do good and lend without expecting anything in return their reward will be great and they will be children of God. But notice there is already a rewarder God here in the earliest sayings. However, what is new for humankind is this *agape* which is totally altruistic and puts the emphasis on praying for one's enemies. Prayer cultivates love and Jesus knew that the more you pray for someone the more you will love them for adoring belongs to praying. And repeating their name each day in loving prayer lets you come to know them better even in their goodness and to understand them more and more as they become daily dearer to you in joyful prayer. And Jesus tells his disciples in this early stage of his teaching that if they love their enemies they will be children of God and that will be their reward which is a natural reward for loving. This Jesus who taught his people in Galilee was a child of wisdom and such a child is spontaneous, playful, loving and loveable. Jesus was childlike and if his people loved as did he they too would be children of God and he said to them

> Be merciful even as your Father is merciful.
> Don't judge and you won't be judged.
> For the standard you use (for judging)
> will be the standard used against you.

A child loves his or her parents with the very love which they receive from their parents and a baby which is not judged does not judge.

Agape and the Four Loves

III,5.2 *Understands natural punishment*

Jesus and his disciples love even those who do evil to them
and they know that the merciful father

> makes his sun rise on the evil and on the good;
> he sends rain on the just and on the unjust.

But there is a natural punishment and if you really understand
the *agape* that loves enemies and sinners you will see that their
non loving and its sinfulness will bring them a suffering without joy.
That is why the agapeic lover will pray for them so earnestly
and love them with such fervor so that they too might come to love.
Thus Jesus explains the results of a self-centered egoism:

> A good tree does not bear rotten fruit;
> a rotten tree does not bear good fruit.
> Are figs gathered from thorns,
> or grapes from thistles?
> The good man produces good things
> from his store of goods and treasures;
> and the evil man evil things.

So the works of agapeic love toward enemies and sinners are at
least twofold in that the disciple of Jesus must love them more and more
and also let them know that any evil doing or lack of love will
only result in suffering not only for other but especially for themselves.
Thus continuing with the theme of the child Jesus says:

> Whatever house you enter, say,
> "Peace be to this house!"
> And if a child of peace is there,
> your greeting will be received.
> But if not, let your peace return to you..

So wherever there is *agape* there is a childlike peace and if *agape*
is absent from a person eventually there will be sorrow without joy.
The Jesus people will love their enemies and because they love them
they will try to show them how to become happy by loving.

III,5.3 *And even hates worldly affection*

The *agape* which loves all persons equally, uniquely and interrelatedly is not opposed to the hatred of any love which denies true love by being a false love that is only a self love. That is why the Jesus of Q¹ tells of a banquet to which many are invited but which many refuse because of excuses such as they have just bought a new farm, or a fine pair of oxen, or have just married a new wife and cannot come to the love feast. That is why Jesus gave that hard saying right at the end of Q¹ and right after the banquet story:

> Whoever does not hate his father and mother
> will not be able to learn from me.
> Whoever does not hate his son and daughter
> cannot belong to my school.

Each form of love: affection, *eros*, friendship and *agape* can be a fundamental attitude and natural affection which can love my father or mother, or my son or daughter more than other persons excludes the *agape* which should love all persons equally. Therefore, to come to the banquet of *agape* I must not make the excuse that I just have a new wife and must care for her. Once I have *agape* and love all persons equally including my wife then I will be able to give her special attention but only relatively. And, of course, it is not easy to leave the worldly ways behind and come follow Jesus to the banquet of *agape* and that is why at the end of Q¹ he also says:

> Whoever does not accept his cross
> and so become my follower,
> cannot be one of my students.

For *agape* to unconditionally love all persons, places and things it must hate and get rid of any excuse making preferential self love that ties it down in an exclusive love of one's own. One must carry the cross of deabsolutizing one's farm, oxen, or wife.

Agape and the Four Loves

III,5.4 *The judgmental love of Q²*

Right away at the beginning of Q² in QS 4 we hear John the Baptist proclaiming:

> You offspring of vipers!
> Change your ways
> if you have changed your mind.
> Don't say, "We have Abraham as our father."
> God can raise up children for Abraham
> from these stones.
> Even now the ax is aimed
> at the root of the trees.
> Every tree that does not bear good fruit
> is cut down and thrown into the fire.

During this period of Q² from 35 C.E. to 75 C.E. Mack tells us that the Jesus people had the two main problems of persecutors and traitors and this early saying seems to be addressing the traitors. Up in Galilee many did have a change of mind and follow Jesus. But then when they were threatened by serious persecution and death they could have started acting and talking like ordinary Jews and simply called themselves children of Abraham rather than Jesus people who would seek to bear the good fruit of unconditional *agape*. You might wonder how this apocalyptic attitude of condemning to hell fire those Jesus followers who would not now bear witness could fit in with an *agape* this is not supposed to resist evil. But John the Baptist like Jesus is not resisting evil rather by telling the whole truth and nothing but the truth he is not in the least a traitor, but he gets himself martyred as did Jesus. Each traitor who is afraid to go out and proclaim the good news will not bear the good fruit of a universal love without fear. Once again unconditional love must explain the misery that comes from any self-centered love and once a disciple understands this he should know if he betrays this love he is entering hell fire.

III,5.5 Must pass judgment on this generation

The Jesus people during the forty year period from the death of Jesus to the end of the Roman war were threatened by a wicked generation. Thus QS 32 says:

> Some said to him, "Teacher,
> we wish to see a sign from you."
> He answered them,
> "A wicked generation looks for a sign,
> but no sign will be shown it,
> except the sign of Jonah.
> For as Jonah became a sign to the Ninevites,
> so will the son of man be to this generation."

Jesus proclaimed his message of love to many and the Q
people changed their attitude and way of life and followed him.
But his example and love message were not enough to convince
the multitude and they wanted a sign or miracle as proof.
During the forty year period from the death of Jesus to the end
of the Roman war the Q community went through difficult times.
Up in Galilee the cities of Chorazin, Bethsaida and Capernaum
saw many loving deeds but that was not enough for them.
All they will get is the sign of Jonah which was simply his
message that the people of Nineveh should repent and change.
The people of Q must love them and pray for them and they
even do more for they perform the works of love of reading and
writing and speaking and listening for the wicked generation in
the wicked cities and the story of Jonah is part of their writing.
As the people of Q pray for their enemies they meditate on
their common Jewish scriptures and the Q^2 text is a
rewriting of that whole sacred story and spiritual reading
and writing is a work of love they perform for their persecutors.

Agape and the Four Loves

III,5.6 As will the Holy Spirit

As the Q community rewrote the great epic-apocalyptic story
they meditated daily on just how to love their traitors and persecutors.
They themselves included the story about the lost sheep and had Jesus
say that if the good shepherd could find it:

> He will rejoice more over that one sheep
> than over the ninety-nine
> that did not go astray.

So they would love and pray for each traitor just as Jesus would
for the lost sheep, but how would Jesus love their persecutors?
In QS 37 the son of man speaks their mind;

> Whoever makes a speech against the son of man
> will be forgiven
> But whoever speaks against the holy spirit
> will not be forgiven.

So even if the Pharisees and the wicked generation speak against
the son of man they will be forgiven as Jesus forgave his persecutors.
But what is the Holy Spirit that all of a sudden appears here in Q^2?
It is also said in QS 37 that when the Jesus people are brought
to trial they should be confident in their love:

> Don't worry about what you are to say.
> When the time comes, the holy spirit
> will teach you what you are to say.

On page 169, Burton Mack says that: "It is obvious that the vision
of standing trial had traumatized the Q community." But the Holy Spirit
will inspire them and so at least the Holy Spirit guides and inspires.
And so as we wonder about the relation between loving and forgiving
in Q^2 there is much forgiveness for the wicked generation might
even speak against Jesus as the son of man and they will be forgiven.
But the Holy Spirit seems to be greater than the son of man and
perhaps is as holy as God the father and the son of God whom we
are now ready to meet as we come to the new period of Q^3.

III,5.7 The agape that reverences God alone in Q³

The Q³ section of the text begins with the words:

> Then Jesus was led into the wilderness
> by the spirit for trial by the *diabolos*.

This spirit must be the same Holy Spirit who inspires
the Jesus people when they are on trial and the last words
that the son of God says to the *diabolos* in this Q 56 saying are:

> It is written, "You shall reverence
> the lord your God and serve him alone."

This reverence must be the deepest core of all *agape*.
Jesus teach that we should love the lord our God with our
whole heart, mind and soul and our neighbor as ourself.
Here in this first Q³ saying there is the lord our God,
there is the son of God and there is the Holy Spirit and they
reveal that we should reverence and serve them alone and we
can do that by loving and serving all of God's children.
Everyone who was, is and will be is a child of the creator.
Jesus, the son of God, is the child of God and reveals the love of God
to all those who are childlike for no one knows the father
except the son who teaches of his *agape* and this agapeic reverence.
In Q¹ Jesus, the child of wisdom, reveals an *agape* for all even enemies.
In Q² Jesus, the son of man, warns sinners about punishment.
In Q³ Jesus, the son of God, reveals how *agape* is rooted in God.
Here with the father, son and Holy Spirit we are only a step away
from the Holy Spirit of the risen lord Jesus revealing that God is love.
This Holy Spirit is almost revealing that she is the love between
the father and the son and that she let Jesus become flesh.
Even the wise of all humankind never knew of this *agape*
that is revealed by the father through the son and the Spirit.
This reverence that the son of God teaches us, by teaching
the *diabolos*, to have for the lord our God now gives us the big
picture that motivates us to love all persons because we love God.

Agape and the Four Loves

III,5.8 Is a reverence that fears God and yet knows

Once their forty years in the desert of being persecuted from town to town by the Pharisees and the wicked generation comes to an end with the conclusion of the Roman war the Q^3 people experience the Holy Spirit revealing to them Jesus as the son of God. In the Q^1 stage Jesus taught an unconditional love with increasing warning about a natural punishment for those who would not love. In the Q^2 stage the son of man emphasized an apocalyptic judgment and justice for any traitors and for all persecutors. Now in the Q^3 stage there is a primacy of loving mercy and yet a punishment of hell fire for those who will not reverence God. When the *diabolos* was tempting the son of God

> He took him to a very high mountain
> and showed him all the Kingdoms
> of the world and their splendour,
> and he said to him,
> "All these will I give you
> if you will do obeisance and reverence me

This pride which the devil had in wanting to be like unto God is much the same pride that egoists have who will not prefer others to themselves and reverence God as greater than themselves. When like the devil we insist on doing our will against God's will we should remember QS 36:

> Fear the one who is able to destroy
> both the body and soul in hell fire.

Reverence for God, even though we know of God's merciful love from Jesus, always includes a fear of the Lord because God in his awesome wonder and mystery makes of us shakers and quakers. Without Jesus' revelation about God's merciful love we might gather as did all the wise among men that God is only just. All religions and philosophies except Jesus' *agape* religion are aware of evil in the world and emphasize God's justice.

III,5.9 That Jesus is like a mother hen with her chicks

Jesus as the son of God in Q³ has set up a new balance between
a merciful love theology and an atonement justice theology with
the primacy given to merciful love in that it will win out in the end.
A mother hen with her sweet, little yellow, peeping chicks
has a great natural affection as you find with all mother
animals for their little babies and Jesus loves with affection.
His *agape* for all that loves and forgives all is also an affection
for all and that is why he says:

> O Jerusalem, Jerusalem, killing the prophets
> and stoning those who are sent to you!
> How often would I have gathered your children
> together as a hen gathers her brood
> under her wings, and you refused.

But Jesus never gives up for as the Q¹ child of wisdom he forgives
his enemies even those who are killing him and as the Q²
son of man he must warn those who betray and persecute
the agapeic love community that there is a just natural punishment.
You cannot be negative to others without living with your negativity.
Now as the Q³ son of God he reveals that God's agapeic affection
even for prophet killers and stone throwers is always calling them.
They will suffer hell-fire but it will purge them and not be forever.
Every detail of the law of love has eternal significance for each
and every person for this Jesus always loves the least of the brethren.
At this point as we think about Jesus as this mother hen we need
to get right to the heart of our meditation in this volume and consider
agape and the four loves in the three stages of this Book of Q.
When *agape* is revealed by Jesus what are the Q approaches
to challenging and renewing affection, *eros*, friendship, and *hesed*?
We already have a beautiful example here with this image of
the mother hen and her affection and we have been told that unless
we hate the objects of our affection and *eros* we cannot be his disciples.

Agape and the Four Loves

III,6 The Gospel of Thomas lacks agape

III,6.1 As do all the Gnostic Gospels

As Burton Mack shows the Gnostic Gospel of Thomas is
more purely a Gospel of the sayings of the Jesus of Q than
are Matthew and Luke and yet the *agape* sayings are lacking.
On page 181 of his book Mack writes that;

> approximately one third of the sayings
> in the Gospel of Thomas have parallels in Q
> and about 60 percent are from the Q^1 layer.

As we think more deeply into the *agape* of the historical Jesus
the Gospel of Thomas can help us by getting us to question why
the Q^1 sayings of Matthew and Luke emphasize a universal *agape*
and how and why that is not part of the Gnostic vision of life.
On that same page Mack writes that

> Three features of the text reveal
> just how independent the Thomas people were.

To understand why their independence kept them from recognizing
the very core of the Q^1 sayings as rooted in:

> I am telling you, love your enemies,
> pray for those who mistreat you

we can begin with what Mack calls the first of the three features
that reveals the Thomas people's independence and that has to do
with the form of Dialogue in which Jesus answers questions.
Thomas, Salome and Mary ask right questions and give right
answers while Matthew, Peter and James do just the opposite.
And this Thomas, Salome and Mary belong to the inner circle that
is privileged by Jesus and the other disciples are seen as foolish.
The Jesus of Q^1 even in Thomas is a wisdom teacher and
wisdom has to do with Gnosis or a special, secret knowledge.
The Jesus of the Gospel of Thomas does not talk about loving all
especially enemies and blessing those who curse you and praying
with love for those who mistreat you for that is all folly.

III,6.2 Lack of agape kept the Gnostic Gospels out of the canon

Just as the Q^1 sayings of Matthew and Luke emphasize the *agape*
which resists not evil and prays lovingly for the enemy
so the Gospel of Thomas emphasizes the secret knowledge that saves.
This secret knowledge belongs only to a few and saying 13
shows that even Peter and Matthew are excluded from it whereas
Thomas is taken aside by Jesus and given the elitist gnosis.
The *agape* that predominates not only in Q^1 but in all
the canonical scripture is not even mentioned in Thomas.
In fact love is mentioned only in sayings 25, 43 and 55
and each of these sayings is more against than for *agape*.
In saying 25 Jesus said:

> Love your father like your soul,
> guard him like the pupil of your eye.

And just before this saying 23 Jesus said

> I shall choose you, one out of a thousand,
> and two out of ten thousand.

So the Jesus in Luke who came that all flesh
might see the salvation of the Lord is the opposite
of this Jesus of Thomas whose saving knowledge
excludes almost all even Peter and Matthew from the few.
Q^2 was all about the future coming of the kingdom and even
the *Our Father* was a prayer of petition for the kingdom to come.
But, for Thomas the kingdom is here and now and within
for the few with Gnosis and will never come for people like Peter.
The canonical writings stress the logic of the both-and
in which the kingdom of love is here and yet is also to come.
In the dialogue of the Gospel of Thomas as Burton Mack shows
any question about a kingdom to come is silly and so is any thought
about the works of love and ritual behavior such as how to pray.
Praying and giving with charity or *agape* are essential in
the canon but are not worth while in gaining secret knowledge.

Agape and the Four Loves

III,6.3 *Thomas lacks both incarnation love*

As Burton Mack explains the independence of the Thomas People
by showing how they differ from all three stages of the Q
community he shows on page 83 how they

> rejected the mythology of the Apocalyptic son of man...
> They took instead, the mythology of Jesus
> as the child of wisdom and the son of God...
> and cultivated his teachings as signatures of
> his self-knowledge as the incarnation of Divine Wisdom.

This Gnostic theme of self knowledge is central for Thomas
and is not only the opposite of the love theme in Q^1 but also
of the grateful prayer of the Son of God in Q^3 who says:

> I am grateful to you, father,
> Master of heaven and earth
> because you have kept these things
> hidden from the wise and understanding
> and revealed them to babies.

The theme of prayerful love runs through both Q^1 and Q^3
and is revealed by Jesus to the childlike who can pray with
a grateful *Yes* and *Amen* for all of existence and as Thomas shows
this is hidden from the wise and knowing Gnostics who deny it.
The Gospel of Thomas does value being like little children
but in the second of the three sayings which speak
of love Thomas speaks ill of love and the Jews:

> You do not realize who I am
> from what I say to you
> but you have become like the Jews,
> for they (either) love the tree and hate the fruit
> or love the fruit and hate the tree.

In this saying 43 Thomas seems to have no appreciation
for the Jews who seem to take ambivalent attributes toward
the tree of the knowledge of good and evil and its good or bad fruit.

III,6.4 And atonement justice theologies

Burton Mack tells us how the Thomas people not only rejected the Apocalyptic son of man but also:

> the notion of the prophets
> as the envoys of wisdom
> or as those who predicted Jesus.

The Gospel of Thomas not only rejects all the *agape* sayings of the Q people but it also rejects the Hebrew Bible and all that led up to the Q interplay of incarnation love and justice. The Mosaic Covenant stressed that the chosen people should love the Lord their God with their whole heart, mind and soul and their neighbor as themselves and any breach of that command or any of the commandments would be punished by the just God. The Davidic Promise theology stressed an everlasting love of mercy for the Kingdom of David and yet punishment for any sin. All of this prepares the way for Jesus' new teaching of *agape* as an unconditional love for all humans and even all flesh. In Q there is the primacy of an incarnation love theology that is further supplemented by Q^3 and the incarnate son of God. In Q^2 the secondary role of atonement justice is presented. So the contrast between the appropriation of the Q sayings in the Gospel of Thomas with Q in Matthew and Luke is very enlightening concerning *agape* for the whole Jewish Christian tradition is rejected as the Gnostic Gospel stresses only a special elite and secret knowledge without any love. No wonder of it that in saying 43 there is no love for the Jews and in fact Jewish love is rejected for the Thomas people are told that if they do not recognize the Gnostic Jesus they become like Jews who had Jesus put to death. Many Jews did not reject Jesus for the first Christians were Jews. So the *agape* of Q and the justice of Q^2 are both rejected by the Gnostics who value instead secret knowledge for the elite.

Agape and the Four Loves

III,6.5 Are true love and justice replaced by endless riddles?

In explaining the differences between the Q text and the Thomas Gospel Burton Mack writes that

> The third feature of the text
> is the riddle like feature
> of the sayings . . .
> the mysterious quality
> of the already enigmatic sayings.

Saying 43 which disparages Jewish love is an example
of this enigmatic riddling with which the Thomas people
distance themselves from the community of Q^1 loving believers.
What is going on with this saying that non-Gnostics

> become like the Jews
> for they either love the tree
> and hate the fruit
> or love the fruit and hate the tree.

Are the Jews like the tree from which comes the fruit of Christianity?
And would the Jews hate the fruit and would the Christians
hate the tree which could be true for the Gospel of Thomas Christians?
When the Q community experienced traitors from the community
and persecutors of the community after the Ascension of Jesus
they called down the apocalyptic message of judgment upon
their enemies and the Q^2 Christ seemed contrary to the Jesus of Q^1.
The Gospel of Thomas rejected the entire Jewish Apocalyptic
movement and its coming of the eschatological kingdom for the good.
The Thomas community would never get involved in such hatred.
The response of the Thomas community to troubled times was
detachment for as Burton Mack says of them:

> whoever finds himself
> of him the world is not worthy. (Saying 111)

Part Two: Sorrowful Proceedings

III,6.6 Does Thomas' hatred of family serve agape?

The difficult saying at the end of Q^1 is used exactly in the Gospel of Thomas at saying 55

> Jesus said, "whoever does not hate his father
> and his mother cannot become a disciple to me.
> and whoever does not hate his brother and sisters
> and take up his cross in My way
> will not be worthy of me.

But the context of this saying is totally different in Thomas
than it is in Q^1 for here it does not have to serve *agape*.
We have a natural egotistic, preferential love for our family,
for our beloved and for our friend and to practise universal
unconditional love for everyone we have to first weed out
our natural love that we might have *agape* absolutely and
then we can love relatively with affection, *eros* and friendship.
To hate then in Q^1 means to weed out our preferential love.
But in the Gospel of Thomas there is no universal *agape*.
Taking up our cross and following Jesus in Thomas means
leaving our family that we might be alone with Jesus
apart from family and society to build up our secret knowledge.
So the three sayings about love in the Gospel of Thomas are
not really about love either as *agape* or even as natural love.
Saying 25 which says "Love your brother like your soul."
in the light of saying 55 and the context of the Gospel cannot mean
loving your natural brother but rather your fellow Gnostic companion.
Saying 43 about the Jews loving the tree or the fruit only shows
that Gnostics should not love in the ways Jews do and thus
even though the Gospel of Thomas builds out of the Q sayings
it is significant that is has no treatment of *agape* so central to Q.
The Jesus of Q teaches an *agape* that is altruistic and thus
builds up a new kind of ethics that prefers the other to the self.
The Jesus of Thomas teaches us to build up self by leaving others.

Agape and the Four Loves

III,6.7 Is Thomas more egoistic than the Greeks and Jews?

When we reflect on what Thomas subtracted from the Q text and what he added to it we are immediately struck by his getting rid of Jesus' new religion and ethics of unconditional love. Thomas develops a self realization ethics instead but when we ponder Gnostic self realization we see that it is more egoistical than the ethics of either the Jews or the Greeks. The Jewish religion is very ethical and Jews are commanded to love their neighbors as themselves especially widows, orphans and aliens. Each Greek system had a self realization ethics and the Platonists, the Aristotelians and the Stoics each considered the political self realization of the city state as well as individual realization. By following the cynical school without the *agape* of Q's Jesus the Gnostics stressed that the kingdom is here and now and within each Gnostic who has discovered true self knowledge. Socrates too saw ethics as beginning with the "know thyself." But the Greek and Roman schools that developed that idea of self knowledge never used it in a totally individualistic way. At the basis of each Greek system was a type of love such as *storge* or affection, *eros* or sexual love and *philia* or friendship. At the basis of the Jewish religious ethics was the *ahava* love of the Mosiac covenant and the *hesed* or everlasting merciful love of the Davidic promise theology and the Gnostics get rid of it all. By totally stressing self knowledge at the expense of any kind of natural love and self realization ethics or of *agape* and its totally altruistic love the Gnostics are totally self-centered. So they will not have a religion and ethics of *agape* and personhood in which all persons are of equal worth, each person is unique and all are interpersonal. They do reverence the Father, Son and Holy Spirit and do not have any subordinationism but human persons are very unequal for the few Gnostics are all good and the others bad.

III,6.8 They do reverence Father, Son and Holy Spirit

In accord with the Q text saying 44 of Thomas reads:

> Jesus said: "whoever blasphemes against the Father
> will be forgiven, and whoever blasphemes
> against the Son will be forgiven,
> but whoever blasphemes against the Holy Spirit
> will not be forgiven either on earth or in heaven."

In the Gospel of Thomas the Father and the Son are both seen
as equally divine but the Holy Spirit could be subordinate.
Jesus is up front in every saying but there is not that much
about the Holy Spirit so this saying helps prevent subordinationism.
But this saying when put into context can also in what it omits
and in what is denied be very instructive concerning *agape*.
In orthodox Christianity which thinks that God is love
the Holy Spirit is thought of as the love between Father and Son.
But this love which is *agape* is totally omitted in Thomas.
Furthermore, the Holy Spirit is thought of as the one who inspires
to pray and to be reverent but in the Gospel of Thomas there
are some very curious statements about prayer for already
in saying 6

> His disciples questioned Him and said to Him,
> "Do you want us to fast?
> How shall we pray? Shall we give alms?
> What diet shall we observe?"

And then in saying 14

> Jesus said to them, "If you fast,
> you will give rise to sin for yourselves;
> and if you pray, you will be condemned;
> and if you give alms, you will do harm
> to your spirits."

So what is this about praying and being condemned
and should the Holy Spirit guide our spirit not to give alms?

Agape and the Four Loves

III,6.9 *But there is no concept of personhood for humans*

The Gospel of Thomas could claim that Father, Son and Holy Spirit
are equal, unique and interrelated but the concept of personhood
that could apply to them could never apply to human persons.
Gnostic elitism is explicitly opposed to the equal worth of humans
and the Gnostics alone are really unique and they are not related
to the masses for whom they would never think of praying.
The belief in *agape* and personhood that Jesus taught in Q^1
of Matthew and Luke and is central to all the canonical texts
is not only rejected by Thomas but any implication is rejected.
That is why we get this peculiar saying that "If you pray,
you will be condemned." for the Gnostics have a consistent
attitude and must rely only on their knowledge that humans
are way too different and only a few will meet the Gnostic standard.
They are cynical about the masses and want nothing to do with them.
Being contaminated by those who love unconditionally and who
pray and give alms as corporal works of mercy could so infect
them that they too might start loving and thus be condemned.
The prayer that adores, repents, thanks and petitions with
agape does imply a faith and hope in love that goes beyond
the Gnostic religion that works within the limits of reason alone.
Are many non-believers who reject faith and hope in love
really Gnostics who are very consistent in their belief
in a secret knowledge that lets them proudly be Gnostic?
Now that the Gospel of Thomas has raised these questions
about *agape* and what it implies we can go now with Mack
and see how he sees Matthew, then Luke and finally Mark
and John accepting the Q^1 Jesus and building on his *agape*.
As we continue to proceed we can explore how true love and true
knowledge might either collide or find ways to support each other.
Does the Holy Spirit give us each the grace to believe in *agape*
and can we reject the Holy Spirit inspiring Holy Mother church?

IV. Affection-Friendship-*Eros*-*Agape*

IV,4 The Augustinian synthesis of agape and John's eros

IV,4.1 Nygren's Luther initiates modernity with pure agape

From 1932 to 1938 Anders Nygren published his 750 page classic *Agape and Eros* and since then many prominent writers on *agape* have considered at length his theses, arguments, definitions and many distinctions and even some Lutherans have been critical of him. From the Catholic point of view the book by Fr. Martin D'arcy S. J. *The Mind and Heart of Love* has given a good defense of the Catholic tradition and has pointed out some key contradictions between Luther and various treatments of *agape* in scripture which Nygren notes. From now on as we ponder *agape* in various New Testaments texts we will keep Nygren in mind for in evaluating him in terms of scripture and in studying his history of *agape* we will be able to get more deeply into the mysteries of love and its variety of kinds. However, as we go along we will ponder not only *agape* and *eros* for if we think carefully there is also the issue of how the natural loves of affection, friendship and natural *agape* might relate to *agape*. Already the word "natural" brings us to a key point in D'arcy's criticism of Nygren for D'arcy think that the natural loves can receive from and contribute to the supernatural love of *agape* whereas Nygren thinks that all things natural are totally depraved because of Adam's fall and thus *agape* and *eros* cannot mix at all. As we have seen the *agape* of the historical Jesus in Q[1] is totally altruistic and loves even enemies as more important than the self. Luther latches on to this and thinks that *agape* is a grace from God and something we should practice toward others but any self love is depraved and only ruins and contaminates *agape*. So when I love my family with affection, or my beloved with *eros* or my friend with friendship I indulge in a preferential love that is really a self love and thus is destructive of pure *agape*. It will now be our task to see how all the implications that make up modernity flow from this first thesis and how the postmodernists get back to the Catholic tradition with a logic of mixed opposites.

Agape and the Four Loves

IV,4.2 Defending Augustine against Luther's pure agape

Nygren's term for what Luther protests in the first fifteen hundred years of Christianity is *The Caritas Synthesis* and by that he means the synthesis of anti-egoistic *agape* and egoistic *eros* for when the Greek *agape* was translated into Latin, *caritas,* that was no longer the pure *agape* that was unlike anything Jewish or Greek. Nygren clarifies his main Lutheran thesis about pure *apape* from page 123 to 133 when he writes about "Love Towards God in Paul" and "Neighbourly Love and Love for God" and argues that Paul in his conversion from being a Jew to becoming a Christian moved from loving God to seeing that we cannot love God as God loves us. God's *agape* for us is spontaneous and unmotivated but our love for God can never be that for our "love" for God is totally motivated and is not spontaneous but is a gift from God that graces us with faith. Thus, we cannot have *agape* or pure love for God for we can only have faith in God's *agape* which can take us beyond our self love to an *apape* for our neighbor for whom we can sacrifice ourself. From pages 91 to 102 Nygren shows why the twofold command to love God and our neighbour is basically Jewish and has not been reworked with the new *agape* of Jesus that Paul and Luther understand. Augustine's *Caritas Synthesis* was more in keeping with the synoptic Gospels and especially John than with Luther's understanding of Paul. When Augustine wrote his *Confessions* quite a few years after his conversion he did say:

> You have made us for yourself, oh God,
> and our hearts are restless until they rest in Thee.

He did believe that loving God could help him share more and more in the happy life so he was motivated to love God and he knew that his *caritas* was not spontaneous but was a gift of grace. So there is a great deal of self love in Augustine's *caritas* but how can Luther get rid of all self love and what else will he have to get rid of including much of the scripture in doing that?

IV,4.3 And with "tota scriptura" against "sola scriptura"

As we are beginning to see Luther not only got rid of philosophy
with his idea of scripture alone but he also got rid of a large
amount of scripture with his idea of a totally unselfish *agape*.
Of course, Jesus did teach a selfless love for others even our enemies.
Nygren points out how already in 1515 in his lectures on Paul's
Letter to the Romans Luther developed his idea of *agape* and self hatred.
On page 512 in volume 25 of Luther's works Luther writes:

> For in accord with blessed Augustine,
> the Master of the Sentences affirms:
> "First we must love God, then our own soul,
> then the soul of our neighbor,
> and finally our own body."

About this statement of Peter the Lombard Luther writes:

> Ordered love therefore begins with itself.
> The answer to this is that this is one of the things
> by which we are led away from love
> as long as we do not fully understand it.
> For as long as we first use each good for ourselves,
> we are not concerned about our neighbor.
> But true love for yourself is hatred of yourself.
> As our Lord said: "For whoever would love his life, will lose it,
> and he who hates his life will find it." Mark 8:35

This is the starting point of Luther's theology and of Nygren's book
on *Agape and Eros* for they are very serious about defining *agape*
as love for the other and thus seeing love for self as hatred of self.
The Catholic tradition with its *Caritas* Synthesis did think that we should
love our neighbor as ourself because we love God who is Love.
Rooted in this notion of *agape* as self sacrificing love Luther
saw no truth in either Judaism or Paganism because with their
self realization ethics they had no idea that true love is hatred of self.

Agape and the Four Loves

IV,4.4 And with works of love against "sola fidei"

Luther does believe in performing the works of love for the neighbor. But he does not believe that we can merit anything from that. Christ's atoning death alone justified and if we believe that with faith alone we will be saved so we do not love God but we have faith in him. We have faith that God's love for us brought Jesus to his death and we should love our neighbor as Christ loved us by self sacrificial love. On page 219 Nygren sets up a chart on the four dimensions of love.

Agape				*Eros*
3	Downward Movement	God's love	Upward Movement	0
2		Neighborly love		1
1		Love for God		2
0		Self-love		3

The self-centred ethics of *eros* and the self hatred ethics of *agape* are exclusive opposites according to the Lutheran theology of Nygren. Contrasting Nygren and Kierkegaard on the issue of getting love right by hating self shows the differences between modernity and postmodernity. Kierkegaard as well as Luther took seriously the saying at Luke 14:26–27:

> If any man comes to me without hating
> his father, mother, wife, children, brothers, sisters,
> yes and his own life too, he cannot be my disciple.
> Anyone who does not carry his cross
> and come after me cannot be my disciple.

For Kierkegaard the aesthetic affection, the ethical friendship and the erotic mystical love have a self preferential basis in them. We must therefore hate these three loves and their objects in order to absolutely love the absolute who loves us and then we can relatively love family, friend and beloved once we first love them as neighbors. Kierkegaard's whole philosophy of the works of love is based on this hate. Luther and Nygren do not correct and restore self-love, love of God and neighborly love with the right kind of a loving self-hatred. But self hatred comes from a faith alone about our total depravity.

IV,4.5 Defending Johannine and Augustinian philosophy

The Prologue to John's Gospel is totally philosophical and in recognizing that Augustine thought that up until it is said: "And the Word was made flesh." it could be seen as Neoplatonic. And for Augustine that event of the incarnation is all important. Augustine even thinks of the sin of Adam as "O Felix Culpa" "oh happy fault" because that original sin could be thought of as the reason for Jesus becoming man and getting his new notion of love started and putting in motion the new world that would result. Nygren, Luther and modernity are totally against Augustine and his *Caritas* Synthesis which combines erotic love and the new agapeic love. Luther and Nygren with their atonement justice theology totally overlook the value of an incarnation love theology which loves all that exists for Platonic and Augustinian philosophers explain how being is good and true and beautiful and if we have fallen from that insight we can rise to it again and Plato's philosophy of the ladder and the cave explain that. The Johannine Augustinian hierarchy of love which Luther quotes is so self evident in its value hierarchy that all of mankind except for protesting, self hating, double predestinationist, atonement theologians like Luther, Calvin and Nygren will see it as most loving. This hierarchy that sees all of existence insofar as it has being as being beautiful, good, true, and holy brings Kierkegaard to his aesthetic, ethical, religiousness A and religiousness B value hierarchy and it brings Max Scheler to his physical, vital, intellectual and spiritual values. No wonder that Nygren is against everyone from John to Augustine right through the middle ages and then against Nietzsche and Scheler. Nygren and Luther see the whole of the philosophic tradition from Plato to John to Augustine and from then on to Kierkegaard and Scheler as trying to perform good works through philosophy and thus they are dead set against it and even if there is the love of wisdom and the wisdom of love in John and the Wisdom literature of the Hebrew Bible they get rid of a great deal of scripture to have only scripture.

Agape and the Four Loves

IV,4.6 And Johannine and Augustinain mysticism

Nygren's treatment of Platonic mysticism is excellent as he discusses "The Doctrine of *Eros* as a Doctrine of Salvation" from page 160 to 200. He begins by asking whether *eros* piety is Christianity's forerunner or rival and intends to show that it is a rival, however, against his own Lutheran position he ends up showing that John can fit with Plato. His treatment of Platonic *Eros* in *The Symposium* and *The Phaedrus* shows that he is a marvelous anti-philosophical philosopher.

In *The Symposium* Plato's idea of the seven stepped ladder which moves from the lower to the higher *eros* in a mystical ascent of purification, illumination and unification has reverberated through nearly all of Catholic mysticism from Augustine to Teresa of Avila to Thomas Merton. The Divine Madness of *The Phaedrus* at 245c and following is the supreme and guiding example of erotic sublimation admired by Mystics from Origen to Dante and to Nietzsche in his sublime creativity.

Just before this chapter Nygren analyzes the Johannine writings especially the first Letter of John that formally states that God is *agape*. On page 152 Nygren quotes John XVI.27

> The Father Himself loveth you,
> *because* you have loved me.

This goes totally against the Lutheran axiom of faith without works. Nygren has shown the Lutheran position that I should love others but not myself and here we see the opposite that by loving Jesus we can help ourselves a great deal by meriting God's love for us. Also Nygren shows how John is against the Lutheran position because there is a brotherly love and particularism for only *the* brethren can become one as the Father and the Son are one (John XVII.11) and so again there is a great self-love for in loving my brethren I also love myself. Nygren on page 157 brings out how this acquisitive love is the opposite of a love that gives and takes, and opposites exclude each other whereas for John and the Catholic tradition they promote each other. Augustine wrote often on John and his mystical *Caritas Synthesis*.

IV,4.7 Modern psychological rugged individualism

On page 470 Nygren writes:

> We now come to the great and fatal
> contradiction in Augustine's view of love.
> He wanted to maintain both *Eros* and *Agape* at once.
> He was unaware that they are diametrically
> opposed to each other and that the relation
> between them must be an Either-or;
> instead, he tried to make it a Both-And.
> But this was not done without tension and conflict.

The reason that Luther admits nothing of *eros* and the philosophy
and mysticism that developed out of its is his view that human nature
became totally depraved with Adam's sin which we have inherited.
No human being can do the least thing that is any good whatsoever
unless he has faith that God's Son became man and died for us.
With faith we can believe in God's *Agape* which is self-sacrificing.
Thus, Luther was the first person ever to believe in this Either-or
for Peter, Paul, the Apostles and all Christians until Luther had this
Both-And view for which Luther and Nygren have no tolerance at all.
Paul believed in The Mystical Body of Christ and the communal
or interpersonal notion of personhood in which we all need each other.
As Martin D'arcy puts it on page 95:

> The full meaning of "Caritas" cannot, however,
> be understood without some reference
> to the doctrine of "incorporation" in Christ.

He then quotes Gerard Manly Hopkins:

> For Christ plays in ten thousand places,
> Lovely in limbs, and lovely in eyes not his
> To the Father through the features of men's faces.

Once Luther stresses his sick notion of self hatred he will not
be able to love Christ playing in lovely limbs and eyes not his
for with modernity's rugged individualism man is already a wolf to man.

Agape and the Four Loves

IV,4.8 And the modern political rugged individualism

The *eros-agape* relation is also very significant for Politics and Augustine wrote his great book, *The City of God*, with this in mind. As Nygren points out he argues that two loves have built two cities. The love of God is building the city of God and the love of self is building the city of man, but Augustine does believe in a well-ordered self love. In his section on *The Campaign Against Self-Love* on pages 709 Nygren shows how Augustine thinks that self-love is evil only when it is selfish and goes against the God who is love and other persons. Because persons are interpersonal self-love can work for others. Against this Luther argues that all self-love is vicious, and needs to be destroyed so that we can imitate Jesus in self-sacrifice for others. Because for Luther each single individual stands alone before God and every man is an island and none of us are part of the main the Lutheran politics of "*cuius regio, eius religio*" developed because psychological rugged individualism implies that politically.
In Modernity state churches become the norm with Lutheran regions, certain Calvinist regions and certain Anglican regions and there were great wars fought between them until in postmodernity there is the attempt to once again get a united states of Europe with peace for all. Augustine's politics of basing our culture on love for God and for the universal common good of all persons describes well the unity of the European peoples before Luther came and protested vehemently against the sinfulness of any self-love and of any common good. Augustine's philosophy of a universal history that makes progress through different periods of history might even look upon Luther and Nygren as contributing to God's plan for human development. Hegel could be seen as a kind of Augustinian pointing out that to the Catholic thesis of the *Caritas Synthesis* the Lutheran Antithesis against any kind of love except pure *agape* even as self-hatred, could bring about the postmodern synthesis beginning with Kierkegaard who went from Luther's Either-or to a Neither-Nor to the Both-And.

Part Two: Sorrowful Proceedings

IV,4.9 By not throwing out Augustine's three p's

As Nygren explains the Lutheran Antithesis to the first fifteen hundred years of Christianity he summarizes beginning on page 594, the ladder-symbolism common to all Catholics and characteristic of *Eros* piety and its ascent by the ladder of virtue, speculation and mysticism. However, as Nygren also points out there was something of this in John's Gospel insofar as he would make much of terms like: "light," "life," "know," "spirit" and "glory" and insofar as he thought "The Father Himself loveth you, *because* ye have loved me." which shows that by the virtue of love we can rise up and even merit God's help.

To think of this from another angle we might notice that the first three things Luther got rid of were the papacy, philosophy and purgatory. Jesus built his church upon Peter and the hierarchy of the other apostles. Jesus was the head of the Mystical Body as Paul put it and we are the members and once Jesus ascended into heaven as we see in *The Acts of The Apostles* Peter was the representative of Jesus upon earth and there was a succession of authoritative Popes right through history. Luther took offence at the church and her Papacy and the Bishops who sometimes were sinful— "*Justus et peccator*" as he would say, and got rid of the very structure of the Church which Jesus had established. He protested against the church in her use of *eros* instead of pure *agape* for that *eros*-piety had at its core the upward ascent from the moral to the intellectual to the theological virtues of Aquinas.

Luther protested against this hierarchy of virtues because they were good works by which one loves God, self and neighbor to grow in love. Luther protested the virtues and then he protested the popes because they were not virtuous and thus he was a great speculator against speculation as is Nygren for their analytic, intellectually virtuous speculation against any synthetic speculation deserves much thanks. And finally Luther got rid of purgatory which enabled Catholics to pray for their blessed dead and the dead to pray for them in a reconciling love even for the self that could love away all sin.

IV,5 The Thomistic synthesis of agape and Paul's friendship

IV,5.1 Nygren also opposes sublimating friendship to agape

On page 650 Nygren writes:

> The Medieval solution of the problem of *Caritas*
> thus consists in the sublimation of acquisitive love
> or self-love into pure love for God.

On the next page he writes:

> The solution was sought
> on the lines of sublimation:
> the initial egocentricity should be
> neutralized by a heightened demand
> for purity in one's love of God.

This sublimation can take one into the realm of the sublime as it did for Plato when all the energy of vulgar sex became reconciled into the creativity and enthusiasm of Divine Madness so that the Platonist would be beyond any sexual temptation in the sublimity of excellence. In the Monastery Luther tried to overcome his sexual temptations but the miracle of transformation never took place in his young life. So he took up a campaign against sublimation and all *eros* friendship and affection as caught in self-love and so whether they were sublimated or not they were equally opposed to self-sacrifice. On page 690 Nygren spells out the difference very clearly:

> The deepest difference between Catholicism and Luther
> can be expressed by the following formulae;
> in Catholicism: fellowship with God
> on God's own level, on the basis of holiness;
> in Luther: fellowship with God
> on our level, on the basis of sin.

So as God sacrificed himself for me a sinner so I must love my neighbor and with pure *agape* and no *eros*, friendship or affection sacrifice myself for any other human who might be my wife or companion or child but I must not love them with any self love which exists in any *eros*, friendship or affection.

IV,5.2 For loving the other half of my soul is also self-love

Nygren places Aristotle, Aquinas and friendship within the context
of Plato, Augustine's *Caritas* Synthesis and *eros* as is clear when
he writes on page 611:

> It is exactly the same fundamental motif
> that find expression in both scholasticism and mysticism ...
> Something similar is also true of the contrast
> between Platonism and Aristotelianism in Medieval thought ...
> If we turn our attention to the basic
> religious and ethical motif
> we find again that it is in both cases the same.

So Nygren does not help us explore the sublimation of friendship into
Agape as we find it in Aquinas and in John as well as in Paul.
When you begin to contrast the love of *eros* and the love of friendship
it is obvious that *eros* is more passionate and powerful with
the energy of sexuality so you can understand an erotic sublimation.
But what would be meant by a sublimation of friendship and would
Aristotle consider such a phenomenon or does it begin with Jesus?
As we have seen Paul does recommend the practise of celibacy
so that if it is one's vocation he or she might dedicate their life
to serving God by proclaiming the good news to all God's people.
Since *agape* is first of all a universal love for all that will even
sacrifice self for them Christian sublimation means the transforming
of *eros* or friendship or affection into that universal altruistic
love that no longer loves just my beloved, my friend or my child.
We see that Jesus practised this sublimation for he did not marry
and thus his *eros* became very powerful toward women many of whom
followed him and cared for him and he said Magdalen's name with love.
The notion of Brethren in John has to do with a universalizing
friendship that seeks to go out and to be friendly to everyone.
Aristotle points out that we have only a few friends but when
agape comes I can be friendly to all who belong to Christ's Body.

IV,5.3 Defending Aquinas' philia against Luther's agape

While St. Augustine was a great erotic St. Thomas was not that at all. At the age of six his parents sent him to the Benedictine Abbey of Monte Casino where he got the best possible education and grew up in the protected atmosphere of the monks with no thought about sex. Whereas Augustine's father took delight in introducing him to sexuality St. Thomas with the Benedictines and then the Dominicans would be a natural Catholic in accord with Nygren's view and would experience "fellowship with God on God's own level, on the basis of holiness." Nygren just does not work with a major distinction between *eros* and *philia* and hence reduces all natural love to vulgar or noble *eros*. But it would never occur to Aquinas to think of the love between Father, Son and Holy Spirit as having to do with *eros* as Nygren thinks Neo-Platonists and Christian Platonists must conceive of God. When Aquinas treats Love or Charity in his *Summa Theologiae* in the second part of the second part in questions 23 to 33 he begins right away in question 23, Article 1, with the question *whether Charity is a friendship* and already in this first article we can begin to see so much about how friendship is sublimated to *agape*. After raising three objections from a strictly Aristotelian point of view to his thesis that *agape* is friendship Aquinas states his thesis:

> On the other hand the Lord's words,
> *No longer will I call you servants*
> *but my friends* (John 15,15)
> can be explained only in terms of charity,
> which, therefore, is friendship.

So, as we have seen already John is very anti-Lutheran and does make a Both-And of, in this case, friendship and *agape* or charity. For, Aquinas the best way to think of *agape* is in terms of friendship. By friendship he means a mutual love as it is between the persons of God and between God and human persons and between human persons as a sublimated friendship makes possible.

IV,5.4 In that sublimated Aristotelian friendship can be agape

While Aquinas greatly appreciates Aristotle's treatment of friendship
he makes it clear right from the beginning that by itself friendship
is not yet *agape* or charity but charity can be sublimated friendship.
As he argues his thesis that charity is friendship he begins by
raising three objections to his thesis from an Aristotelian point of view.
We can examine these one at a time to see how natural friendship
is not yet charity and just what the sublimation is as it becomes charity.
In objection one Aquinas asks "Is charity a friendship?" and then
he writes:

> It seems not. For according to Aristotle,
> *nothing so marks friendship as dwelling together.*
> Now man's charity is with God and the angels
> *whose dwelling*, as Daniel puts it
> *is not with creatures of flesh.*
> Therefore charity is not friendship.

Friends love to spend time together, to live together and as Aristotle
says: *"To eat a peck of salt together."*
But we cannot do this with God or the Angels who are not physical.
We cannot live with God outwardly in space but we can live
with Father, Son and Holy Spirit inwardly in time so in answering
objection one after distinguishing inward time and outward space
he concludes:

> And so here our charity is imperfect
> but will be made perfect in heaven.

Throughout eternity we will be able to dwell in a love of friendship
with the resurrected Jesus so the natural friendship of Aristotle
is sublimated and transformed into a sublime friendship with God
by our faith and our hope that let us believe and hope in
those words of Jesus:

> No longer will I call you servants
> but my friends.

Agape and the Four Loves

IV,5.5 *And Paul lived out this agapeic friendship*

To understand the added elements that let charity be a friendship we can now consider Aquinas second objection in which he writes that it seems that charity is not friendship because:

> according to Aristotle, friendship is not
> without love returned.
> But the evangelical command, *Love your enemies*
> embraces even those who make no such return.
> And so charity is not friendship.

So charity according to Aquinas is God's love for us and our love for God in which there is friendship and it is also our love for all other persons including our enemies even though they do not love us as Aristotle's natural, mutual friendship demands. In his response to this objection Aquinas writes:

> In this way charity, which above all is friendship,
> reaches out to sinners whom we love for God's sake.

So friendship is made sublime first when we love God whom we know only through faith and hope and secondly it is more sublime when for the sake of God we love our enemies. Aquinas explains this by writing:

> Now there is a sharing of man with God
> by his sharing his happiness with us,
> and it is on this that a friendship is based.
> St. Paul refers to it in I Corinthians 1,9
> *God is faithful by whom you*
> *were called into the fellowship of his Son.*
> Now the love which is based
> on this sort of fellowship is charity.
> Accordingly it is clear that charity
> \is a friendship of man and God.

So Paul lived in this friendship of *agape* with God and not only with those who worked with him but even with those against him.

IV,5.6 By going out to sinners in friendship as did Jesus

In his third objection to the thesis that *agape* is *philia* Aquinas writes:

> Besides, for Aristotle, there are three kinds of friendship,
> friendship for utility, for pleasure, for worth.
> Now Charity is none of these.
> It is not useful, nor is it pleasurable . . .
> Likewise, charity is not Aristotle's friendship for worth,
> for that is for the virtuous alone,
> whereas charity extends to the wicked also.
> Consequently charity is not friendship.

However, when Aquinas answers this objection he writes:

> In a friendship of true worth
> we love principally a man of virtue,
> though out of regard for him
> we love all who belong to him,
> even if they are not virtuous.
> In this way charity, which above all is friendship,
> reaches out to sinners whom we love for God's sake.

So when our friendship for others is charitable it is sublimated
in a threefold way for, it becomes holy in loving the three persons
who are God and, it becomes universal in loving all persons
and, it becomes all forgiving in loving sinners for God's sake.
Paul's *agape* was constantly friendly in these three ways for he
believed that God the Father sent God the Son to die for us when
we were sinners and so God will always love us even as sinners.
At Paul's sublimating moment of conversion he came to love
the Father, Son and Holy Spirit as having an equal, divine worth,
and each in their uniqueness and in their being interpersonally related.
And so, even before these ideas were defined at Nicea Paul already
lived them out in a friendly charity for all persons, in their equal
worth, and each in his or her uniqueness and in their interrelatedness.
Aquinas' ideas on *philiac agape* fit perfectly with Paul's practice.

Agape and the Four Loves

IV,5.7 *Friendly charity does not detract from agape*

Nygren's book is about two opposed fundamental motifs and as he writes on page 30 originally they had nothing to do with each other but as they intermingled:

> *Agape* was bound to lose
> something of its original force.

This is the main point of the Protestant Reformation and of Modernity. *Agape* as the new self sacrificing, altruistic love met with *Eros* the upward aspiring love of a self realization ethics and throughout the fifteen hundred year tradition the *agape* of scripture lost its power. On page 621 Nygren puts it simply

> For Mediaeval thought it is self-evident
> that fellowship with God is a fellowship on God's level.
> Man must ascend above his present position,
> mount to the higher world,
> and in some way be conformed to that world.
> he must— to use the expressive word of Aquinas—
> become "deiformis."

As Nygren says the aim of the Catholic was to become holy and there are three heavenly ladders that make this possible:

(1) he ladder of merit;
(2) the analogical ladder of speculation;
(3) the anagogical ladder of mysticism.

For Aquinas these have to do with the three ways of sublimating *Philia* to *agape* or friendship to charity for the ladder of mysticism lets it become holy, the ladder of speculation lets it become universal and the ladder of merit or of becoming virtuous lets it be forgiving. In article 3 Aquinas argues that charity is a virtue and he writes:

> on the other hand Augustine says that charity
> is a virtue and, as our most completely ordered affection,
> joins us to God and makes us love him.

So here we see the third term, affection, for this virtue of charity.

IV,5.8 But agape contributes to philia as friendship does to charity

As we are seeing Aquinas is a great scripture scholar and he
uses scripture to prove every point that he demonstrates theologically.
Augustine has shown how John the Evangelist is a philosopher
and a mystic contrary to Nygren's thesis that merit, speculation
and mysticism are not a part of the agapeic scriptural tradition.
Now Thomas is showing us how John and Paul write of a friendship
that is also part of that scripture that grew out of an oral tradition.
In the loving view of Aquinas *agape* contributes greatly to *philia*
with its threefold sublimation but according to Aquinas and other
Catholics mystics, philosophers and virtuous persons can also
contribute with their enlightened *eros*, friendship and affection to *agape*.
There is much merit in the works of humans that grace reveals and
that can contributes to *agape* as they climb their ladders of sublimation.
The Jesus whose *agape* is altruistic in a new and revolutionary way
so loves others that he lets their worth and work contribute to his *agape*.
When Paul went to the Acropolis he let the Greek philosophers speak
through him to explain the *agape* of Jesus to the loving Greeks.
There is much of Stoic philosophy and friendship and affection
in his writings such as his notion of conscience which is Greek.
So in the sublimation process by which Christian *agape* and Aristotelian
philia synthesize they each contribute to each other for the *agape* lets
the friendship become holy, universal and forgiving already in scripture
for John and Paul present *agape* in terms of Greco-Roman friendship.
Just as Paul could say: "I make up in my suffering what is lacking
in the suffering of Christ." so the mystics, the philosophers and the
holy Christians are going to add to *agape* as they make their synthesis.
The revolutionary *agape* of Jesus that altruistically loved others more
than the self went out and learned from Socrates and from Plato,
Aristotle, the Stoics, Epicureans and Sceptics and *agape* unfolded
with the help of the merit of mystics, philosophers and virtuous people.
As Thomas shows Jesus helps Aristotle and Aristotle helps Jesus.

IV,5.9 *By not throwing out Aquinas' three m's*

In Nygren we see how Luther in not accepting the *Caritas Synthesis* and in order to keep *agape* pure got rid of the papacy, philosophy and purgatory but also he got rid of mysticism, monasticism and Maryology for these too corrupted *agape*. The monastery from Benedict on had to do with a community of those who sought to become holy through practicing the vows of poverty, chastity and obedience and through prayer and work. The priests would say mass each day and sing the Divine Praises of Matins, Lauds, Prime, Terse, Sect, None, Vespers and Compline in which they would sing the 150 psalms each week all year long. Many would live the intellectual life and teach such students as Thomas Aquinas and they also practised and taught agriculture. When the Franciscans and Dominicans initiated their new type of spirituality in the 12th century even though they did not live in a monastery they still kept a life of prayer and their new work. They practiced love and care for the poor in the new cities. St. Dominic initiated the Rosary and instead of the 150 psalms a devout lay person might pray instead the 150 *Hail Marys*. The monastic and religious ways of life had within them the ladders of mysticism, merit and speculative philosophy and all of this had to do in Luther's eyes with a built in self love. This was all part of the *Caritas* Synthesis that watered down and corrupted the self sacrificial, altruistic love of Jesus according to the perception of Luther who saw no self sacrifice in asceticism. If monasticism and mysticism help one to become holy through living a virtuous meritorious life then that is contrary to *agape*. Concerning Mary Thomas in the third part of his *Summa* wrote about the Incarnate word and the Grace of Christ and the one Mediator and our Lady and the childhood of Christ. There was more art about Mary than Jesus and the Cathedrals were each a Notre Dame and Luther was opposed to all of this.

IV,6 The Franciscan synthesis of agape and Luke's affection

IV,6.1 Nygren's loving treatment of Fransciscan love

In treating the Analogical Ladder of Speculation from pages 626 to 633 Nygren lovingly explains Bonaventure's *Itinerarium Mentis in Deum*. In this treatise of *The Journey of the Mind into God* the mind finds traces of God in the sense world, our soul and in the eternal world. Nygren writes on page 627

> Under the living influence of the piety of St. Francis,
> which detected traces of God's power and love
> everywhere in the world, Bonaventura
> was able to fuse all this traditional material
> into an independent unity.

Nygren shows how Bonaventure neatly put together the ladder of love from Augustine, to Pseudo-Dionysius, to Bernard of Clairvaux to Hugo of St. Victor but the main point is that Francis lived all this out. In Francis and the Franciscans we find a new kind of agapeic synthesis not in terms of *eros* or friendship but in terms of affection. When Francis detected traces of God's power and love everywhere in the world he did not just detect it with his mind but in his heart with a warm affection so that he loved Brother Sun and Sister Moon and the Wolf of Gubbio and the Doves for whom he built nests. Just as Augustine came to a sublimated *eros* and Aquinas to a sublimated friendship so Francis made clear a sublimated affection. It is interesting that when Nygren gives his list of key Greek terms he does not include *storge* or the Greek word for affection and Nygren does not thematize and make explicit the notion of affection even though he seems to greatly appreciate Francis and the Franciscan Spirituality. Of course, deep down Nygren the Lutheran still believes that self love is in Franciscan love and this takes away from the pure altruistic *agape*. However, the perfect joy of St. Francis is to be found in suffering with Christ for others and the Stigmata shows Francis to find holy joy in imitating Jesus whose *agape* was new according to Luther because it had no self love so maybe Nygren finds Francis to be Lutheran.

Agape and the Four Loves

IV,6.2 *Begins to reveal a sublimated affection*

A certain Pascal Robinson wrote that:

> Thomas extended the Kingdom of God
> by the love of theology,
> Bonaventure by the theology of love.

Agape does seek to extend the kingdom of love and each spirituality had its way of doing that by meeting the special needs of the times. Noble friends might tend to stand side by side and appreciate the world together by philosophizing together or theologizing together. Their *agape* as sublimated friendship might see the three persons of the Trinity as being lovers of wisdom in their mutual friendship. Augustinian mystics on the other hand might stand face to face with Jesus enraptured in each other with a sublimated *eros* that might begin with the likes of Dante and Beatrice and include also the Bridegroom mysticism of Bernard of Clairvaux and the Carmelites. But if we ponder Franciscan affection in comparison with the *eros* of Augustine and the friendship of Thomas we might even think of the Father and the Son as loving each other with more affection than either friendship or *eros* and Francis centers on the human Christ who became flesh like all animals and could suffer with love. In his book *The Early English Lyric and Franciscan Spirituality* David L. Jeffrey writes on page 8:

> The Franciscan school characteristically finds
> the source of its rhetoric in the commonplaces
> of ordinary life—the love of son for mother,
> of mother for child, of brother for brother,
> St. Francis of Assisi's love of animals—
> encouraging the effort to transfer these
> or similar emotions to higher and nobler objects.

Jeffrey is discussing here the Franciscan poems *Stabat Mater Dolorosa* and *Dies Irae* and his mentioning of transferring these or similar emotions had to do with what we will explore as sublimating affection.

Part Two: Sorrowful Proceedings

IV,6.3 Francis' sublimated affection goes out to all

Francis knew natural affection with his mother, father and brother
but he never married and had a family of his own so all the affection
he could have had for his wife and children he was free to give to others.
So the sublimation of affection frees one to serve others as Paul put it.
The famous prayer of St. Francis shows his agapeic affection:

> O Divine Master,
> Grant that I may not so much seek
> To be consoled … as to console,
> To be understood … as to understand
> To be loved … as to love,

Ideal *eros* and ideal friendship both have a mutuality that lets
the lovers stand face to face and friends stand side by side but as
Francis brings out in this prayer affection can be empathetic
rather than even sympathetic or compassionate for the *sym* of the Greek
and the *com* of the Latin etymologically refer to a mutual togetherness.
But as Francis brings out his understanding of the other need not be
understood and his consoling of another can be without being consoled.
His loving is like a mother's affection that goes out to her child
and with Francis every living creature is his child just as would be
the child Jesus for he loves each needy creature as Mary loved Jesus.
Just as Mary stood by the cross loving her son so Francis loved the Wolf.
When Francis visited the town of Gubio

> There appeared in the territory of that city
> a fearfully large and fierce wolf
> which was so rabid with hunger
> that it devoured not only animals
> but also human beings.

Francis went out to the wolf against the advice of the citizens and made
the sign of the cross over the wolf and showed him great affection.
The wolf was tamed and lived in the town with such affection for all
that the townsfolk always saw in him the very affection of Francis.

Agape and the Four Loves

IV,6.4 Affectionate names are prayed in his heart forever

When you read *Fioretti* or *The Little Flowers of St. Francis* you notice all the dear names of all the beloved who were touched by the affection of Francis and brought that affection to others. Part one tells of The Deeds of St. Francis and his first companion. Just as Jesus chose twelve disciples so Francis

> had twelve chosen companions who
> were followers of the most complete poverty.

and

> It was also very inspiring to see
> the affection and awe and humility
> with which St. Francis
> treated and spoke to Brother Bernard.

St. Francis spoke to each individual with the kind of affection with which Jesus spoke to Magdalen so that after his resurrection and he was not recognizable she knew him in the way he said her name. He prayed for others always and so when he spoke to them it was as if he were praying their name with an awesome wonder and with an humility before them that let them know their great worth. In the section on *How St. Clare ate a meal with St. Francis and His Friars* we read that when they ate around their humble table:

> St. Francis began to speak about God in such
> a sweet and bold and profound and divine and
> marvelous way that he himself and St. Clare
> and her companion and all the others . . . were
> rapt in God by the overabundance of divine
> grace that descended upon them.

If St. Augustine and his mother had a mystical experience of *agape* that sublimated the power of *eros* this is a mystical experience of *agape* that sublimates Franciscan affection with its sweet, holy, profound and marvelous way of feeling. "The fire of divine love was burning in the souls of those friars and nuns."

IV,6.5 Franciscan-Lukan agape had a mother-child affection

If there is one Biblical text that is the basis for Franciscan affection it is Luke 3:6 in which he writes that Jesus came

> that all flesh might see the salvation of the Lord.

The Franciscan love of animals is rooted in this passage for Francis who sought to imitate Jesus in every way wanted to rescue all animals. He even became a vegetarian out of love for animals and his affection especially sought to save and rescue any who might be suffering especially all the new poor who were coming into the new cities to work. Just as St. Augustine opened the New Testament and read the passage of Paul that brought him to conversion and erotic sublimation so St. Francis and Brother Bernard opened the Bible three times and read three Q^1 passages in Luke that converted Bernard to agapeic affection. The passages were:

> If you wish to be perfect, go, sell all you have,
> and give to the poor, and come, follow me.

and then when Jesus sent them out to preach he said:

> Take nothing for your journey, neither staff,
> nor wallet, nor bread, nor money.

In that way they should place all their hope for support in God and concentrate entirely on preaching the Gospel and finally they opened the Bible a third time and read:

> If anyone wishes to come after me,
> let him deny himself and take up
> his cross and follow me."

These passages are at the heart of the Franciscan and Nietzschean love for Jesus and the mother-child affection which they signify for Francis has to do with Mary's affection for her suffering son and especially for Francis in wanting to save and rescue all the suffering. The Wolf of Gubbio, the doves without a nest and the cities' poor called forth from Francis and the Franciscans the *agape* of Jesus for others even at the expense of self and an affection of mother for child.

Agape and the Four Loves

IV,6.6 *That was foretold by Joachim of Fiore*

Joachim of Fiore, a Cistercian abbot who died in Colabria in 1202, found in the apocalypse of John three stages of sacred history. For God the Father worked through the patriarchs and prophets. God the Son worked through the apostles and other apostolic men. Since Christ God the Holy Spirit has worked through religious orders. This age of the Holy Spirit also has three stages beginning with Benedict. Out of the Benedictines came the Cistercians but now there will come twelve holy men prefigured by the twelve patriarchs and twelve apostles. As David Jeffrey puts it on page 70:

> The opening of the Fioretti may suggest
> that the Franciscan Spirituals thought
> they knew the identity of that final dozen.

As Joachim pondered the mystery of revelation throughout Biblical history and through the age of the Holy Spirit he saw how the faith hope and love of one period could be totally new in the next period. To indicate this he used the ancient Stoic philosophical term of *rationes seminales* which the Greek called *Logoi Spermaticoi*. As Joachim thought of it this sperm or seed could give rise to a totally new kind of plant and fruit unlike seeds as we know them. There might be an idea in scripture such as the promise to David that the Davidic line of Kings would last forever and the line was destroyed as when the Babylonians killed the last of the David kings. But then there emerged the new idea of a kingdom of priests that let the line continue in a totally new and unforeseeable manner. Then Jesus and his *agape* could be seen as the new Davidic Messiah who was a child of the line of David again in an unforeseeable way. Like a seed giving rise to a totally new plant and fruit Jesus could have unpredictably sprouted forth as a *ratio seminales*. Every person is filled with unforeseen new possibilities and when St. Francis loves someone his affection is humble and goes out even to animals seeing within them untold, mysterious, lovable seeds.

IV,6.7 Whose rationes seminales inspired Bonaventure

Franciscan affection goes out to each individual flower, leaf
or pebble for in every creature there is a reflection of God's wisdom.
In his *Hexaemeron* Bonaventure developed a new theology
of history which differed from that in Augustine's *City of God*.
In doing this he used Joachim's *rationes seminales* again to show
the unknowable richness of each scriptural text and of each historical
event and for Franciscans it indicated the richness of each creature.
Francis' love went out with affection to each such mysterious creature.
Each flower, leaf and pebble, the doves without a nest, the wolf,
each of the Franciscan Brethren, St. Clara and her nuns and
each of the poor of the cities reflected the suffering Son of God whom
Francis with his Mary-like heart would love in their mysterious worth.
These seeds of semen and sperm that carry the hereditary traits
mix with a variety of eggs that carry innumerable hereditary traits
and who could ever guess the marvelous variety of possible offspring?
Augustine found many contradictions in the Bible if you only read
it literally but from Ambrose which helped him immensely he
saw that there were also the moral, the mystical and typological senses.
From the viewpoint of the *rationes seminales* Bonaventure also read
the Bible in a Franciscan way in the literal way and then with three
kinds of spiritual sense: allegorical, tropological and anagogical.
The tropological found a moral meaning in a variety of passages
and the allegorical referred to what is to be believed in faith.
As Jeffrey puts it on page 90:

> All four senses of exegesis were applied
> to the study of Nature.
> St. Bonaventure asserts of all creation
> that "as faith, hope and charity bring us to God,
> likewise all creatures suggest what
> is to be believed, expected and done."

Nature reveals believing allegory, hoping tropology, and loving anagogy.

Agape and the Four Loves

IV,6.8 To see affection's history so as to aid Scotus

Bonaventure saw Francis living out the four senses of scripture
by literally imitating the Q[1] Jesus with an affection always growing
in allegorical faith, tropological hope and anagogical charity.
The Greek word anagogical comes from *ago*— to lead and *ana*— upward.
Franciscan love led up the mystical ladder not of Platonic *eros* but
of Franciscan affection and as he ascended with the nine choirs of
Angels so his love saw more deeply into each creature's loveliness.
Higher still and higher his affection led him upward and deeper
still and deeper it let him see the *logoi spermaticoi* of each
creature in the mystery of a new beauty just around every corner.
When Duns Scotus, the English Franciscan philosopher, thought of
the complex being of each individual creature he called it *haecceity*.
Aristotle had tried to account for the individuality that Plato lost
and argued that matter is the principle of individuation letting
each horse, for example, be this unique horse unlike any other horse.
But, since the rational souls of humans can know immaterial ideas
they must be immaterial since action follows being and you know
the immaterial soul because of the immaterial abstraction it performs.
But, since our human soul is immaterial we are not individuated
by matter and at death we live on in the soul moving the inner sphere.
So, to accomplish what Aristotle wanted, Scotus posited *haecceity*
or the principle of *thisness* that would individuate each unique creature.
Thus to account for the *rationes seminales* of each unique being
Scotus formulated the theory that is the very basis of postmodernity.
As Kierkegaard, Nietzsche, Hopkins, Dostoyevsky and all the rest
developed their existential philosophies and poetries of the individual
that Kierkegaard built his philosophy around they went back to Scotus.
Hopkins read Scotus, became a Catholic, and celebrated *haecceity*.

> in the dearest freshness deep down things . . .
> Because the Holy Ghost over the bent
> World broods with warm breast and with ah! bright wings.

IV,6.9 To see the haecceity that led Ockham to nominalism

Levinas wrote that all postmodern philosophies are nominalistic. But what is that theory of knowledge which came forth from Franciscan love claiming that true knowledge knows its inadequacy? Before Ockham there were ultra realists, realists and conceptualists. Platonic ultra realists argue that when our mind conformed to the form of things our ideas were true but Aristotle argued that the forms are only in the things and that things do not participate in an eternal form.

So Aristotle, the realist, saw truth to be the conformity of our mind to the forms in things and the conceptualists developed instead a coherence theory arguing that when our idea of something is adequate and consistent then in an idealistic way we can know it truthfully. The skeptics from Socrates on could argue with them that "I am the wisest man in Athens because I alone know I know nothing." However if we claim to know something, or predicate a universal name to some thing, we should remember that that name is only a name on our lips and we cannot adequately know a thing because there is always more to it than any universal name realizes. So nominalism arises out of the Franciscan *rationes seminales*, haecceity and respects "the dearest freshness deep down things." Jeffery on page 92 quotes Alain de Lille as saying:

> *omnis mundi creatura*
> *quosi liber et pectura*
> *nobis est in speculum:*
> *nostrae vitae, nostrae mortis*
> *nostrae status, nostrae sortis*
> *fidele signaculum.*

All the world's creatures, as a book and a picture, are to us a mirror: in it our life, our death, our present condition and our passing on are faithfully signified. Scotus developed the metaphysics and Ockham the epistemology of this insight.

Agape and the Four Loves

Bette Jo and Dad

Tom, Bobby, Bette Jo, Cliff, Dad and Mom

Part Two: Sorrowful Proceedings

Dad and Bobby   Tom and Dad

Daddy fly fishing

Agape and the Four Loves

Our grade two class

Our grade three class

Part Two: Sorrowful Proceedings

The report card

Part Three

Glorious Finishings

Agape and the Four Loves

I. Father

I,7 Of agapeic eros with his wife

I,7.1 In their sacramental love making

From the moment Mother and Father met their love was made
in heaven and Gramma Coates, their shamanic cupid,
knew that her Joneva Mae was emerging into a loveliness
beyond her understanding though she felt its coming glory.
She had always been taken with young Joe and his dancing
dark brown eyes even back then when with his ever smiling
face he told her about his family and about training for sports.
Daddy who could always read people knew when he met Leona that
she was an intelligent, loving woman with just the right questions.
In growing up with his sisters and their friends Daddy was perfectly
at home with the opposite sex and they fostered his masculinity.
We know already in High School he was an accomplished kisser.
Mother too went through a healthy dating process by coming
to know wonderful young men but never completely knowing any.
Mother sensed in Daddy a reverent, Catholic adoration that she
had never known in the youth of her wholesome Mormon community.
From his first night out with Joneva Mae, Joseph Manuel knew
her totally virginal innocence and as their love making began
step by step it took on the sacramental holiness of the Sacred Mass.
There was the liturgy of the word as they told their stories to each other.
There was the Good News that they shared in aspirations together.
Daddy told Mother of his creed and she was at once attracted
to his Catholic Agapeic world not only of Father, Son and Holy Spirit
but also of the Virgin Mary, the Queen of the Angels and the Saints.
Then in the liturgy of the Eucharist they offered their hands
to each other and then slowly their lips and even their mouths.
And then there was the sacred sacrament of their matrimony
and they took each other into the joy of the total consecration.
And finally there was the bliss of heavenly ecstatic communion.
And in that year of 1965, after thirteen years with the garbage route,
Daddy sold it and he and Mother entered their glorious older age.

I,7.2 And the sharing of physical exercises

From 1952 until 1965 Daddy got an abundance of physical exercise as each week with hardly a break he would clean up the town. Mother helped to get him ready with clean clothes, good food and lots of tender loving care as they slept in each other's arms and side by side in various loving positions through each night. She also had her routine as she did the laundry each Monday and had special days for baking, for ironing and for shopping. She lit the wood and coal stove each morning and cooked three meals each day and with her children had the dishes always to do. She prayed her rosary each morning, each afternoon when she took her nap and each evening before sleep and she always said that after a good night's sleep one should arise bright and eager for a new day's work and be ready for a good sleep each evening. Wilhelmina was expecting a baby in early February of 1966 and Daddy said to me on the phone:

> What are you going to name that little boy, anyway?

And without having discussed it with Wilhelmina I answered "Joseph." He thought that was a good idea and just one day before his birthday on February 4, little Joseph Robert was delivered by caesarian section. They could have had the same birthday and been a birthday present for each other if it were not for the caesarian which saved Wilhelmina. Mother and Daddy were married on Nov. 12, 1936, so that November 12 of 1966 was their thirtieth wedding anniversary. He often helped her fill the washing machine and the laundry tubs when she did her Monday laundry which was so much less now. Only Cliff and Tom were still at home and they were often busy so Daddy began to help Mother with the dishes and the housework. By the time of their 30th Anniversary their sacramental love making had within it the three great sacred things of sex, death and religion. Their bliss was so ecstatic that it took them into the little death.

Agape and the Four Loves

I,7.3 *And the sharing of vital exercises*

The four exercises into which Daddy's agapeic world took him
have to do with the four levels of Plato's cave and the four stages
on Kierkegaard's life's way and also deep down to the four loves.
Physical exercises produce health. The Vital produce happiness.
The Intellectual Produce wisdom. The Spiritual produce holiness.
This value hierarchy has to do with the four loves in that
affection and physical values are the most basic followed by
friendship and the vital values and then *eros* and the intellectual values
and finally *agape*, and the spiritual values which integrate them all.
Mother and Father's *agape* not only let their *eros* flourish
in a sacramental *eros* that let their love-making fulfill
the sacrament of their matrimony just as a priest's saying of Mass
fulfills his sacrament of holy orders with more grace each time
but it also let their friendship flourish with more and more vitality.
Mother was always a very modest lady who as a Mary-Like Crusader
would not let her daughter wear a dress or skirt above her knees.
Her modesty had to do with her innate sense of appreciation for
all the values that included the physical but went beyond the physical.
One can get bogged down in physicality to the exclusion of
the other exercises that promote and make flourish the other values.
Mother was as modest as Daddy's mother and his sisters and
her modesty had to do with her practice of the exercises of vitality.
By being very ethical even in her Mormon way Mother attended
to right diet, right virtue, right peace and joy which all contributed
toward a happy friendliness with all especially with her husband.
She lived a life of moderation and the golden mean that kept
her high vitality from any bi-polar mania or depression and
in spite of his smoking and drinking she helped Daddy's vitality.
Mother and Daddy were each other's best friends and by 1967
the fruit of their work together on raising their family was becoming
more and more abundant as Bette Jo married a wonderful man.

Part Three: Glorious Finishings

I,7.4 And the sharing of intellectual exercises

While Daddy was mathematically gifted and read the newspaper and
some sports magazines it was Mother who in loving each day
to do her spiritual reading also delighted in the intellectual life.
In reading *The Dark Night of the Soul* by St. John of the Cross
she not only discovered the poetry of ideas for her own meditation
but she came to understand the agapeic *eros* of her husband and
herself much better for she read such lines as:

> upon my flowery breasts
> kept only for him alone
> he reclined his head
> and all his cares
> were forgotten among the lilies.

Such beautiful lines she memorized and thought about them
in terms of St. Teresa of Avila, St. Therese the Little Flower, *The
Devout Life*, St. Augustine, *The Imitation of Christ* and The Bible.
Even though discussing such books with Daddy was not in
keeping with his taste she still felt she shared her intellectual
exercise with him for as he reclined his head upon her flowery
breasts she felt that the poetry of St. John of the Cross must have
in some way been there making their love-making more divine.
In the Fall of 1968, Cliff left for Assumption College in North Dakota.
Mother loved their Benedictine Spirituality with its work and prayer.
Bobby graduated from Loyola of Chicago and met the lovely Genie
Leahy who was studying literature at Northwestern and when
she and he finished studying in Chicago they moved to Salt Lake City.
She grew up there and Bobby started to study law there after
wanting to be a monk, then a poet, then a psychiatrist and at last
with the advice of Mr. Kelling he decided to become a lawyer.
Bette Jo and Bob's daughter, Lynn Marie, was born and Mother
and Daddy were so happy to see all their children doing so well.
The wisdom of the big picture was falling into place for their family.

Agape and the Four Loves

I,7.5 *And the sharing of spiritual exercises*

Daddy and Mother shared a shamanic background which initiated both of them into the practise of spiritual exercises from childhood. When Daddy's father died his prayer life with his mother and sisters began in earnest and it increased in fervor with each Dark Night. Gramma's mother died when she was eight and her father's mother died when he was five so both of them awakened to the spiritual and Mother identified with each of them and with their union. As Mother grew in the Catholic world and received special help from each priest who became her spiritual director she grew in the many spiritual exercises of her daily prayers, rosary, three Masses a week, constant spiritual reading and discussion. She found that her daughter's husband, Robert Wunderle, had a philosophical mind like herself and her son, David, and she loved talking with him when possible and with each of the priests. Mother said the blessing before each meal and they felt together that their prayers had been answered for Tommy was already in his last year of High School and doing very well and he too applied to Assumption College and, of course, was accepted. Joe Larrigan who bought the trash route had hired another Basque, Joe Goitandia, to run it and Tommy helped him. But Joe broke his leg and Tommy took care of it by himself. He was earning plenty of money to go to college and then some. Mother and Father began to discover the meaning of the glorious mysteries and even their agapeic love making allowed Daddy to continue to feel for the next day his wife's glorious loveliness. Now that he was retired his gambling was going better than ever. All their children were now succeeding just as he had wanted. This glory of their totally beautiful marriage and of their children's wonderful success turned all his sorrow into joy. The God of love became much more manifest to him as he prayed with a renewed praise and thanksgiving and with continued petition.

Part Three: Glorious Finishings

I,7.6 And of being helped by Holy Mother Church

Daddy and Mother both knew very clearly that the great success story
of their children's education was much aided by Holy Mother Church.
The holy men who became priests and took the vow of celibacy
were able to dedicate their loving attention to their flock and already
in grade school they made an educational difference with their teaching.
Even though there was no Catholic school in Ketchum we each
memorized the answers to the questions of the Baltimore Catechism.
Learning how to memorize was already an important acquired skill.
My eighth grade teacher motivated me to memorize the Prelude
to *Evangeline* by reminding me that I memorized so much at church.
The Holy Sisters came each May for two weeks of catechism school
and they were a grace which inspired our family in untold ways.
My Mother always loved them and the priests and we came to love
them partly by identifying with her and also having Daddy's backing.
When I went to Mt. Angel with the Benedictines and then Bobby went
we were a poor family, but the tuition was very low because
the holy fathers took their vows of poverty, chastity and obedience
and thus did not need any salary and were free to teach and pray.
Aunt Claudia and Uncle Pete, my godparents, gave me $500.00 each year.
I was able to earn $500.00 each summer and the Diocese of Boise
paid $1000.00 each year for me as a seminarian which I later paid back.
Holy Mother Church at the Monastery and in the Diocese gave me
the best imaginable of educators and helped my parents
tremendously in getting started the education for all the children.
Perhaps each of us children came to love Holy Mother Church so much
because she was like our Mother who loved Daddy and each of us
with the same devotion with which priests and sisters loved everyone.
And we came to love our Mother also because of the way Daddy loved
her and was so happy to see her to become a Catholic and a saint.
No family in Ketchum was like ours in getting the education we got
and we are all extremely grateful to our second Mother and Father.

Agape and the Four Loves

I,7.7 *And of belonging to the Mystical Body of Jesus*

Daddy's shamanic sensitivity to the spirit world was always nourished by Holy Mother Church and as the blessed dead among his family and his friends increased so did his prayerful love. But also his own family was rapidly increasing with his children getting married and bringing forth many grandchildren. He definitely felt some kind of connectedness with his family and also especially with his Basque people but also because he was so much a part of his wife's very being her world was also a part of his and he was a proud American and Democrat. What Daddy and Mother felt together was that they were members of the Mystical Body of Christ for they grew in a greater sense of the community of all persons with a spectrum of intensity beginning with themselves, going to their children and to all loved ones. "The eye cannot say to the hand: "I do not need thee." And in being so helped by Holy Mother Church, the love of priests and sisters who gave themselves for others graced them to love all others. That we should love our neighbors as ourselves became so real for them that they loved each other first as persons with all other persons and then as man and wife in their special love. In her spiritual reading and carefully listening to sermons Mother came to love Jesus in such a way that she loved all poor sinners in just the way he did including her own beloved father. For Grandpa Coates had become an alcoholic who squandered all his money and whom Grandma Coates had to divorce in order that she might save some of what he had worked so hard for. Mother's love for her father let her realize the everlasting merciful love with which Jesus died for sinners because they were part of his body and needed him so much to save them. Daddy knew how Mother loved her father and he tried to help her to help him but in some earthly, temporal way it was to no avail. But, in their loving faith they knew he was a member of Jesus's body.

Part Three: Glorious Finishings

I,7.8 In a love stronger than death

From the moment Mother and Daddy first met they knew they would
love each other forever and their love made eternity self-evident.
Their love gave them a joy that wanted itself over and over forever.
Their love had about it a glory that manifested the unmanifest
even in its unmanifestness for that is the very nature of glory.
Daddy went through many Dark Nights: when his father died,
when he was put in jail and couldn't finish college, when his
boxing career was brought to an end, when gambling became
illegal and he had no job, when he was shot and when
he became an alcoholic and then finally the garbage man.
But all of that now had a glorious joy about it because
the whole story seemed to be the turning out so well as he
and his wife could live on in their children and their happiness.
But the eternity their love made self evident was not only one
lived on vicariously in the generations of all their children to come.
When they felt their "I love you." which they felt all the time
there was always in parenthesis with it a "forever and forever."
Their *agape* was a love of the God of Love forever and a love of all
his creatures who became members of Jesus' body when he
became the God-made-flesh for the salvation of all their flesh.
Their *agape* gave a context to their *eros* that let it become
that sacramental love making and that eternal face to face delight
that flowered forth in their children and in their faith in eternity.
Their *eros* also contributed to their *agape* in a glorious mutuality.
The *agape* brought their *eros* into realms it never would
have dreamed of without the Son of God becoming lovely flesh
to save all flesh and every moment of beautiful fleshly love.
Their *eros* brought their *agape* into a unique realm that was
only theirs in that their erotic love and their love making
was unique in all the world just as their union was unique.
They knew they would love each other more and more forever.

Agape and the Four Loves

I,7.9 With flesh as instrument of salvation

The world, the flesh and the Devil can lead us into temptation and
into the suffering of the rods of men, but the flesh can also be
the instrument and the means of our salvation once it is saved.
There is the battle between the flesh and the spirit but when the God
became flesh spirit had a victory that can let flesh be spiritual.
That is what Daddy discovered throughout his fifty years of marriage.
As Mother became a Catholic she learned that sex in marriage had
the threefold purpose of bringing forth children, of sanctifying
the couple and of lessening the dangers of concupiscence in that order.
After about eight years into their marriage when Mother became
Catholic Daddy could notice Mother's new agapeic sexuality.
Now that she knew that sex could be a sacramental sanctifying
of the couple her touch became more angelic as she delighted
in giving Daddy delight for she felt its healing power for him.
She thought of her poor father who was a kind of lost soul and
thought that maybe it had to do with his being also a lost body.
She had seen him cry and sob when beauty reached the glory point.
When he was in the Insane Assylum and she and David went
to visit him his gift of tears before glorious beauty broke
forth when he beheld his grandson who was named after him
and whom he had not seen for years and she felt sorry for him
that he never knew the power of the sacraments which could heal.
After Mother had her hysterectomy and the bearing of children
was no longer a part of their sexuality their agapeic *eros* was
now able to take them into new realms of a more joyful wisdom.
Mother came to know of the "Yes, Yes, Yes" of Molly Bloom and
she learned how to so delight the flesh of Daddy that
his conscious mind went into an ecstatic trance that
bloomed forth into a "Yes, Yes, Yes" even for all of existence.
And their fleshly love once saved by the *Agape* of Jesus even
took Daddy into the glorious praising joy of "Jesus, Jesus, Jesus!"

Part Three: Glorious Finishings

I,8 Agapeic friendship with his children's spouses

I,8.1 Standing side by side with David's Wilhelmina

In 1974, Tommy graduated from the University of North Dakota
and on May 28 of that year he and Annette were married.
Now all of his children were through college and each was married
and each had a good job and they were each starting their families.
Daddy's world of shamanic, Basque *agape* let him become
very quickly true friends with each of his children's spouses.
His and Mother's children were the best of friends having grown
up praying and working and playing and fishing and hunting together.
The four boys ate their peck of salt together as they sweated
it out with Daddy and Bette Jo was the best of friends with each.
From the moment Wilhelmina arrived in Ketchum and sat
down for supper Mother and Daddy knew they were birds of a feather
who flock together just from the way she prayed with devotion
when Mother asked me if I would like to pray the grace before meals.
Having been in the seminary for nine years I had missed that
many years of growing up with girls and thus I did not know
how to take a sexual leading role which girls of my age expected.
Wilhelmina being eleven years older than myself knew how
to guide me along and right away when we met she liked me,
even though she keenly felt the age discrepancy, because she
felt the agapeic kinship of her Limburg and my Basque culture.
Sometimes she affectionately called me Basquey, rhyming
with key, and like Mother and Daddy's Mother and sisters
she liked to say the Rosary and she and Mother went to weekday
Mass as I watched Josje and David Scott who was now five.
Because of her way of praying and because of her culture
that went back to Roman times Daddy felt that she was
like the women he held most dear with genuine values.
She was a kind and caring nurse and talked with Daddy
about the sores on his face and he came to think of cancer.
And she told him she would pray for him and he prayed for her.

Agape and the Four Loves

I,8.2 *Standing side by side with Bette Jo's Bob*

At Tacoma, Washington, there was an Air Base and when Bette Jo went
there to work it didn't take her long to meet Robert Wunderle who
was in the Air Force and with whom she fell in love immediately.
Bob was from a Lutheran family and majored in philosophy in college
with the thought that he might go into the ministry so he also had
a strong agapeic background and was a perfect soul mate with Bette Jo.
Daddy didn't like plane flights so I gave Bette Jo away at their wedding.
Daddy who was always so proud of his daughter and felt bad that
he could not go to her wedding threw a lovely yard Party for them as
on their Honey-Moon they came back to Ketchum and Bette Jo's world.
Even Aunt Simona and Uncle Martin came up from California.
Bob was able to meet Bette Jo's friends Jeaney Flowers
and Vergie Gunderson and they had fun exploring Sun Valley.
But most of all Bob really hit it off with mom who shared
his philosophical interests and she loved to ask him questions
and listen to his well expressed answers and he explained to her
how there were different types of Lutherans and how his group
believed in the real presence of the body of Jesus in the Eucharist.
He felt just like a Catholic and went to Mass with them and
he did seem to be more Catholic than the Episcopalians she knew.
Bob didn't really get into Dad's world of fishing and hunting
even though Dad wanted to teach him if he wanted to learn.
Dad was especially happy that Bette Jo and Bob both had
such good jobs and were already buying a house in Tacoma.
He did notice that Bob always called Bette Jo only Bette but
Bette Jo didn't seem to mind and so that was just fine with him.
He was very happy to see Bob's excellent character that was kind,
happy, intelligent and without the slightest short temper like his.
He took Bette Jo and Bob downtown and introduced Bob to his friends
and they all remembered well what a terrific student Bette Jo had been.
Daddy and his new son-in-law stood side by side enjoying all together.

Part Three: Glorious Finishings

I,8.3 Standing side by side with Bobby's Genie

In Daddy's eyes Bobby did very well by becoming a Lawyer
and marrying a doctor's daughter from Salt Lake City, Utah.
As Daddy watched Bobby grow from training to be a monk,
to become the Editor of *Cadence*, the Loyola Student Poetry Journal
and writing in it a beautiful poem in a very contemporary style
on a Western Cowboy out there in the Desert Daddy knew so well,
to then studying psychology and wanting to be a psychiatrist
he was glad that he proved to be practical and study the Law.
Just as Mother became friends with Bob Wunderle because
the were kindred philosophical spirits in sharing ideas
so Gramma Coates saw Genie as a lady of the highest class.
Gramma always loved good literature and the Great Books
and that was exactly Genie's interest and what she majored
in at that excellent University of Northwestern and then taught
for years at the college in Elko, Nevada, where she and Bobby
and their three children: Amy, Jesse and Tom resided.
Just as Daddy became better friends with Bob through Mother
so also he became better friends with Genie through Gramma.
Through Gramma's friendship with Genie Daddy knew her better.
Daddy had always liked Elko and wanted to move there when
gambling closed down in Idaho as did his friend, Leon Bilboa.
Elko is a center of Basque culture and Bobby and Genie got
their children involved in Basque Dancing and Daddy loved
seeing his grandchildren and even Bobby dressed up in Basque
costumes and in looking so Basque and maybe Genie Leahy
was what they call black Irish and had Basque blood in her.
For at the time of the Armada many Basques were saved in Ireland.
Daddy began to see that Holy Mother Church not only helped
in educating his children but also in bringing them together
with the perfect mate for Bobby and Genie are the other half
of each other's souls in loving literature and the arts so much.

Agape and the Four Loves

I,8.4 *Standing side by side with Cliff's Bim*

On November 12, 1976, Mother and Father celebrated their 40th wedding anniversary and now all their children were settled. Cliff and Tom both lived in Idaho even though Cliff and Bim lived in Burley, but still they were close enough to visit often. Ruth or Bim, as she was called came to Assumption college from the little town of Mott, North Dakota, and she and Cliff met in their classes for they were both studying for the medical profession. Cliff was training to be a medical technician and Bim a nurse. So after Wilhelmina Bim was the second daughter-in-law to be a nurse. As a tall and beautiful blond she is the perfect match for Cliff who is the tallest in the family and she likes sports and the outdoors. Bim was such an empathetic and loving lady that Daddy felt that he could confide in her and he could talk with her even as if she were his nurse who could understand his life's story. Bim's family owned a tavern in Mott and as she told him that he felt a bond of non-prohibitive openness with her as if she knew the value of socializing with friends through the night. In 1969, as Tommy was accepted at Assumption College Daddy quit smoking and drinking and he shared all of that in detail with Bim. Cliff had already told her how he went to one of Cliff's basketball games in an intoxicated and staggering state and Cliff and Tom were embarrassed as they were another time when he was drunk and road a horse sitting on it backwards right down main street. He told Bim that he was glad that his grandchildren would never know him as a drinker and even a smoker and he was proud of that. As Cliff and Bim's children: Jody, Tobby and Heidi grew up Cliff became their basketball coach at school and Bim would cheer them on and Daddy was happy that Cliff fulfilled his wishes. For when Daddy was in High School he wanted to be a teacher and a coach and his children were now in health, education and welfare with Bobby as a Lawyer looking after justice.

Part Three: Glorious Finishings

I,8.5 *Standing side by side with Tom's Annette*

In 1976, Tom got a job teaching at Wood River Junior High.
Late that Summer Tom and Annette parked their camper near
Mom and Dad's lawn and then when Tom would go to school
Mom and Annette would often go to Mass and do house work.
In the afternoon Dad and Annette would do things together such
as go fishing at various beaver ponds with worms for brook trout.
Daddy had stopped fly fishing because wading around in streams
with hip boots was getting to be a bit difficult and he did like
taking his grandchildren and Annette fishing in such a way
that they as beginners could learn to fish and soon catch some.
In 1977, they took their camper to Mormon Bend on the Salmon River.
Dad stayed there for a month from early July until early August.
During July of 1978, they camped out again and Annette who was
pregnant caught a beautiful, big Chinook in the Dutchman Hole.
She and Daddy had lots of time to talk and become the best of
friends and Annette told me:

> I don't know how Dad felt about me
> but you could tell he was genuinely good.
> It was very black and white.
> He told me that he and Brian were drinking
> on the day Dad was shot.

Because Annette was able to be with him so much they got to be
friends in a very special way and he shared his heart with her.
He made the comment that he never went to any other of his
children's weddings and Annette asked: "Why not?" and she
could not remember his answer but you knew he was remorseful.
He told her that he used to like to dance and he would often
click his fingers when a song that he liked came on the radio.
Annette said that when she and Dad were camping together
he used to pray hard and you could see his lips moving and
you could almost hear him as he drank his morning coffee.

Agape and the Four Loves

I,8.6 More with Annette as mom and dad move to Gooding

Annette asked Dad many questions as they camped together.
He told her the story of how he quit smoking and drinking.
The read blotches on his face began to turn into skin cancer.
In 1969, he had is ear removed and he said the pain was severe.
He said to Annette:

> What the hell am I doing?
> I threw the pack of cigarettes away
> and I never wanted another drink.

All that happened ten years before just as his last child was
ready to go away to university and all pressure was then off.
The scare of cancer, the ear operation and the pain must
have been a kind of shock treatment that motivated him to
stop his two addictions which were very strong and dangerous.
He told Annette all about his gambling and how he had
saved $80,000 in coffee cans so that now he could give
each child $10,000 and now with their share she and Tom
could start building a new home down at Bellevue which
was fairly close to Tom's work and there was land for a good price.
Ketchum had become a Boom Town and the little old house
and lot that Daddy and Mother had bought for $3,500.00 they
were now able to sell for $80,000.00 and with that they could
buy a lovely home in Gooding where dad grew up and get
away from Ketchum and its icy cold winters and even
the gambling which did keep Daddy awake until late at night.
They were all set now and Daddy had been a good provider.
The new home cost them $75,000.00 so now they had enough
to live on with their Social Security and the extra $25,000.00.
Mother could make interest on that at the bank and if anything
happened to Daddy she would have enough to get along on.
Mother was very happy now to have a lovely home and to be
away from those many years of smoking, drinking and gambling.

Part Three: Glorious Finishings

I,8.7 *David's new wife Carolyn*

I had often done things that Daddy just couldn't understand,
such as telling lies and staying out so late in that Summer of '61.
But when Mother told him that I had twin daughters with another
woman he really didn't know what to say so when he called me
about the $10,000.00 he said that perhaps I could give the exchange
from the American dollars into the Canadian to Wilhelmina.
That would be a couple of thousand and he really felt bad for her.
By that time Wilhelmina had left me so that I could be
with her God-Daughters, Angela Joy and Charity Marie,
and Josje and I were living together before I moved in with Carolyn.
So some kind of a closer, silent bond grew up between Daddy
and Wilhelmina as he pondered her agapeic love that cared so
for others that she became the God-Mother to David's twin girls.
Bette Jo, Bobby, Cliff and Tom were all such good and holy persons
and their family life was all going so well, but David who had
studied to be a priest and who had a Ph.D. in the love of wisdom
and taught philosophy to others seemed to cause so much trouble.
He could savvy the game and knew the rods of men so what would
happen to Wilhelmina and the boys and to Carolyn and the girls?
He knew that his drinking made it hard for those whom he loved
but this adultery he could see would be far worse and he began
to pray in a new way for David, Wilhelmina, Carolyn and the children.
He had always thought of guys who messed around with women
as punk kids with no sense of responsibility but his love for David
didn't let him do that and all he could do was be silent about it all.
Mother would ask me questions about how I could do such a thing
but Daddy didn't do that as if he knew that I didn't know.
He met and loved all of his children's spouses but now
he could not meet Carolyn for David came to visit without her.

Agape and the Four Loves

I,8.8 *The three great secret things*

While Daddy was an extrovert and loved to socialize with others
he kept a reverent silence before the three great secret things of
sex, death and religion though others discussed them so much.
The reality of an interpersonal relation between a male and a female
is only something people can speculate about and often when
you listen to the speculation in can sound almost mean or shallow.
As a gambler in all of his thinking Daddy always wanted to make
the best bet possible and thus he approached sex, death and religion.
Perhaps that is why he was always silent about myself and Carolyn.
He just didn't want to get into the whole thing and say anything
that would lead him to take offence or to be offensive to anyone.
A man never knows a woman in her passionate depths until
he sexually knows her and so also a female does not know
a male and all of his ghosts until she sexually know him.
Daddy knew that and as an artist he knew that true art
was always a creative exploration of those great shamanic secrets.
In the same vein Daddy never really told others the hidden depths
of his own prayer life and of his thoughts and feelings about religion.
He would say his mother was a good Catholic without going into it.
Concerning his own death Annette told me:

> He had great respect.
> He did not want anyone to see him die.
> He wanted morphine. – He knew it would
> shut down his system. – Cliff knew it.

Annette said that Dad knew what was going on. He could read people.
He had a sixth sense. And the great respect that Annette had sensed
no doubt began for him when his father died and he identified
with his Mother's and Sister's feelings and loved their reverence.
The mysteries of sex and of death brought him to the mystery of prayer.
What could he do before David, Carolyn and Wilhelmina and before his
own death but place a prayerful bet on God's loving kindness.

Part Three: Glorious Finishings

I,8.9 What Is agapeic friendship in a family?

The agapeic sacrament of marriage took Mother and Father's *eros*
even in the intimacy of lovemaking into new sacred dimensions
and Daddy definitely became friends with his children's spouses.
But was there a special agapeic dimension to that friendship?
Was friendship with them different from his other friendships?
Perhaps we can detect the agapeic dimensions in his friendship
with Wilhelmina and in the complexities of the Carolyn relation.
His *agape* gave the primacy to love and though he knew there
would be the justice of the rods of men his silent love even
of friendship manifested a belief in the God of love that would win out.
His belief that love would conquer all governed all his friendships.
The affection he had within his family for his wife and children
had a familiarity about it that he would also have with his
grandchildren but could never be there with his children's spouses.
If we think of Annette as the archetypical example of a daughter-in-law
who is his friend, we can see how they stood side by side
sharing their worlds together and how they ate their peck of salt together.
As Annette even became a fishing partner for trout and for salmon
Annette said of him:

> You got a sense he was liked.
> He was a party guy.
> He was good at sports and in acting.
> He was a Renaissance man
> with many different talents.

Dad's respect for women had a certain distance about it that
let him relate to his children's spouses in a unique friendship.
There was a special closeness with them because they were the beloved
spouses of his children and the parents of his grandchildren to be.
But that distance between them had to do with the sacred
that was opposed to the profane of an untoward familiarity.
That distance and that closeness made for their unique friendship.

Agape and the Four Loves

I,9 Agapeic affection with his grandchildren

I,9.1 Being grandfather was different than being father

As Grampa came down to the last five years of his life he was
deep down happy and very proud of his large Goicoechea family.
As the only son of his father he kept the family name alive
with his own four sons and now with his seven grandsons.
He also had seven lovely granddaughters and the two sets of seven
seemed to have an almost secret symbolic significance for him.
His four children had a college education, good jobs and great lives.
He had shared his hunter-gatherer fishing life with his grandsons
and his granddaughters knew his special love as had his daughter.
As he prayed for his grandchildren each morning and each night
he realized that they had a special agapeic affection together that
was quite different from that which he had shared with his children.
For his children he had the pressure of being provider and disciplinarian.
Now in his leisure and freedom from those parenting responsibilities
he could just do fun and yet valuable things with his grandchildren.
Annette called him the fishing baby sitter for he would call her
in the evening and say:

> You get those kids ready.
> I am going to be there at 7: a.m.
> to take them fishing.

They were very eager and knew how the trout bit so well so early.
They would be gone the whole day up Dogwood or Fishcreek
or down to Magic Dam and he had everything well planned.
In her book, *How to Build the Grandma Connection*, Susan Boyok
has an abundance of wisdom that is often pertinent to Grandpa.
She explains 5 steps to building the Grandma-Grandpa connection:
(1) Feel it (2) Think about it (3) Plan it (4) Make time for it (5) Enjoy it.
Whenever his grandchildren came to visit he did exactly this.
He saw his wife being the perfect Grandmother and his feelings
and thoughts in their shamanic, agapeic affection reached back
to the mourning for his lost father and to Uncle Pete fishing with him.

Part Three: Glorious Finishings

I,9.2 He took them into his bigger than life connection

When Grampa was five years old and his father died he was
taken into the connection with the spirit world of the blessed dead
by the successful mourning process with his mother and five sisters.
The prayers he learned as a child he said each morning and night
everyday of his life and he taught them to his children who were
taken thereby into the faith of their father without any doubt.
It was into this larger than life connection that he also took his
grandchildren who had already been initiated by their parents.
Whenever he took them fishing he would tell them stories and those
stories continued to grow with them as they matured so that
the older they became and had children of their own he was with them
and his grandchildren told his stories to their spouses and children.
Up Fishcreek he told them about Uncle Pete's sheep-camp,
about catching brook trout in the beaver ponds and running
up into the hills and back to train for track as he tended the sheep.
His grandchildren studied his three high school and one college annual.
As they came to know him they asked their parents more about him.
Their bigger that life connection took them into the five dimensions
of his world with: (1) The Father, Son and Holy Spirit (2) The Blessed
Virgin Mary (3) Queen of the Angels (4) and of the Saints
(5) and of all the living in his earthly world of time and of space.
As each grandchild made *The Sign of the Cross,* said *The Hail Mary*
The Angel of God and *The Our Father*, there always would be
a connection with Grampa Joe whose faith lived in each of them
just as his father's spirit had been with him since he was five.
Uncle Pete had cooked sheepherder spuds even with fresh trout
and as they went fishing that became a kind of near sacred meal.
Grampa with his missing teeth, missing ear and limping leg
would live on in the memory and hearts of each of his grandchildren.

Agape and the Four Loves

I,9.3 *The legacy he left is as strong as the love he gave*

Grampa's legacy was beautifully expressed by Annette and children.

FISH ON   –   FISH ON

If ever there was a pond or stream to fish,
There was Grandpa holding his pole in his hand.

If ever a mountain to climb, any person's wish,
There was Grandpa chasing game over the land.

We didn't know Grandpa when he was young and felt ten feet tall,
but legend has it that he was the finest track star of them all.

We will never forget the look that could kill, followed by a tease,
the five dollar bill presented on sight to each of us.

Mommy and Daddy would say "No, too generous!" but Grandpa saw
our begging, bright eyes that said, "Yes, Grandpa, thank you please."
He would never hesitate even though we were always creating a fuss.

We had some great times together, and it hurts to say good-bye.
But Grandpa . . . you made each of us proud to be a Goicoechea,
even though now we must cry.

Yet as we look up in the sky, our hearts sing,
for we know one star up high will never, ever fall.
The most famous star heaven now brings,
lights up our pathways to the everlasting call.

So now Grandpa, as always before, we send our love.
We hope the next time you say, "Fish on. Fish on!" you will
remember the "Idaho Mountains" and rushing Salmon River waters
and keep one eye on us from above, Paul, Kali, Cory Goicoechea.

Part Three: Glorious Finishings

I,9.4 Memories of him belong to the stories of their lives

Whenever Grampa drove his grandchildren fishing it was a time for telling them stories and often there was a moral to the story. His stories aimed at instilling a sense of excellence in them. His neice, Fern Cenarrusa, asked him to tell her his story and she wrote out what he said that we might all reflect on it and he told his story with an emphasis on his sister, Claudia, and her husband, Uncle Pete, because Fern was their daughter-in-law.

> My mother, Eulalia, brought her two children, Claudia
> and Mary, from Spain. Their father had died in Spain.
> My mother came to Boise to live with her aunt, Mrs. Mendiola.
> Three years later she married Euleterio Goicoechea
> who was born in Lekeitio, Spain. My mother was born
> in Elanchove, Spain. Angelus was their first child.
> Then I was born, followed by Dorothy, then Simona.
>
> My father bought a ranch in Tuttle. He raised sheep
> and milk cows. He died when I was five years old
> and is buried in the Shoshone cemetery. I have
> never been able to find his grave. Mother sold the ranch
> and outfit and bought a home in Gooding.
> My five sisters and I went to school in Gooding.
> We were a poor family and all of us worked
> to help mother make a living. When I was in high school,
> every morning at 5:00 o'clock I ran up town
> to clean a drug store and poke up a furnace.
> Then I went upstairs to a lawyer's office
> and cleaned it and built the fire in a pot belly stove.
> I got $20.00 a month from the drug store
> and $10.00 a month from the law office.

Grampa's story is about turning hardships into opportunities and being a winner through physical, vital, intellectual and spiritual exercises.

Agape and the Four Loves

I,9.5 *And his genes belong to their inheritance*

Grampa had a great confidence based upon his ability and his constant training and exercise which were at the heart of his stories. His grandchildren inherited that confidence and his habits of hard work. As he went on with his own story he said to Fern:

> Joe and Uncle Pete were partners on a ranch out of Carey near Fish Creek. They raised sheep. Claudia went to work for Ramona helping in the kitchen during lambing time and with farm work. That is when she and Pete were married. I was about eight or ten years old when Uncle Pete started taking me to the sheep camp. Uncle Pete gave me a white Arabian horse that was easy to ride. I thought I was a real cowboy, I tried to run wild horses down, but I never caught any.
>
> Then Uncle Pete and Joe split up their outfit and Claudia and Pete moved to Picabo. I think each one had two sections of land up Fish Creek.
>
> When I was 14, Uncle Pete got me a job driving derrick for the McGlockin brothers in Tikura. I worked two summers for them, helping with moving of hay, milking cows, and odd jobs for 75¢ a day.
>
> When I was 16, I was playing football and basketball I won first in the State in the 880 ½ mile and received a gold medal. That summer I worked in the hayfield for Kirkpatrick's in Picabo. On Leona's birthday I remember buying her a little present at the Picabo store. I got $1.50 a day working in the hayfield and when I stacked hay, I got $2.00 a day.

His grandchildren inherited his spirit of excellence and hard work.

Part Three: Glorious Finishings

I,9.6 His story passed on to them his Basque culture

The Basques are a hunter-gatherer tribe that because of the protection of their high mountain homeland were able to endure with their culture in tact for at least the past 40 thousand years and Grampa's story shows that with his family he still lived in that culture in Idaho. Thus he went on to tell Fern who married into that culture:

> When I was 17 years old, I played quarterback on the Gooding High School football team. We played ten games against Twin Falls, Burley, Jerome and seven other teams. We never lost a game; then we went to Boise for the championship game of Idaho. They beat us with a score of 13 to 7.
>
> I was forward on the basketball team. We lost to Twin Falls in the district meet. I won another gold medal in the 880 that year.
>
> In my last year of high school, in 1929, I didn't go out for track, but still played quarterback on the football team and forward on the basketball team.
>
> In 1930, I went to Gooding College. We didn't play football. I played guard on the first string basketball team. I ran ten different races. After running the 880 and winning, a half hour later I entered the mile race and won. I never lost a race.
>
> When the Depression came I couldn't find a job and never finished college.
>
> Mary was married and lived in Portland. Angelus and her husband lived in Emmet. Mother Dorothy and Simona went to California.

Daddy doesn't mention going to jail so the depression is his third trial.

Agape and the Four Loves

I,9.7 *With its physical, vital, intellectual, spiritual values*

As Grampa took his grandchildren fishing and told them stories and as he told Fern his story he was passing on the wisdom of the Elders. There was the time of childhood joy and the prowess of youth but wisdom must know how to deal with even The Great Depression.

> With only three dollars in my pocket, I got on a freight train
> in Gooding and traveled through 22 states looking for work.
> I almost starved to death. When I came back, I went to Picabo
> and whet to work for Uncle Pete in the lambing sheds at Tikura.
> I got $45.00 a month – big money!
> In the spring, I and a young sheep herder from Spain took
> the sheep out on the range. We didn't get along with each other,
> so I quit and joined the CCC. I only stayed with the CCC
> for six months and then I went to Richfield to help Uncle Pete
> with the lambing. That summer I worked for Joe Cenarrusa
> on his ranch in Carey.
>
> Louie Arian Sr. bought Bill York's pool hall in Carey.
> He had trouble with some of the people, so he hired me
> as a bartender and bouncer. I had a few fights, but
> afterwards got along real good.
>
> On November 12, 1936, Joneva and I were married
> in Hailey. Uncle Pete and Claudia were there.

When Grampa was a boy in grade school he already ran uptown each morning to work and he ran up the hills at the sheep camp. Physical exercise was always a big part of his value world and it led to the vital values of team work and being energized in community. He always told stories about education and the values of reading, writing, speaking and listening for he felt the wisdom of an intellectual life. But what was there with him at the center of his culture from beginning to end was his prayer and keeping in touch with spirit.

Part Three: Glorious Finishings

I,9.8 *And its optimistic view of love's glorious power*

Glory is a making manifest of the unmanifest even in its unmanifestness. The more of a an elder Grampa became the more it was natural for him to take others into the realm of mystery even as he knew it in prayer. He felt it important to tell the story of his mother and father and their importance for him and so he continued with Fern:

> Your grandfather, Euleterio Goicoechea, my father, was a tall man – six feet, 2 inches tall. My mother told me that he could out broadjump all the Basques in Boise and outlift them in raising weights.
>
> Your grandmother, Eulalia, was a very religious person, a real good Catholic. We lived close to the Gooding Catholic Church. My mother kept it clean and I helped her. I started the fire in the pot belly stove and had the fire going for the Priest every Sunday morning when he came from Jerome.
>
> I don't remember my mother spanking me. She used to pull my ear when I disobeyed.
>
> When I was a very young boy and stayed with the sheep herder up Fish Creek, there were a lot of grouse. I can remember killing them with rocks. Uncle Pete ordered a 22 rifle from Montgomery Ward Catalog. They sent him a 270 rifle. I borrowed that gun from Uncle Pete when I was working at Louie's pool hall. I shot and killed the largest deer that ever came out of Little Wood River with it. I had it mounted and it was in the Carey Pool Hall for years.

Nietzsche and Grampa both lost their fathers when they were five. And they both got in touch with the spirit world as they sensed their fathers continuing to be with them and their holy mothers had much to do with that as they prayed for the fathers with their children.

Agape and the Four Loves

I,9.9 *That for him did change all sorrow into joy*

Once Grampa experienced the miracle of his absent father being present he knew how joy says Yes and Amen to all sorrow as well. The love of others lets that joy be and Uncle Pete was like a father for Grampa, or was he not more like his grandfather?

> Uncle Pete was like a father to me when I was young, and I loved him. He was very kind, had lots of patience and seldom got angry. His word was his bond and he was honest and true. When he died, I was sick with the flue and unable to go to his funeral. I was really sorry that I couldn't be there.
>
> When I had the deer hunting accident and was shot in the ankle, I was in the Hailey hospital for a long time. Uncle Pete and Aunt Claudia would come often to see how my family and I were getting along. They were really wonderful people and were always ready to help. Last year when we stopped at the Richfield Cemetery, we were happy to see their graves decorated and taken care of. Keep up the good work. Your Uncle Joe, The Gambler

And so Little Joe and David Scott; Lynn Marie and Ritchie; Amy, Jesse and Tom; Jody, Tobby and Heidi; Paul, Kali and Cory; Angela Joy, Charity Marie, Jonathan Luke and Carolyn Crystal, Grampa had great dreams for all of you.
You and your families are still part of his dreams as he prays for you and your families with his mother, sisters and wife.
From him you inherit much of your ability but for success your attitude is equally important and his value system forms our attitude. He signed his letter as The Gambler, and he did savvy the game. And so with him let us always make the bet of the leap of faith in humankind's highest affirmation of affirming all in love.

II. Nietzsche

II,7 Reconciling the Buddha with the Evangel on the Cross

II,7.1 *The Buddha too is an enlightenment lion*

What Zarathustra says about the enlightenment lion in Part Two
has to do with the modern enlightenment of the French and Kant
but also with the axial age of ancient Greece and also of India.
The Pre-Socratics were enlightenment figures who wanted to move
from myth to logos and Heraclitus was Nietzsche's favorite Pre-Socratic.
Buddha in India also had a skepticism and a keeping within
the limits of reason alone that that let him critique Hindu culture.
After he treats Luther, Leibniz and Kant in *The Anti-Christ*
in sections ten and eleven he treats the Buddha and Buddhism
in sections twenty through twenty three so that we can think of
the rest of Part Two in *Zarathustra* in relation to what he says
about Buddhism in these four sections of *The Anti-Christ*.
Nietzsche begins section twenty by writing

> with my condemnation of Christianity,
> I should not like to have wronged
> a kindred religion which even preponderates
> in the number of its believers: *Buddhism*.
> They belong together as nihilistic religions -
> they are *decadence* religions –
> but they are distinguished from one another
> in the most remarkable way.

From the viewpoint of the child in *Zarathustra* and the childlike
Jesus in *The Anti-Christ* Nietzsche says Yes to both Kant and
the Buddha who as enlightenment lions went beyond the camel.
For Nietzsche both Platonists and Hindus are despisers of
the body who live for the afterworld for the Hindu also thinks
that we are here under a veil of maya or illusion and that
true knowledge will let the jiva or human become atman
or the world soul and wisdom will show that atman is Brahman.
The Buddha began by teaching that he knew nothing of atman
and as an enlightenment lion he too focused on the here and now.

Agape and the Four Loves

II,7.2 *He too believes in justice, equality and revenge*

In Part Two of *Zarathustra* in the chapter *On the Tarantulas*, we are shown this poisonous spider in whose soul sits revenge and this applies to both Kant and the Buddha and is the reason why they are both still nihilistic and decadent even though they are beyond the camel. To make the ethics of his practical reason work Kant still had to posit freedom of the will, immortality of the soul and a judging God. Kant believed in liberty, equality and freedom and a rewarder-punisher God who with proper revenge would properly punish evil. Because the good here are often not properly rewarded and the evil are not properly punished Kant had to posit a judging eternal God. Now while Nietzsche wants to be fair to Buddhism and sees that it does not have a rewarder-punisher God there is still the law of Karma and the wheel of rebirth and so Nietzsche writes:

> Buddhism is a hundred times
> more realistic than Christianity-
> it has the heritage of a cool and objective
> posing of problems in its composition.
> It arrives after a philosophical movement
> lasting hundreds of years;
> the concept of "God" is already
> abolished by the time it arrives.

Buddhism is caught up not in a struggle against sin for it is
beyond good and evil but its concern is a struggle against suffering.
The first Hinayana Buddhism like Hinduism and Platonism
still believed in the law of Karma and the wheel of rebirth which
we can finally escape when we reach Nirvana with total enlightenment.
Buddhism always had a compassion for those abused by the caste system.
And the compassion of the Bodhi Sattva in Mahayana Buddhism
is even greater; but as Zarathustra has argued compassion
is connected with pity and what has caused more suffering
than the follies of the compassionate and its hidden pity?

II,7.3 But he is a free spirit and not a famous philosopher

In his chapter *On the Famous Philosophers* Zarathustra begins to distinguish different kinds of enlightenment lions when he writes:

> Hungry, violent, solitary, godless:
> that is how the lion-will wants to be.
> Free from the happiness of serfs,
> redeemed from gods and worship,
> fearless and fearful, great and solitary:
> that is how the will of the genuine man is.

In his *Critique of Pure Reason*, Kant freed himself from gods; but in his *Critique of Practical Reason* he took back what he gave up. But the Buddha went into the wilderness and became a free spirit.

> The genuine men, the free spirits,
> have always dwelt in the desert,
> as lords of the desert;
> but in the towns dwell
> the well-fed famous philosophers-
> the draught animals.
> For they always, as asses,
> pull- the people's cart.

Nietzsche can remain a Neo Kantian in his Yes saying to *The Critique of Pure Reason*'s no saying but he has to reject *The Critique of Practical Reason* with its vengeful atonement justice. The Buddha would also go along with *The Critique of Pure Reason*. This being a free spirit is something that the child-like Jesus and the Buddha share and we get a clue to this in section thirty-one when Nietzsche writes:

> the mountain, lake and field preacher
> whose appearance strikes one
> as that of a Buddha
> on a soil very little like that of India.

How does Nietzsche reconcile his Jesus and the Buddha?

II,7.4 Deep down the Buddhist is a preacher of death

Why does Nietzsche see the Buddhist as nihilist even though he admires such a free spirit so much especially in his cheerfulness? In section twenty-one of *The Anti-Christ*, Nietzsche writes that for the Buddhist:

> The supreme goal is cheerfulness,
> stillness, absence of desire,
> and this goal is *achieved*.
> Buddhism is not a religion in which
> one merely aspires after perfection:
> perfection is the normal case

But in spite of this already back in Part One of *Zarathustra* in the chapter *On the Preachers of Death* Zarathustra says:

Yellow men or black men: that is what
the preachers of death are called . . .
They encounter an invalid
or an old man or a corpse;
and straightway they say
'Life is refuted!'
But only they are refuted,
they and their eye that sees
only one aspect of existence . . .
'Life is only suffering'-
thus others of them speak.

There are the black robbed priests and monks of the West and the yellow robbed Buddhist monks of the East and the Buddha did leave his palace and wife and child when he encountered the invalid, the old man and the corpse that he might go and seek enlightenment. All sentient creatures do suffer and that is rooted in desire but desire can be eliminated through the eightfold Buddhist path. That is also the elimination of bad karma and the need for reincarnation so we end in the nirvana of nihilistic emptiness.

II,7.5 His will to power sublimates with celibacy

In section twenty three of *The Anti-Christ* when writing about
Christianity and Buddhism Nietzsche takes up the question of celibacy
which both the black robes and the yellow robes share as they
advance along their mystical way and he writes:

> The requirements of chastity increase the vehemence
> and inward intensity of the religious instinct-
> it renders the cult warmer,
> more enthusiastic, more soulful.

Nietzsche is here writing about sublimation which is the way that
the will to power works as the lion goes beyond the camel and then
the lioness goes beyond the lion and the child goes beyond the lions.
In the middle of Part Two after the three songs of the lioness
Zarathustra begins to explain the will to power which he first
introduced in Part One in the section on *A Thousand and One Goals*.
In Part Two in the chapter *On Self Overcoming* he writes:

> Whatever I create and however much I love it-
> soon I have to oppose it and my love:
> thus will my will have it.
> And you too, enlightenment man are only
> a path and footstep of my will,
> my will to power walks with
> the feet of your will to truth.

So Kant and the Buddha became totally dedicated to the truth
and even though Kant was like St. Paul in not being married
the Buddha and many Buddhists make celibacy part of their practise.
What Nietzsche says about making their cult warmer, more
enthusiastic, more soulful goes back to Plato's *Phaedrus*.
At 245c with the myth of the charioteer all the energy of
the vulgar sexuality of the black horse is channeled with celibacy
into the enthusiasm and divine madness of the white horse.
All the energy of the camel and the lions let the child be creative.

II,7.6 *His sublimation is beautification*

In his next chapter *On The Sublime Men* Zarathustra discusses the enlightened men who become sublime:

> If he grew weary of his sublimity
> this sublime man,
> only then would his beauty rise up-
> only then would I taste him
> and find him tasty.

The Buddha has become beautiful in the sublimation of both his eros and his thanatos for the sex drive and the death drive have become reconciled to his higher drives, instincts and tastes and he is not tense about desiring a women or fearing death. Those who have not overcome themselves and reached an integration but grow weary of their disintegrating forces

> Stand there like a tiger about to spring;
> but I do not like these tense souls,
> my taste is hostile towards all these withdrawn men.
> And do you tell me, friends, that there is
> no dispute over taste and tasting?
> But all life is dispute over taste and tasting!

What makes up the will to power of each living creature are these tastes and the dispute among tastes and sublimation is an ordering of tastes. The classical saying is:

> *De gustibus*
> *sed non disputandum est.*
> Tastes should not be disputed.

But Zarathustra says:

> Taste: that is at the same time
> weight and scales and weigher;
> and woe to all living creatures
> that want to live without dispute
> over weight and scales and weigher!

II,7.7 But unlike the child lions do not believe in belief

In the next chapter *On the Land of Culture* Zarathustra further discusses the enlightened men of the future and their new age Buddhism and he has them say:

> we are complete realists
> and without belief or superstition.

In the previous chapter when speaking of these lions in relation to beauty and goodness he said:

> when power grows gracious
> and descends into the visible:
> I call such descending beauty.
> And I desire beauty from no one
> as much as I desire it from you,
> you men of power:
> may your goodness be
> your ultimate self overpowering.

The modern men and the New Age women are lionlike in their power and they do not believe in grace and a gracious descent of beauty into their own bodies and attitudes and relationships. So in being critical of the lion the childlike Zarathustra says:

> But he who had to create
> always had his prophet dreams
> and star - auguries -
>
> and he believed in belief.

Zarathustra as a child is willing to take a leap of faith and place a bet on love, on amor fati, on our highest affirmation. The lion wins the freedom from the belief system of the camel and that prepares for the child's creativity but that creativity also depends upon a new kind of belief in the worth of all flesh. So, as there is a struggle of forces, drives, instincts and tastes within the will to power we will now have to understand how the highest sublimation comes from believing in love.

Agape and the Four Loves

II,7.8 *Men of pure knowledge do not love the earth*

As Zarathustra tells the story of his journey through history
ever since he first started thinking in terms of the opposites he
first believed in the value of the reverent spirit that took upon itself
heavy burdens as in the cultures of Christian Platonism and Hinduism.
Then he saw the enlightenment critique of that mythology which
told the similar story of the cave and four levels of the caste system.
He became a believer in the enlightenment and men of pure knowledge.
In the chapter on *The Immaculate Perception* he says:

> Once I thought I saw
> a god's soul at play in your play,
> you of pure knowledge!
> Once I thought there was
> no better art than your arts.

But things changed and the shortcoming of pure knowledge began
to become evident as the lioness and the child began to evolve.
Zarathustra says:

> Truly, you do not love the earth
> as creators, begetters, men joyful
> at entering upon a new existence!

The lion is a good critic of afterworldlings and despisers of the body
but he himself does not become a loving creator;

> But now your emasculated leering
> wants to be called 'contemplation'! . . .
> But it shall be your curse,
> you immaculate men, you of pure knowledge,
> that you will never bring forth.

In order to reconcile all the urges and tastes within oneself one
has to include the beautiful, the good, the true and the holy.
If one lives for only the truth of pure knowledge without any belief
one cannot really have a sublimation and beautification that lets
there be an integrated personality with a vibrant functionality.

Part Three: Glorious Finishings

II,7.9 They do not love it as innocent creators

Right from the beginning of *The Prologue* Zarathustra has compared his love to the sun's gifts of warm light and now he says:

> For already it is coming, the glowing sun-
> *its* love of the earth is coming!
> All sun-love is innocence and creative desire.

So Zarathustra's childlike criticism of the Lions of the Enlightenment has brought us not only to *The Twilight of the Idols* but to *The Daybreak* of a new day of innocent creative love. Kant and the Buddha who do not believe in belief and want only pure knowledge are also criticized by the lioness who is the image of Romantic Love and we have her songs in the middle of Part Two: the Night, Dance and Tomb songs. But in the chapter on *The Poets* Zarathustra's disciples ask him why he says that the poets lie too much and after telling them that he too is a poet he says:

> Alas, how weary I am of all the unattainable
> that is supposed to be reality.
> Alas, how weary I am of the poets.

Zarathustra has four great temptations which indicate to him that he has not attained the reconciliation of a full sublimation. They are shame, pity, weariness and disgust and they have a certain order in that the camel caste brought about shame. The compassion of the lions contains a hidden pity and the promise of the lioness about romantic love can make the loves weary insofar as it is supposed to be real but is not attainable. All of these go against Zarathustra's taste so that his disgust brings him to overcome the shame of the camel, the pity of the lion and the weariness of the lioness that as a child he might love the earth and all flesh with an innocence that believes in their beauty and goodness with a Yes and Amen.

II,8 Reconciling the romantic lioness with the here and now

II,8.1 *Besides enlightenment lions there is the romantic lioness*

In the very first chapter of Part Two, *The Child with the Mirror*, we already here from Zarathustra about his lioness wisdom:

> Ah, if only I knew how to lure you back
> with shepherd's flutes!
> Ah, if only my lioness wisdom
> had learned to roar fondly!
> And we have already learned
> so much with one another.

Kant did not really have a love of wisdom; rather he was concerned with reason- pure reason, practical wisdom and judgmental reason. Strictly speaking the Buddha too is not really a lover of wisdom. These lions of the enlightenment sought a pure and practical knowledge within the limits of reason alone without any belief. But, the lioness is connected with a certain love and wisdom. Nietzsche learned so much with Schopenhauer and Wagner but they never learned to roar fondly for Schopenhauer remained a pessimist and even though he wrote beautifully about a metaphysical love of the sexes the individual was not real. With the Hindus he believed we have fallen into the realm of *maya* or illusion so that each *jiva* or human is atman and atman is Brahman so that the here and now is illusion. When Nietzsche underwent his conversion in October of 1881, he clearly saw the melancholic lack of joy in this romanticism. So also was he now totally clear about Wagner with whom he had learned so much about Schopenhauer and The Tragic Greeks. Nietzsche with Wagner came to see Greek tragedy and music as a redemption from Schopenhauer's pessimism, but in 1881 Nietzsche was redeemed even from Wagner and Dionysian pessimism and with Jesus came to a Yes and Amen for the here and now. The child will go beyond the lioness but she is his mother as a *"praeparatio evangelica"* or preparation for the Good News.

Part Three: Glorious Finishings

II,8.2 *And her eros gives gifts to the child*

At the end of the chapter, *On the Child with the Mirror* Zarathustra says:

> My wild Wisdom became pregnant
> upon lonely mountains;
> upon rough rocks
> she bore her young, her youngest.

In October of 1881, when Nietzsche underwent his conversion, high
up there in the mountains of Upper Engadi amidst all those
great rocks of Surlei he became pregnant with his inspiration.
This was for him the great moment of sublimation for now all
of his writing about the child's love is conceived within him.
As a Romantic with Schopenhauer and Wagner he longed for a
beautiful, mutual erotic love with Lou Salome and other lovely ladies.
But, as those pessimists showed it just couldn't be and he felt
devastated and fell into the depths of nihilism which he describes
in *The Night Song*:

> It is night: only now
> do all songs of lovers awaken.
> And my soul too is the song of a lover . . .
> Light am I: ah, that I were night!
> But this is my solitude,
> that I am girded round with light.

These first opposites of the original Zarathustra, light and night
are now getting a new meaning in the history of Zarathustrian legacy.
The sun of light gives as does this lioness for her new child
but to receive with a Yes and Amen can be a higher affirmation.
Nietzsche and Zarathustra went beyond enlightenment knowing
and became romantic, lioness lovers but that giving did not work.
Nietzsche wished with all his might that he and Lou could be
suns of mutual giving to each other; but then he discovered
that even as the ugliest man he could be a receptive thankful child.
Most of all with a childlike gratitude one can live in Joyful Wisdom.

Agape and the Four Loves

II,8.3 *But receiving can be more blessed than giving*

The lioness in her romantic affection and *eros* will do anything for her child in a selfless giving that brings Zarathustra to say:

> Now she runs madly
> through the cruel desert
> and seeks and seeks
> for the soft grassland-
> my old, wild wisdom!
> upon the soft grassland
> of your hearts, my friends!-
> upon your love she would like
> to bed her dearest one.

This lioness would like to build up a romantic love in the hearts of all just as Schopenhauer would with his writing and Wagner with his music and Nietzsche was one of them until October of 1881.

> It is night: only now
> do all songs of lovers awaken.
> And my heart too is the song of a lover.

But the night and its song taught him of a new and different love than that of the sun that wants to give gifts as the lioness would selflessly give her life for her child for the hand grows callous in giving.

> Oh, it is only you, obscure, dark ones,
> who extract warmth from light-givers!
> oh, only you drink milk
> and comfort from the udders of light.

Nietzsche was left in a dark night of the soul when he was rejected by Lou Salome; but there he learned of the highest love of the child. In the sublimation process of his conversion Nietzsche found that he could say Yes and Amen even to the eternal return of Lou's rejection. He could now sing the song of the obscure dark one and that would become the song of his Zarathustra and his other writings. The Night Song of his childlike writing could be for his lioness of light.

II,8.4 From the dance song's romantic pessimism

In *The Dance Song* Zarathustra and his disciples are walking
through the forest in the evening when they come to a meadow
and beautiful young girls are dancing there but begin to flee
when they see Zarathustra but he urges them to stay and dance.
He says he will sing a song for them if they remain dancing.
His song is about a conflict between Lady Life and his wild wisdom.
The whole setting is very romantic and Zarathustra loves the ladies.
He loves Lady Life and Lady Wisdom even in their conflict.
He sings his song about the deep down conflict within Romantic love:

> But when the dance had ended
> and the girls had gone away,
> he grew sad.

And that is the way Romantic love was for Nietzsche and for Wagner
and Schopenhauer in their music and in their philosophy.
Romanticism was seen to be as pessimistic as Christianity.
For the Jewish priests saw most of existence as profane and
then Paul stressed the inherited sin of Adam for all and Augustine
continued that and then Luther and Calvin saw depravity everywhere.
Nietzsche sees Christianity as a pessimistic misinterpretation of Jesus.
Zarathustra ends the dance Song with the words:

> Ah, my friends, it is the evening
> that questions thus within me.
> Forgive me my sadness!

Zarathustra wonders if it is folly to go on living, for what he
wanted so much, namely, a successful Romantic Love failed him.
That was the whole message of Schopenhauer and his idea
that everything here is illusion and of Wagner and his operas
that had a melancholic sadness deep within Tristitia.
Up until 1881 Nietzsche only knew of this kind of pessimism.
But with the sublimation of his conversion he was able
to find a joy that could even will the eternal return of his sorrow.

Agape and the Four Loves

II,8.5 *To the funeral song's Dionysian pessimism*

As Zarathustra step by step explicates the history of how we came to the highest love he shows in *The Funeral Song* how he moved from Romantic pessimism to Dionysian pessimism which with Jesus can affirm all of life even the most painful in a special glory. He says at the beginning of this tomb song:

> O, you sights and visions of my youth!
> O, all you glances of love,
> you divine momentary glances!
> How soon you perished!
> Today I think of you as my dead ones.
> A sweet odour comes to me from you,
> my dearest dead ones,
> a heart-easing odour that banishes tears.

As the shamanic child Nietzsche learned to find the presence of his dearest, dead and absent father so now he learns how to go through a successful mourning that lets sorrow be joy. He sees that his will can sublimate and reconcile the worst. He ends the Song by singing:

> Yes, you are still my destroyer of all graves:
> Hail, my will!
> And only where there are graves
> are there resurrections.
> Thus sang Zarathustra.

This Dionysius who is like Jesus and can look at Tragedy and turn it artistically into a Joyful Wisdom is the guide for Nietzsche and his Dionysian pessimism is at the same time a glorious optimism that believes in a resurrection of love. The pessimist sees that the best of times can be the worst of times, but this can be redeemed by seeing that it is better to have loved and lost than not to have loved at all and Zarathustra in his chapter *On Redemption* explains such a healing sublimation.

II,8.6 On redeeming romantic pessimism with sublimation

In *The Anti-christ* in section twenty three when discussing further Christianity and Buddhism Nietzsche writes:

> So that love shall be possible,
> God has to be a person.

This connection between love and personhood is central for Nietzsche and his thought about it is developed in *Zarathustra* Part Two, chapter 20 in *On Redemption* where he discusses the task of becoming what we are and how it is accomplished through sublimation. In this chapter Zarathustra says:

> I walk among men
> as among fragments of the future:
> of the future which I scan.
> And it is all my art and aim,
> to compose into one and bring together
> what is fragment and riddle
> and dreadful chance.

Zarathustra is a person with great purity of heart and he wills one thing – to bring the sublimational integration of amor fati to all. He has found that most persons are poor suffering disintegrated wrecks. In the many drives, instincts and tastes of their will to power they they are fragmented and a riddle of contradictory values fighting against each other with one dreadful throw of the dice after another. His task is to bring the great love to each person for as he says at the end of that same section twenty three of *The Anti-christ*:

> One endures more when in love
> than one otherwise would,
> one tolerates everything.

The whole point of Zarathustra's mission is to teach redemption that can transform every 'It was' into an 'I wanted it thus!' Nietzsche discovered in 1881 how to transform every sorrow into joy and in this chapter *On Redemption* we move from lioness to child.

Agape and the Four Loves

II,8.7 A sublimation based on faith, hope and love

In that section from *The Anti Christ* Nietzsche goes on to write:

> The point was to devise a religion
> in which love is possible:
> with that one is beyond
> the worst that life can offer-
> one no longer even sees it. –
> So much for the three Christian virtues
> faith, hope and charity:
> I call them the three Christian shrewdnesses.
> Buddhism is too late, to positivistic
> still to be shrewd in this fashion.

Schopenhauer based his pessimism on the Hindu and Buddhist belief that we are caught here in the wheel of rebirth and living in illusion and samsara as long as we think we are individuals. There is no personhood with the atman that is Brahman and with the anatman or no self that we get beyond in the mystical unification. Romantic pessimism also believed that love never lasts and thus with Wagner we can only mourn but never be redeemed from our suffering and the sadness of erotic love that can only fail. Nietzsche himself is very shrewd and he totally believes in these three theological virtues that can endure and tolerate anything. As long as we are caught up in Romantic Pessimism we are still a prisoner in the wheel of rebirth as it were and thus Zarathustra says in *On Redemption*:

> Will – that is what the liberator
> and bringer of joy is called:
> thus I have taught you, my friends!
> But now learn this as well:
> The will itself is still a prisoner.

As long as we are a camel or an enlightenment lion or a lioness of Romantic Pessimism we are not integrated by the great love.

Part Three: Glorious Finishings

II,8.8 A sublimation higher than reconciliation

Zarathustra is very clear about atonement justice theologies and their rewarder-punisher Gods and for him all these Gods are dead. The postmodern child of love believes in them no longer and thus he says in *On Redemption*:

> Can there be redemption
> when there is eternal justice?
> Alas, the stone "It was"
> cannot be rolled away;
> all punishment too must be eternal.
>
> This madness preached.

Plato, Paul, Augustine and Luther all carried this heavy burden of only justice as did the lions, Kant and the Buddha, and as did the Lioness, Schopenhauer and Wagner, but Zarathustra sees through this madness and replaces eternal justice with eternal love.

> Has the will become its own
> redeemer and bringer of joy?
> Has it unlearned the spirit of revenge
> and all teeth-gnashing?

Nietzsche unlearned justice and its revenge in October of 1881 and The Drama of Zarathustra is now reaching the stage of the child where this joyful wisdom will be explained as the birth of the child. Zarathustra goes on:

> Who has taught it to be reconciled with time,
> and higher things than reconciliation?
> The will that is the will to power must will
> something higher than any reconciliation –
> but how shall that happen?
> Who has taught it
> to will backwards, too?

It is now our task to clearly understand this childlike sublimation that is even higher than reconciliation and that wills backwards.

Agape and the Four Loves

II,8.9 *Sublimating the "It was" into "Thus I will it"*

Enlightenment and Buddhist Lions and the Romantic Lioness became free from the weight-bearing and reverential spirit and they create freedom for themselves with a sacred No even to duty. Zarathustra asks at the end of *The Three Metamorphoses*:

> Why must the preying lion still become a child.

He answers by saying:

> The child is innocence and forgetfulness,
> a new beginning, a sport, a self-propelling wheel,
> a first motion, a sacred Yes.
> Yes, a sacred Yes is needed, my brothers,
> for the sport of creation.

We must now see what this Yes is and why it is a sacred and how it can bring one to a sublimation that is even greater than reconciliation. What is the child's creative will that says: "Thus shall I will it."? It was the case that Nietzsche's father died when he was only five. It was the case that Lou Salome left Nietzsche all alone again. But with a fruitful mourning process with his family of women Nietzsche was able to say a sacred Yes to the death of his father. And now all of his writing is a sacred creative Yes to the departure of Lou Salome so that all of his negative reactions are sublimated into a creative Yes that is even more than a reconciliation. Throughout Part Three of Zarathustra and throughout Part Four we see how spirit or the forces of the will to power become child. By pondering in detail three chapters: *The Vision and The Riddle*, *The Convalescent* and *The Intoxicated Song* we will be able to see the essence of this transformation into the physiology of the child. As we go to Part Three we read in *Of Involuntary Bliss*;

> For one loves from the very heart
> only one's child and one's work.

We must now see how Zarathustra came to create himself as a child that he might be creative with his Yes saying and Joyful Wisdom.

II,9 On becoming Zarathustra's child with Jesus

II,9.1 *By courageously believing in eternal life*

In *The Anti-Christ* in section 29, as Nietzsche begins to tell us why he loved Jesus so much, he writes:

> What are the 'glad tidings'?
> True life, eternal life is found –
> it is not promised, it is here,
> it is *within you*, as life lived in love.

The Drama of Zarathustra culminates in the child who like Jesus knows the true and eternal life that is lived here and now in love. In Part Three, Chapter Two, *On the Vision and The Riddle*, Nietzsche poetically tells us of his own conversion when he was climbing in the high mountains of Switzerland in October of 1881, and he tells the story of Zarathustra and of his most tragic moment. Zarathustra tells of a young shepherd who was sleeping with his mouth open when a serpent came and bit him deep inside the throat. The shepherd was writhing in terror and pain and Zarathustra tried to pull out the snake but he would not let go his bite. Finally Zarathustra yelled out:

> Bite! Bite! Bite its head off!
> The shepherd into whose mouth
> the snake crawled bit
> as my cry advised him;
> he bit with a good bite!
> He spat away the snake's head
> and sprang up.
> No longer a shepherd, no longer a man –
> a transformed being, surrounded with light,
> *laughing!* Never yet on earth
> had any man laughed as he laughed.

Such is the vision that opens the way for the lioness to metamorphose into the child and the riddle is: "who is this shepherd and what is this serpent whose head is here bit off?"

Agape and the Four Loves

II,9.2 With a love beyond wisdom that praises folly
The very last words of Zarathustra's *Prologue* are:

> I wish I were wise! I wish I were wise
> from the heart of me, like my serpent!
> But I am asking the impossible:
> therefore I ask my pride
> always to go along with my wisdom!
> And if one day my wisdom should desert me -
> Ah, it loves to fly away!
> - Then may my pride fly with my folly!

At this point in the drama when the shepherd bites off the head of the serpent we see the departure of wisdom which lets there be a place for folly which Zarathustra's great love can also embrace. The camel of Christian Platonism, the lion of the enlightenment and the lioness of romanticism each loved a wisdom that excluded folly in its laughing, innocent, childlike play with all of existence. When the riddle is answered in Part Three, Chapter Thirteen, it turns out that the shepherd who bit off the serpent's head is Zarathustra. Now he is very ill from the monster's bite who crept into his throat and choked him but he hears the birds and animals singing:

> Everything goes, everything returns;
> the wheel of existence rolls for ever.
> Everything dies, everything blossoms anew;
> the year of existence runs on for ever.

Zarathustra hears them sing about the eternal return of everything and he says:

> The great disgust at man – it choked me
> and had crept into my throat.

Zarathustra could not will that he would be the ugliest man again and again; he could not will the return of the little man. That is disgusting and wisdom is against it but these foolish animals in their joy are bringing joy and laughter to the convalescent.

Part Three: Glorious Finishings

II,9.3 Goes beyond survival of the fittest with a will to power

When Darwin thought about evolution he tried to understand it in terms of the survival of the fittest, but Nietzsche sees that the unfit too will survive and he is disgusted with such existence. Nietzsche seeks to understand all living things by seeing in them a will to power which is not only a will to survive but to prevail. Each living thing wills to have the best life possible and anything less is against its taste or is disgusting and thus Zarathustra is disgusted that life with its same problems keeps returning. However, Zarathustra as a convalescent is discovering two ways of employing the will to power which have to do with negative reactions to disgusting situations or one can love positively. Nietzsche's basic philosophy has to do with the will to power that can with ressentiment have negative reactions or with an amor fati or love of destiny that is proactively positive. As Zarathustra metamorphoses into the child while he goes through his convalescence he comes to love what disgusted him. He distinguishes the lower men from the higher men and especially the lower men disgust him and they have made him ill. As Zarathustra puts it when he is convalescing:

> Alas, man recurs eternally!
> The little man recurs eternally!
> I had seen then both naked,
> the greatest man and the smallest man:
> all too similar to one another,
> even the greatest all too human.
> The greatest all too small! –
> that was my disgust at man!
> And eternal recurrence even for the smallest!
> That was my disgust at all existence.

Zarathustra is still resentful and is expressing his negative reaction against existence, but now he is about to be healed.

Agape and the Four Loves

II,9.4 That goes beyond ressentiment with an amor fati

As Zarathustra said in Part Two, Chapter Two verse 20

> It is my art and aim,
> to compose into one and bring together
> what is fragment and riddle and dreadful chance.

We are here dealing with a riddle for who is the shepherd who
has been made deathly ill by the snake bit and who is the snake?
We do have a fragmented Zarathustra who is disgusted by little men.
He has all this hatred and disgust and it is making him deathly ill.
His wisdom which disdains fools is at war with his love within him.
While he is so ill with disgust the birds and animals are singing and
playing around him and their joy begins to touch and to heal him.
He does not just get rid of fragment and riddle and dreadful chance.
but their negative energy condensed into disgust is sublimated.
A joyful love sparked by nature begins to harness all of his
negative energy and he is able to use it for positive purposes.
Nietzsche can be very thankful that his father died, that he
got ill and could not teach, that women rejected him because
all that sorrow through a productive mourning and sublimation
process let him become the great lover, philosopher, and poet he was.
He became a true overman by overcoming the negativity
within himself as he received the gift of amor fati from
the joyful birds and animals who taught him a joyful wisdom.
Zarathustra has had to face the four great challenges of pity,
weariness, shame and disgust and now he overcomes the last.
Great love can overcome each of them as the will to power becomes
the will to truth that works with the forces of things as perspectival.
Throughout Part Four Zarathustra will try to be a missionary
who wants to bring truth, love and joy to the higher men.
He cannot be satisfied with them because they are not satisfied with
themselves and with the morality of mothers they care for others.
He has gone beyond the lioness to her cub and so should they.

II,9.5 Beyond good and evil with a yes and amen for all

After convalescing Zarathustra through sublimation has grown
into the great health of the child who dances in playful laughter.
This brings him to a new ethics that goes beyond good and evil
as the camel saw it with his self-realization ethics and as
the lion saw it with his categorical imperative and as the lioness
practiced it with compassion for her child and his or her world.
Part Four begins with a quotation from *Of the Compassionate:*

> Alas, where in the world have there been
> greater follies than with the compassionate?
> And what in the world has caused more
> suffering than the follies of the compassionate?
> Woe to all lovers who cannot surmount pity!
> Thus spoke the Devil to me once: Even
> God has his Hell: it is his love for man.
> And I lately heard him say these words;
> God is dead; God has died of his pity for man.

So the key distinction is between lovers who go beyond compassion
and those who cannot surmount it or suffer for and with another.
No person and no thought, word and deed are simply evil for they
all have something of the good in them for all that is is good.
Zarathustra finds that there is plenty in the little man to love.
Good and evil are in the eye of the beholder and Zarathustra comes
to say Yes and Amen to everyone and everything because he sees
perspectives that are good and his love can see good in everything.
However, Nietzsche does say No to No saying just as he
is here saying no to compassion and pity that contain No-saying.
The ethical attitude of Amor Fati or love of all destiny unmasks
ressentiment and shows that is suffers with an impotency
and brooding that result in a value reversal and make good look bad.
As a convalescent Zarathustra went beyond his impotency and
brooding in pity, weariness, shame and disgust to a joyful love.

Agape and the Four Loves

II,9.6 And beyond nihilism with an eternal return

Zarathustra finished the story about *The Vision and the Riddle* by writing:

> No longer a shepherd, no longer a man –
> a transformed being, surrounded with light,
> *Laughing*! Never yet on earth
> had a man laughed as he laughed!
> O my brothers, I heard a laughter –
> and now a thirst consumes me,
> a longing that is never stilled.
> My longing for this laughter consumes me -.
> Oh how do I endure still to live!
> And how could I endure to die now!

When he addresses The Higher Men this theme of laughter together with that of dancing becomes predominate and he urges them to laugh at themselves as a man ought to laugh for as he says in Part 19 in of *The Higher Men*

> Better to be foolish with happiness
> than foolish with misfortune,
> better to dance clumsily than to walk lamely.
> So learn from me my wisdom,
> even the worst thing has two good sides.

This is the way to get beyond nihilism for the will to truth loves the inner forces of each things will to power as perspectival. Every person, place and thing; every thought, word and deed even at the worst of times has two good sides to be loved. If like playful, creative children we can laugh at ourselves even in all of our misfortune and weakness we will have the higher love together with Jesus and the child of the drama of Zarathustra. The whole point of Nietzsche's poetic, philosophic vision is to love to will the eternal return of even the sorrowful with joy.

II,9.7 In a loving joy that wills eternity

As *The Intoxicated Song* begins, the higher men are speaking with Zarathustra about humankind's highest affirmation – the great love of the childlike Jesus – and the ugliest man snorts out:

> 'My assembled friends,' said the ugliest man,
> 'what do you think? For the sake of this day –
> I am content for the first time
> to have lived my whole life . . .
> It is worth while to live on earth:
> one day, one festival with Zarathustra
> has taught me how to love the earth.
> "Was *that* – life?" I will say to death.
> "Very well! Once more!"'

The ugliest man who has suffered greatly for being so terribly ugly has discovered with Zarathustra that:

> All joy wants the eternity of all things,
> wants honey, wants dregs, wants
> intoxicated midnight, wants graves,
> wants the consolation of graveside tears,
> wants gilded sunsets, what does joy not want?

With the joy of the singing birds and the playing animals Zarathustra the ugliest man even loves himself as the ugliest man. Through the ages of history Zarathustra has been the one who distinguished the light and the night and all the different opposites. Zarathustra became the Christian Platonists who lived for the afterlife. Then he became the enlightenment lions who lived for a better future. Then he became the romantic lioness who loved especially her child. But now he is the child who like Jesus wants the salvation of all flesh just as it is in this life for the ugliest man and for Nietzsche who lost his father, his job and his beloved but who learned of joy. Zarathustra so loves that he wants the same life for ever and now the ugliest man and his friends have come to the same great love.

Agape and the Four Loves

II,9.8 And can say yes to all sorrow as well

Zarathustra and the higher men have been gifted with love
so great that they say the grateful prayer of Yes and Amen for every
existing reality and can affirm it by willing its eternal return for as
the ugliest man says:

> My friends, what do you think?
> Will you not, like me, say to death:
> "Was *that* – life?" For Zarathustra's sake
> very well! Once more!

The ugliest man can now say – very well, let me be this same
ugliest man over and over again forever, for that is the test of love.
How is it that the ugliest man is able to pass this test of love?
It is possible because he has learned the trick of sublimation
that can take any bad trick and turn it into a good trick.
That is precisely the creativity of the child who in all innocence
can take any aliment such as being born crippled and unable
to walk and through compensation be better because of just that.
This way or method of creative illness toward the great
health is philosophical in its genealogical method that
recoils with counter-memories against negative reactions.
It is psychoanalytic in working out weariness, shame
disgust and pity with a talking cure and is successful mourning.
It is literary just as this very book *Thus, Spoke Zarathustra*,
creates, in dramatic acts, value with authority.
It is historical in manifesting the three metamorphoses
of western culture and in the journey of every individual.
In section 11 of *The Intoxicated Song* they sing:

> so rich is joy that it thirsts for woe,
> for Hell, for hatred, for shame, for the lame,
> for the *world* – for it knows,
> oh it knows, this world.

Yes, Zarathustra as the child Jesus can say Yes to all suffering.

Part Three: Glorious Finishings

II,9.9 In a glory that wants deep, deep, deep eternity
Zarathustra and the higher men believe in

> The Holy Spirit of the Risen Lord Jesus,
> the Holy Catholic Church, the communion of saints,
> the forgiveness of sins, the resurrection of the body,
> and life everlasting.

This is exactly what the best love imaginable affirms
as Zarathustra and the higher men become inspired by
the Holy Spirit of the child Jesus who is the very love that is God.
All persons will keep living just as they have been in a great
communion of saints and of all flesh that are saved by love.
Sublimational love lets all sins be forgiven with a love that
doesn't pity the suffering but loves him just as the ugliest man
is loved by Zarathustra just as he loves his father and Lou Salome.
Our very body in all of its infirmity is loved with all the beautiful
good that the lover such as Zarathustra can behold and love.
With this great love that sees that love is God and that God
is love Nietzsche goes beyond modernity into that postmodern
love that can let lovers like Therese the Little Flower love Hitler.
People who like to take offence and be scandalized might
blame Hitler on Nietzsche but Nietzsche is teaching us how
to love Hitler just as Zarathustra would love all the higher men.
If our Holocaust studies would bring us always to pray for
Hitler and to love him then we would have Zarathustra's great health.
In the veritas of vino we might come to sing with Zarathustra
and The Retired Pope and the ugliest man and Hitler:

> The world is deep
> Deeper than day can comprehend.
> Deep is its woe,
> Joy – deeper than hearts agony
> woe says: Fade! Go!
>
> But all joy wants eternity.

III. Q³

III,7 Matthew's Gospel of agape for Jewish converts

III,7.1 Which he explains to his Jewish audience

Matthew writes his gospel for the Jews who have become Christian
and for the Jews whom he wants to interest in the Messiah Christ.
As he writes he has before him Mark's gospel and the book of Q.
He constructs his story with an introduction, five parts and
a conclusion as a dramatic account in seven acts of the coming kingdom.
He takes Mark's synoptic narrative of Jesus' life story and divides
it into five parts like the Pentateuch and then inserts the
62 Q sayings which he also divides into five suitable parts.
It is our task here to examine how the *agape* of Q fits into the
context of Matthew just as we examined the same in Thomas' gospel.
In the book of Q proper the incarnation love theology of Q^1
is primary for the historical Jesus and then the atonement justice
theology of Q^2 needs to be reconciled with that as secondary.
As we ponder the sayings of the book of Q in Matthew we can ask
if the justice of the apocalyptic Son of Man is primary
and if the agapeic sayings of the Jesus of Q^1 became secondary.
Throughout his gospel Matthew is constantly showing how the
many events of Jesus' life are foretold by the Jewish prophets.
For the Jesus of Matthew all the Law of Moses is contained in
the double command of loving the Lord, your God with your
whole heart mind and soul and your neighbor as yourself.
If Jews follow the teaching of Christ they will be fulfilled Jews.
But if they are like the scribes and the Pharisees of Matthew 23
then the apocalyptic son of man will judge them and find
them wanting because they have taken offence at the fulfillment
of that which is the very best in their own religious culture.
Jesus the Messiah King is founding a new kingdom in order to
fulfill the kingdom of the Jews by taking it to the ends of the earth.
Matthew's gospel is divided into five parts like the Torah of Moses
and is his *agape* not more like the *ahava* of Mosaic justice
than the *hesed* of the Davidic promise theology and its mercy?

Part Three: Glorious Finishings

III,7.2 And introduces with his birth and infancy narrative

On page 173 Burton Mack writes:

> If one were to ask which of the narrative gospels
> most nearly represents an ethos toward which
> the community of Q may have tended
> it would be the Gospel of Matthew.

Matthew does build on Q³ which thinks of Jesus as son of God, as focused on the temple in Jerusalem and as stressing the authority of the scripture which all has to do with a new kingdom. In his birth and infancy narrative Matthew begins his Gospel with a genealogy of Jesus Christ, son of David, son of Abraham. He divides Jewish history into fourteen generations from Abraham to David, fourteen from David to the Babylonian deportation; and fourteen from the Babylonian captivity to Christ and quotes the Hebrew scriptures as foretelling each event in Jesus' life. What Mack says here and what we clearly see is that Matthew is not primarily concerned with the *agape* sayings of Q¹. With the destruction of the Temple of Jerusalem right after the death resurrection and ascension of Jesus the Christians of Matthew's day were concerned about his second coming and the new kingdom. The kingdom of David which according to the Davidic promise would last forever was destroyed at the time of the Babylonian captivity. The Jews then thought of themselves as being a kingdom of priests and the temple was rebuilt and their belief was justified. But when the second temple was destroyed and priestly sacrifice came to an end the main concern of Matthew and of Jewish Christians was with Christ the King and his new kingdom which Matthew's gospel is about from beginning to end. From the moment of his birth Jesus is already related to kings for King Herod wants to kill him because Jesus is a threat to his kingship and the three Magi bring those gifts fit for a king as the Star of Bethlehem leads them to their new king.

Agape and the Four Loves

III,7.3 *The kingdom of justice and agape is announced*

On page 185 Burton Mack writes:

> One notices that the aphorisms of Q^1
> although they had lost all their bite
> by landing in the Gospel of Matthew, were
> scarcely able to carry the weight assigned them.

The aphorisms of Q^1 have bite insofar as they stress *agape* as an unconditional love of God for us that makes justice secondary and as an unconditional love that we too should practise. In Luke's gospel the unconditional *agape* of Q^1 is right up front and stressed as that which differentiates Jesus love from all others. In ordering Mark's synoptic narrative in five stages of repenting for the kingdom of heaven is at hand Matthew gives the justice of apocalyptic judgment theology the primacy and in this way the unconditional *agape* theology of Q^1 is made secondary. After Matthew completes the narrative section of the first of his five parts on proclaiming the kingdom he has Christ give The Sermon on The Mount in chapters 5, 6 and 7 and here he introduces his first material from Q but without any emphasis on the *agape* sayings of Q^1 even though he mentions many. On page 184 Burton Mack writes:

> Jesus' teachings captured the best intentions
> of the Jewish ethical codes based on the Torah
> and made them available even for gentiles.

This balances what Mack says about Matthew above and it could be said that the new kingdom of justice and *agape* for Matthew fulfills the Law and the Prophets and as we go along we might ask if Matthew's model of fulfillment does not work also for *agape* and the four loves insofar as it fulfills them. Likewise we can ask if Luke also has a fulfillment model and if it differs from Matthew's by making justice secondary. Does the *agape* of Q^1 fulfill affection, *eros*, friendship and *agape*?

Part Three: Glorious Finishings

III,7.4 The kingdom of justice and agape is preached

As we ponder how the new kingdom of Jesus will fulfill
the Law and the Prophets for Matthew it seems Mack is right
when on page 212 he writes:

> Matthew uses the prophet motif merely as
> a predictive device, and reinterprets the teaching
> of Jesus as thoroughly compatible with Pharisaic law.

So in terms of the relation between *agape* and justice how does
Matthew see Jesus as preaching the fulfillment of the Law?
How is God not only a loving Father but also a just judge
for the Jesus of Matthew and how does that love demand justice?
Right after Jesus proclaims the Beatitudes in his Sermon on
the Mount Matthew has Jesus say in chapter 5, verse 17:

> Do not imagine that I have come to abolish
> the Law or the Prophets. I have come not
> to abolish but to complete them.

Throughout the rest of chapter five Matthew clarifies his model
of the fulfillment of the law and he gives many examples of new laws.
As Jesus preaches his new kingdom to the crowds he says:

> In truth I tell you, till heaven and earth disappear,
> not one dot, not one little stroke,
> is to disappear from the Law
> until all the purpose is achieved.

As the new love of *agape* fulfills the love of *ahava* and *hesed*
the law connected with each of these forms of love also needs
to be more specific so Jesus explains that just desiring a woman
is already to commit adultery and divorce too is made more strict.
The *ahava* of the Mosaic Covenant theology is the love of God
with your whole heart, mind and soul and loving neighbor as self.
If you really do this you will keep all of the Mosaic laws.
Hesed is the everlasting merciful love promised to David
and to his and with it is the punishment of the rods of men.

Agape and the Four Loves

III,7.5 *The mystery of the kingdom of justice and agape*

As soon as we begin Matthew's treatment of the kingdom
we are taken further into the interplay of love and justice for
at Matthew 11:11 we read:

> In truth I tell you, of all the children born to women,
> there has never been anyone greater than John the Baptist.
> Yet the least in the kingdom of Heaven is greater than he.

So the whole of the Law and the Prophets reach their point of greatest
excellence in John the Baptist and yet he can hardly compare
with those of the new kingdom of love and justice which fulfills him.
The new *agape* that fulfills the old *ahava* and *hesed* has
an amazing and mysterious new value that we might better
understand by going back to our section on fulfillment where
at Matthew 5:23 we read

> So then, if you are bringing your offering
> to the altar and there remember that
> your brother has something against you,
> leave your offering there before the altar,
> go and be reconciled with your brother first,
> and then come back and present your offering.

Here we have the essence of Matthew's Good News about *agape*.
This kind of reconciliation with your brother and sister which
now includes all of humankind would never have occurred
to John the Baptist and to the Law and the Prophets which he fulfills.
This context of reconciliation belongs to Matthew alone of
the four evangelists and it is in terms of it that he gives a primacy
to getting justice just right before there can be a true love.
The saying above about John the Baptist is a Q^2 saying and
Matthew does put some Q sayings in the narrative part of each
of his five sections but part B of section 3 in chapter 13
gives many Q^2 like parables of judgment which separate
the good from the wicked and continue to emphasize justice.

Part Three: Glorious Finishings

III,7.6 *The church is the first fruit of the kingdom*

The kingdom of Heaven which fulfills the Law and the Prophets
and of which John the Baptist is not a member began on earth
with those who love and pray together and in chapter 16 Christ
forms his church upon Peter:

> You are Peter and on this rock
> I will build my community.
> And the gates of the underworld
> can never overpower it.

If anyone wants to follow Christ and belong to his church
Jesus in Matthew 16:14 tells us:

> Let him renounce himself
> and take up his cross and follow me.

Jesus is the Good Shepherd and in his discourse on the church
in Part B of section four at Matthew 18:24 we are given
Q's 54 from Q^2 which says:

> Suppose a man has a hundred sheep
> and one of them strays;
> will he not leave the ninety-nine
> on the hillside and go in search of the stray?

If we begin to enter the kingdom of Heaven by entering the church
of Christ justice is very important for we can become unjust
and sin against the love that binds us together and go astray.
But our loving Father who is a just judge will go out in
search of us and help up to reconcile with our brothers and sisters.
The son of man came to save what was lost but according
to Matthew some can refuse to be members of his saving church:
Matthew uses QS 49

> O Jerusalem, Jerusalem. . . . How often would I
> have gathered your children together as a hen
> gathers her brood under her wings,
> and you refused.

Agape and the Four Loves

III,7.7 *The approaching advent of the kingdom*

Already in the original book of Q there are at least 8 sayings about the coming of God's kingdom as we first see in QS 8:

> How fortunate are the poor;
> they have God's kingdom.

But the sayings about the kingdom in Q^2 are very different from what they are in Q^1 which does not stress an exclusivistic, apocalyptic view in which the kingdom will come at end time. Of course, the eight sayings about the kingdom of *agape* are in Matthew but his overall context stresses an apocalyptic view of the kingdom soon to come that concludes his his five stage coming of the kingdom with his treatment of the last judgment at Matthew 25:31–46:

> When the Son of man comes in glory,
> escorted by all the angels, then he will take
> his seat on his throne of glory. All nations
> will be assembled before him and he will
> separate people one from another as the
> shepherd separates sheep from goats.

Paul had an apocalyptic view of the second coming and he thought that it was imminent but while Matthew also stresses the threefold apocalyptic battles between angels and demons, a psychological struggle and a moral war his view of the second coming of Christ and the final coming of the kingdom is that we do not know when it will happen. As Matthew's apocalyptic Christ brings persons to consider how best to love God and their neighbor he stresses:

> In truth I tell you, in so far as
> you did this to one of the least of
> these brothers of mine, you did it to me.

So in Matthew there is a great stress on *agape* but if its standards are not met the punisher God will get non-lovers.

Part Three: Glorious Finishings

III,7.8 Concludes with the passion and resurrection

The passion of Jesus begins on Holy Thursday at the last supper.
In Matthew 26:26 and following he transforms the bread into
his body and the wine into his blood and he tells them that
this is the blood of the covenant which:

> is poured out for many
> for the forgiveness of sins.

The Eucharist prefigures Christ's passion and death and for
the rest of time will refigure it bringing the church to salvation.
As we partake of his body and blood in communion we
can receive his loving grace preparing us for resurrection.
Mark has a strong treatment of the passion, death and resurrection
of Christ which Matthew and Luke both synoptically follow.
Both Christ and all humans will partake of this resurrection.
It is our task here to ask about the resurrection for the Q community.
The coming of the kingdom according to Q^2 does have to do
with death, judgment and heaven or hell for this is part of
the apocalyptic vision as we see, for example, in QS 32:

> The men of Nineveh will arise
> at the judgment and condemn this generation.

In Q^1 there are sayings that imply an afterlife but perhaps
not a resurrection for as QS 36 says:

> Don't be afraid of those who can kill
> the body, but can't kill the soul.

and QS 52, another Q^1 saying, says:

> whoever tries to protect his life will lose it;
> but whoever loses his life
> on account of me will preserve it.

So the Jesus of Q^1 is a saving teacher whose kingdom can come
on earth as it is in heaven and in heaven as it is on earth.
With Matthew the kingdom becomes the church and with Peter
as its leader the apostles are commissioned to make it universal.

Agape and the Four Loves

III,7.9 And reveals one form of orthodox Q¹ agape

All the *agape* sayings of the Q¹ Jesus are, of course, in Matthew
but they do not have the same agapeic role to play that they will
in Luke who, in writing for the Gentiles, will emphasize a kingdom
of universal, forgiving love and a salvation to be seen by all flesh.
We will explore how Luke reconciled the apocalyptic judgment
of the Q² Son of man with the loving and forgiving Jesus of Q¹.
But now as we conclude our reflections on Matthew we can see
why Burton Mack says that the all forgiving *agape* of the Q¹ Jesus
loses its bite in Matthew who identifies more with the Son of God
sayings of Q³ and emphasizes also judgment and non-forgiving justice.
To think further about *agape* in Matthew we might notice how he
does keep and use it rather than deny it as does the Gospel of Thomas.
It seems that Matthew's judgmental attitude would be very hard
on Thomas and his Gnostic approach of negative love and prayer.
As we continue we will reflect upon how the Jesus of Luke might
relate to the Gnostic sayings of Thomas differently than Matthew.
However, before we further explore *agape* from these angles
it is important to notice that Burton Mack does discuss
the Gospels of Mark and John in relation to the Q community.
So to examine the full picture of the many voices of *agape* we
must also ponder the attitudes and visions of these two Gospels.
Much of Matthew and Luke is shaped by the synoptic plan of Mark.
So even though the Q sayings are not directly included in Mark
we must wonder about the *agape* of the Q¹ Jesus non only in Mark
but in John, Luke and even Paul in order to understand Jesus' love.
Is everything important about the new Christian love already
there in the Q¹ sayings of Jesus and if that *agape* does have
implications for our understanding of personhood and the four loves
it is not our most important task to examine that Q¹ *agape*
from the perspectives of the other writings of scripture and tradition?
Can we spell out the traits of Q¹ *agape* and see if there are others?

III,8 And whether Mark and John's have Q¹ agape

III,8.1 Does Mark use the agape of Q³ and of Paul?

In the beginning of Mark's Gospel at the baptism of Jesus

> He saw the heaven torn apart and
> the spirit, like a dove, descending on him.
> And a voice came from heaven,
> 'You are my son, the Beloved;
> my favour rests on you.'

The word here for beloved is *agapete* and so we have all that is important about *agape* and personhood right here is this passage. We have the three persons of the one God in their special *agape*. This Jesus of Mark is the Son of God as he was for Paul and Q³ and as Burton Mack writes on page 177:

> Q was the most important text
> in the hands of Mark, Matthew and Luke
> as they composed their narrative gospels.

That this is true for Matthew and Luke is plausible but how is it true for Mark who does not present Jesus as the teacher of the Q¹ sayings? On page 180 Mack writes:

> One can see why Mark left out
> most of the Q¹ instructions.
> There was no place in his story
> for Jesus to be instructing people
> in the ethics of the Jesus movement.

This ethics of Q¹ is the ethics of *agape* that loves even enemies as more important than the self and gives to them and forgives them. What Jesus teaches in Q¹ he does practise throughout Mark's gospel. He is the Good Samaritan for widows, orphans and aliens in the first half of the Gospel before the midpart of the Transfiguration and he does offer his life out of love in atonement even for his enemies. But Mark's attitude toward the Jews and the destruction of the Temple is different from even that of Q³ so to be precise about the *agape* of Mark and of Q³ we now need to attend to Mack's further distinctions.

Agape and the Four Loves

III,8.2 And how does Mark differ from Q^1 And Q^3?
On page 177 and 178 Mack writes:

> Mark wrote his story of Jesus some time after the war
> and shortly after Q and been revised with the Q^3 additions.
> If we date Q^3 around 75 C.E. to give some time
> for the additions obviously prompted by the war,
> Mark can be dated between 75 and 80 C.E.
> Mark's community also had been confused by the war,
> but it drew a conclusion about the war's meaning
> that was quite different from the position
> taken by the people of Q.
> Mark thought that the destruction of the temple
> was exactly what the Jews deserved.

In Mark's judgmental attitude the Jewish leaders had rejected Jesus.
It was thought that the first temple was destroyed by the wrath of God
because the Jewish leaders had been unfaithful to Yahweh and so
Mark is very Jewish in his thinking in believing that God is
punishing the Jews because the Scribes and Pharisees not only
failed to listen to Jesus in all of his goodness but put him to death.
The Lament over Jerusalem in Q^3 S 49 is, on the contrary, quite loving.
Jesus like the mother hen tried to gather her chicks under her wings
and because they refused the Son of God says:

> Look, your house is left desolate.
> Now, I tell you, you will not see me
> until you say, 'Blessed is the one
> who comes in the name of the Lord.'

This love for the Jewish leaders as if they were the hen's chicks
and the non-condemnation that waits for their return shows that
the *agape* of Q^3 is closer to Q^1 than the judgmental wrath of Q^2.
And even though Mark's Gospel is one of *agape* from beginning
to end it still has a Jewish condemnation of the enemies of the God-man
and does not have that other realization ethics of Q^1 and even Q^3.

Part Three: Glorious Finishings

III,8.3 And how does Q's agape aid Mark's synoptic vision?

When we think of Matthew and Luke writing their Gospels we think of them as having Mark's Gospel and the Q document before them and putting those together for different audiences each in his own way. But Burton Mack is telling us that already Mark was strongly influenced by the Q document and so we must consider how its *agape* together with that of Paul plays a role in Mark's narrative. Neither Q nor Paul give us a narrative about Jesus or the Christ but they do each develop a teaching about Jesus' special new love for us. Right in the middle of Mark's Gospel at the story of the Transfiguration once again a voice from above says:

> This is my Son, the Beloved.
> Listen to him.

In Greek, the term is *agapetos* and in Latin *charissimus* which is the superlative degree of the adjective meaning my most beloved Son. At the end of the Gospel the centurion has a similar saying when he sees how Jesus died:

> In truth this man was Son of God.

So this is the structure of the Mark's Gospel which at beginning, middle and end stresses that this Jesus is the *agapete,* the most beloved, who dies in such a noble loving fashion that he is the Son of God. Paul's universal *agape* because of which there are no longer Jews nor Greeks, male nor female, masters nor slaves but all are persons who are equally lovable shows itself through Mark's Gospel. At Mark 15:40–41 we see that many women followed him just as did men:

> These used to follow him and look after him
> when he was in Galilee. And many other women
> were there who had come up to Jerusalem with him.

Mark takes note of this *agape* that gives women a new place and role. On page 187, Burton Mack says that Luke "read Mark and Q together as saying essentially the same things." Is Mark's *agape* that of Q^3?

III,8.4 Does Mark join the agape of Paul's Christ and Q's Jesus?

Just as Luke read Mark and Q together as saying much the same thing can we say that Mark read Paul and Q together as saying the same thing? Burton Mack thinks that Mark did fuse Paul and Q together.
But because the Q people do not have Jesus and the Kerygma of the incarnation, crucifixion, resurrection and coming of the Holy Spirit Mack thinks that only the Jesus of Q^1 is historical and that Paul and it would seem that also Q^2 and Q^3 are making up the rest as fiction. One could argue that given the *agape* of Q and of Paul and thus of Mark there is more truth in their fiction than in Mack's facts. However, the writings of Paul and of Mark, for that matter, were read by many who were contemporary with Jesus and the events of his life. There are many kinds of evidence to suggest that what Paul wrote is true and thus also what Mark wrote in conjunction with Paul. Burton Mack does a wonderful job of helping us to understand Q and of explaining the influence of Q on the Gospels and Thomas. But when he tries to assign the Kerygma to the realm of myth I think his argument is preposterous for there would be all kinds of writing against Paul and Mark by eyewitnesses to Jesus.
How could Paul who was preaching Christ's death and resurrection get away with it just ten years after the death of the historical Jesus? What is really most important to the Jesus of Q and the Christ of Paul and Mark is the brand new *agape* of Jesus which is the core of Q^1, Q^3, Paul, Mark and the entire New Testament writings. Mack in spite of being such a good scholar hardly focuses on *agape*. When Mark puts together the Son of God of Q^3 and Paul's Son of God he emphasizes throughout the one and the same *agape* that is there in Q^1 and Paul so strongly and thus becomes the core of his own Gospel. The *agape* which Jesus explains in Q^1 and then modifies with justice in Q^2 and then exemplifies as the Son of god in Q^3 fits well with the *agape* of Paul's suffering and rising Christ and with Mark. Did any Christian in the first century deny that story as Mack does?

Part Three: Glorious Finishings

III,8.5 Is there Q agape in John as well as in Mark?

The Q sayings are found in Matthew and Luke but as Burton Mack shows Mark and John are also heavily influenced by the Jesus of Q. On pages 222 and 223 Mack writes:

> Mark's reduction of the Christ myth
> to terms compatible with the Jesus myths
> was an intellectual and literary accomplishment
> of truly historic proportions.
> It was not, however, the most imaginative
> combination of the two traditions possible.
> That achievement took place
> in yet another Jesus tradition,
> one that I have not mentioned until now.
> The author of the Gospel of John,
> wrote his novel account of Christian origins
> toward the end of the first century.

The truly new *agape* of Jesus that loves others more than self is the great message of the sayings of Q^1 and Christ becomes the medium for that message in Paul and beginning with Mark the synoptic Gospels each with its own emphasis put the two together. But the Gospel of John has its own unique, non-synoptic way of relating the *agape* of Q and of Paul in terms of a new structure of Life, Light, Love and Logos that actually explains how the continuing revelation by the Holy Spirit of the Risen Lord Jesus is not mere myth or fictionalized story telling as Burton Mack sees it but is the Holy Spirit continuing to teach just as did Jesus. On page 194 Mack writes:

> It has already been shown that the authors
> of early Christian texts felt free
> to attribute new sayings to Jesus.

He talks about an appropriate and inappropriate way of doing this and we might now ask if John clarifies the distinction between the two.

Agape and the Four Loves

III,8.6 Does John distinguish his Gospel from the Gnostics?

On page 224 Burton Mack writes:

> Like the Gospel of Thomas, the Gospel of John
> represents a community that was
> very close to becoming a gnostic sect.

John's audience like that of the Gnostics did include philosophers and mystics for as Augustine said the Prologue of John could have been written by a Neo-Platonist until it reaches that point when "the word became flesh" with an incarnation love that made possible the crucifixion and the resurrection of the Son of God and then the coming of the Holy Spirit who continued the process of inspiration. From chapter 13 through chapter 17 of John's Gospel Jesus gives his farewell discourses and explains how the Holy Spirit will guide the church in a process of continuing inspiration and revelation. At John 14:15-17 we read:

> If you ask me anything in my name
> I will do it.
> If you love me
> you will keep my commandments.
> I shall ask the Father
> and he will give you another Paraclete
> to be with you for ever,
> the Spirit of truth
> whom the world can never accept
> since it neither sees nor knows him;
> but you know him,
> because he is with you, he is in you.

This text is all important because it is a response to the Gnostic's anti-love and anti-prayer way of getting their secret knowledge. It can also be a response to Burton Mack's way of thinking that all but Q^1 are only fictionalized stories falsely attributed to Jesus. All the canonical scriptures are inspired by the Holy Spirit.

Part Three: Glorious Finishings

III,8.7 Does the Holy Spirit of love and truth distinguish them?

At the bottom of page 224 Burton Mack writes:

> From Q^1 to the Gospel of John is a long, long way
> for the imagination of any movement to journey
> in such a short period of time.

Between 30 and 33 C.E. Jesus taught his new revolutionary
doctrine of *agape* and seventy years later the Holy Spirit of Jesus
gave his farewell discourses explaining more fully that same *agape*.
With the help of these words in John's Gospel we need to think about
what Burton Mack calls "the imagination of a movement" for
the Gnostic movement and even the movement of Burton Mack
tend to reduce inspiration as it is in John to mere imagination.
The Spirit of Jesus said:

> I shall ask the Father,
> and he will give you another Paraclete
> to be with you for ever,
> the Spirit of truth
> whom the world can never accept
> since it neither sees nor knows him.

So Holy Mother Church under the guidance of the Holy Spirit
would say that "the imagination" of the gnostic movement
would not know and be guided by the Holy Spirit.
It seems to me that Burton Mack also is part of the world
that does not accept the revelation of the Spirit of Jesus
but rather tends to reduce what Jesus says in John's Gospel
to the mere imagination of a community producing mere myth.
True revelation takes place through a conflict of interpretations.
As Burton Mack so clearly points out the child of wisdom
in Q^1 and the Son of Man in Q^2 and the Son of God in Q^3 and
the Christ of Paul and the mix of all that in Mark and then
in Matthew and now in John does teach *agape* in different ways.

Agape and the Four Loves

III,8.8 Is the Jesus of John truly the Jesus of Q^1?

As Burton Mack concludes his treatment of John at the bottom of page 225 he writes:

> But as it turns out, in was hardly the myth
> or the message that generated Christianity.
> It was the attraction of participating in
> a group experimenting with a new social vision.

But there is no great separation between the so called "myth" or "message" or "new social vision" for each one of them in its essence is centered on *agape* which the Gnostics rejected and which Burton Mack does not focus on as the key point. In thinking of everything after Q^1 as mere myth and imagination he does not believe in John's view that the Spirit of Jesus is guiding the tradition of the church so that its social vision of a new politics of *agape* is its message and Jesus and his communities are the media of that message for it is not myth but the greatest story ever told that only God could tell. The Johannine community focused on this God of Love who is Love and this true Love for what belonged to the creed code, cult and canon and what did not such as Gnosticism. Burton Mack writes on page 224:

> As any church historian knows,
> the Johannine image of Jesus at the center
> of a universe pulsating with the powers
> of light and darkness, the miraculous and the banal
> is a very early projection of the mythic mentality
> that became characteristic of medieval Christianity.

John's logic of mixed opposites rooted in the paradox of the God-man and the belief in the truth of both scripture and tradition was thrown out by the reformers who wanted to keep scripture alone and get rid of tradition but as Mack shows tradition is already in scripture though he calls it myth.

III,8.9 John's revealed agape is philosophical and mystical

According to John the Word of God became flesh that we might have life
and have it more abundantly because of a newly revealed love
for others as more important than the self and this love's new
light can take us out of darkness and let us live happily ever after.
The Greek philosophers quested to know the source of all becoming
and they thought that *arche* might be water or air or the infinite
or many other kinds of cause out of which things could come to be.
The first words of John are classically philosophical:

> In the beginning was the Word
> and the Word was with God
> and the Word was God.

For Christian philosophers this became a certain truth not only for
Augustine and Medieval philosophers but also for Descartes.
As a philosopher and as a mystic John centered everything around
agape and went back to the spirit of Q¹ and included the key ideas
about the Q¹ *agape* as they were in Paul, Mark, Matthew and Luke.
The first part of his Gospel organizes seven signs of *agape* and
the second part seven moments of *agape's* glory so that both
manifest the God who is *agape* even in his unmanifest mystery.
The Last Supper and the Farewell Discourses are all about *agape*
and the Paraclete who will come to continue to reveal it not only
conceptually but also experientially or in accord with the mystic way
of a purgation away from darkness to illumination and unification.
John calls himself the beloved disciple and at chapter 19:19-27
the disciple whom Jesus loved is given to his mother and she to him.
So now John is the *agapete* or beloved just as Jesus was in Mark.
In John there is already a mix of scripture and tradition in that John
has included many traditions within his scriptural Gospel and he
has explained how this works because Jesus assures his followers of his
continuing presence in his Spirit who will inspire them with his truth.
Now we can see how this Spirit isat work in Luke's Gospel of *agape*.

Agape and the Four Loves

III,9 Luke's history of agape from its Q^1 beginnings

III,9.1 *As the Holy Spirit's well founded teaching for Theophilus*

On page 188 Burton Mack writes:

> Jesus, for Luke, was a man
> who "went about doing good"
> because the spirit of God
> was upon him.

Luke's Jesus is not only the clearest teacher of Q^1 *agape* but he also practices love with a mercy and forgiveness that always makes incarnation love theology most primary and does not at all let apocalyptic judgment theology have the last say in any way. The introduction to Luke's Gospel in *The Bible of Jerusalem* says:

> Luke's gospel is very warm and human,
> concentrating on Jesus' mercy and forgiveness,
> his call especially to the poor and underprivileged,
> inviting both Jew and gentile to salvation.

Whereas the writer of John's Gospel was a mystic and philosopher writing for those who could follow a conceptually ordered account, Luke is an historian who wants to help others believe in Jesus and thus he writes for the one who would love God or Theophilus. Thus he begins his Good News by writing:

> I in my turn, after carefully going over
> the whole story from the beginning,
> have decided to write
> an ordered account for you, Theophilus.

So Luke did make a careful study of the accounts of others which were handed down from the outset by eyewitnesses. He constantly writes about how the Holy Spirit was with Jesus and all those connected with Jesus so we can be sure that he thinks that the scripture he writes will all of its tradition is Spirit inspired. Anyone who reads his Gospel as a Theophilus or lover of God will see how he puts together so smoothly the self sacrificing of the Q^1 Jesus and Paul's universal *agape* with its joy and Peace.

Part Three: Glorious Finishings

III,9.2 Guides Luke's infancy story through its 5 Joyful Mysteries
As Luke tells the love story of the incarnation of the Son of God
through: (1) the Annunciation (2) the Visitation (3) the Nativity (4)
the Presentation and (5) the Finding in the Temple he constantly
has the Holy Spirit playing the key role in the drama for:

> The Holy Spirit will come upon you
> and the power of the Most High
> will cover you with its shadow.
> And so the child will be holy
> and will be called the Son of God.

This loving activity of the Holy Spirit continues when Mary
visits her cousin, Elizabeth, and when she sings her magnificat.
When Zechariah sings his *Benedictus* he is filled with the
Holy Spirit and he sings of God's faithful love to our ancestors.
So according to Luke the story of *agape* begins thirty years
before Q¹ when out of love Jesus, the Son of God, became flesh
that according to John the Baptist quoting Isaiah at Luke 3:6

> All flesh will see the salvation of God.

This shows the total universality of Luke's understanding of *agape*.
Not only will all humans be saved by this Jesus whose very
name means savior but it seems that all loving animals will too.
As soon as Jesus begins his public ministry at Luke 4:18
his words are filled with the spirit of Q¹ *agape*:

> The spirit of the Lord is on me,
> for he has anointed me
> to bring good news to the afflicted.
> He has sent me
> to proclaim liberty to captives,
> sight to the blind,
> to let the oppressed go free,
> to proclaim a year of favour
> from the Lord.

Agape and the Four Loves

III,9.3 And presents the Q¹ agape sayings first and in order

In distinguishing Luke's treatment of Q¹ *agape* from Matthew's Burton Mack on page 188 writes:

> Luke also followed the Q sequence
> by inserting the first block of Q¹ material
> into the story as the "sermon on the plain"
> before introducing the dialogue
> between John and Jesus.

So, from Luke 6:20 to Luke 6:50 Jesus presents the bulk of the Q¹ *agape* teaching which in its revolutionary way centers on the love of enemies:

> But I say this to you who are listening:
> Love your enemies; do good to those who hate you,
> bless those who curse you
> pray for those who treat you badly.

Matthew placed the Q¹ *agape* sayings within the context of the apocalyptic judgment dialogue between the son of man and John the Baptist whereas Luke gives the primacy to *agape* and makes atonement justice secondary to incarnation love. This has to do with what Mack referred to as the Q¹ sayings losing their bite in Matthew and one would think that they would keep their bite in Luke but Mack goes on to write:

> So Luke incorporated Q into his gospel,
> but he was not overly interested
> in using its contents as instruction
> applicable in his own day.

So, Luke throughout his gospel is giving an orderly account of the events and the teachings of the God-man to Theophilus. Luke is very interested with a great passion to tell this love story to anyone who is the least bit interested in loving God and his love. Once again Mack is telling us that for himself he does not believe in the Kerygma and no stories for him are Spirit inspired.

Part Three: Glorious Finishings

III,9.4 And in presenting the historical agape of the historical Jesus
Agape as a brand new revolutionary kind of love with nothing like it
anywhere is an historical phenomenon arising at a definite time
and in a definite place with the historical incarnate son of God.
Burton Mack questions the historian Luke's historical Jesus.
Again on page 188 he writes:

> And Q was simply interspersed
> as the instructions Jesus gave on the way.
> The historian's sense of distance
> put Q in its place, albeit as a historian's fiction.

So what is Burton Mack getting at when he writes about Luke's
historical fiction when obviously Luke thinks he writes historical truth?
In the development of the higher biblical criticism Rudolph Bultmann
wrote a well known book called *Myth and Kerygma* and he thought
of the Kerygma with is incarnation, crucifixion, resurrection
and coming of the Holy Spirit as the true historical basis for the
Christian belief and he thought of the various stories as fictive myth.
Now Burton Mack thinks of the Kerygma and everything in the Bible
except the Q[1] sayings of Jesus as fictive myth and he only believes
in the *agape* that the Q[1] Jesus taught as being an historical fact,
and even then he does not emphasize *agape* as the historical event.
So if we prefer to think of Luke as writing historical truth rather
than mere historical fiction how are we to understand the
historical *agape* of the historical Jesus so that we can appreciate
the analysis of the Q scholars and Burton Mack without agreeing
at least with Burton Mack that anything except Q[1] is mere fiction?
The historian can describe events that happen at a given time and
in a given place but when Luke tells the story of the God-man he
can describe the imminent man but not the transcendent God.
When the Holy Spirit comes over Mary and enables her to conceive
the God-man within her womb the event is partly historical and
partly not for the Holy Spirit is not material though her work can be.

III,9.5 He also presents the historical Holy Spirit

Again the introduction to Luke in *The Bible of Jerusalem* says:

> Luke also brings out the importance
> of individual spiritual qualities,
> especially prayer, joy and praise of God,
> and the essential part played
> by the Holy Spirit in the Christian life.

So Luke is writing a history of the Holy Spirit and the spiritual gifts of the Holy Spirit the first of which is the attitude of *agape*. The historian can spot *agape* as it comes into human history but while Luke can experience the fruits of the Holy Spirit it is his faith that lets him know the Holy Spirit whom he cannot see. How can Luke write a history of the Spirit when the subject matter of history is that which is experienced in time and space? For Luke the Holy Spirit is not only the object of his history but also the source of his history as the one who reveals its mystery. It seems that Burton Mack is very different from Luke for Mack will think of Jesus as a wisdom teacher who is the historical Jesus responsible for the sayings of Q^1; but all the other sayings and deeds attributed to Jesus in the Gospels and Paul are only fictive. They are invented by the followers of Jesus who claim he said and did them even though the historical Jesus did not say or do them. Luke on the other hand believes in the Holy Spirit of the Lord Jesus and he thinks that this Spirit of Jesus and of the Father is inspiring the followers of Jesus to speak and act according to the Spirit of Jesus. Is it the case that Mack does not have any faith in the unseen source of the seen and the heard but he only believes in what he sees? On the other hand do not believers have a faith and hope in *agape* and whatever is consistent with and adequate to *agape* is true. Were not the canonical writings selected as true on this basis and were not writings rejected when were not in keeping with *agape*? Is not Luke writing a history of the historical Spirit of Jesus?

III,9.6 Who guides the historical Holy Mother Church

Again on page 188 Burton Mack writes:

> The importance of the teachings of Jesus for Luke
> was not their relevance for all time,
> but the record they left of a marvelous teacher
> and prophet whose effectiveness was only that
> he enlarged the congregation of the people of God
> to include gentiles. Thus the church was born.

The record of what that marvelous teacher and prophet taught was in some parts not relevant for all time and yet the *agape* teaching of Q^1 has been most certainly the very heart of the church at every stage of her history as Luke shows in The Acts of the Apostles. With Matthew Luke knows of the institution of the church by Jesus when he said: "Thou art Peter and upon this Rock I build my church." Through the church's history the gates of hell have tried to prevail against it and thus in the second stage of the church's history there were the Q^2 sayings against the scribes and Pharisees and all those who threatened the church as either persecutors or traitors. That phase did pass and was not relevant for all time for Luke's Jesus as Mack says "had dinner with a Pharisee" for after the Roman war and the destruction of the temple Pharisees were no longer a threat and the Jesus of Luke gets along well with all. But the *agape* which Burton Mack does not focus on is the very reason why the new congregation of the people of God enlarges. The church history Luke gives begins with Peter and the twelve. For Luke it includes many women for at Luke 8:2 we read:

> With him went the Twelve,
> as well as certain women
> who had been cured of evil spirits.

Luke well knew the church of Paul and how it is the Bride of Christ. Luke knows that the history of the church is the history of *agape* which is relevant at each new time and place of church history.

Agape and the Four Loves

III,9.7 And her historical Holy Scriptures

So far we have seen a history of the many different scriptures about Jesus and his love which began with Q^1 and went to Q^2 and to Paul and to Q^3 and to Mark and to Matthew and to John and to the Gospel of Thomas and to the many Gnostic Scriptures and now to Luke who is writing a history of the Holy Spirit's work. By 165 C.E. Marcion clearly saw that the Gnostics from their beginning had rejected the *agape* of Jesus and replaced it with an *eros* not only between Jesus and Magdalen but which was woven right into their creation stories with various versions of Sophia and a good and bad divinity who was mystically known. Following the lead of Marcion Holy Mother Church under the lead of the successors of Peter and of the Apostles set up a canon of truly revealed and inspired scripture in accord with the criterion of the *agape* which went beyond a self-realization ethic with Jesus. Many groups of Jesus people who belonged to the churches of Paul, of John and there was Luke's audience and once a canon was defined that did not accept Gnostic or other heretical writings there historicality came into existence the one, holy, catholic and apostolic church with its common creed, code, cult and canon. All of this can be followed historically step by step as Luke begins to do it in his *Acts of the Apostles* and hence we can see how the Holy Spirit guiding Holy Mother Church is there bringing forth the scripture and defining what truly is scripture and what is not. So what will eventually emerge in history are three views about *agape* and its relation to the four loves for Holy Mother Church has always had right from Q^1 on an agapeic synthesis which for example, would see Jesus loving Magdalen with *agape* as he loved every person but then loving her in her uniqueness even with *eros* but the second view of the Gnostics left out the *agape* and had pure *eros* just as modern Reformers will want only a pure *agape* and deny the agapeic synthesis.

Part Three: Glorious Finishings

III,9.8 As they present the historical Sorrowful Mysteries

Whereas Luke's Gospel alone presents the five joyful mysteries
all four of the canonical Gospels present the five sorrowful mysteries:
(1) the garden agony (2) the pillar scourging (3) the crowning
with thorns (4) the carrying of the cross and (5) the crucifixion.
Luke gives us these five historical moments of Jesus loving us
as more important than himself in accord with the *agape* of Q^1.
This agapeic sacrifice of Jesus even for his enemies is also
connected with the Eucharist which the scriptures reveal as a
continued historical way in which our sufferings can be offered up
with those of Jesus in each sacrifice of the mass as continued loving.
The Gnostics did treat the death of the God-man and they did ponder
the Eucharist but the five sorrowful mysteries were not recapitulated
in each sacrifice of the Mass as they are for Holy Mother Church.
At that first supper of *agape* Jesus said:

> This is my body given for you . . .
> This cup is the new covenant
> in my blood poured out for you.

The covenant of love is renewed in every sacrifice of the mass
and Jesus' love on Calvary lets all of our suffering be loving.
The Reformers who saw the first sacrifice of Jesus as complete
in their vision of a pure *agape* without any mix of good works
at first still believed in a real presence of Christ's body in
the bread and his blood in the wine but the logic of their faith
alone, and *agape* alone without erotic mystical good works
eventually led most of them to a remembrance without real presence.
Each day the person who prays the Rosary can meditate through
the five historical moments of the sorrowful mysteries and pray
for his or her loved ones that they might be graced by the
love of Jesus who suffered for them each then and loves them now.
Our loving suffering for others with Jesus can turn our
suffering into joy and can as Luke shows even become glorious.

Agape and the Four Loves

III,9.9 And the five historical Glorious Mysteries

In the Kerygma of the incarnation, the crucifixion, the resurrection
and the coming of his Holy Spirit upon the apostles Jesus lived out
the *agape* for others which he first explained in the Q^1 sayings.
Out of love for others as more important than himself the son of God
became man and then he went through the five historical moments
of suffering and dying for us not only to atone for our sins, but
also to teach us how to imitate him in our suffering with love.
Now the Holy Spirit inspires Luke to teach and guide us through
the three glorious mysteries of: (1) the resurrection, (2) the ascension
(3) the descent of the Holy Spirit upon the Apostles and then later
in the tradition he will further guide us with (4) the Assumption
of Mary into heaven (5) and the crowning of Mary as our Queen.
Since Jesus is the Messiah King of heaven and earth it is fitting
that his mother be bodily assumed just as he ascended into heaven.
And once she is there again it is only fitting that she be crowned
with our love and prayer as our interceding Queen of heaven and earth.
The resurrection from the dead is the most glorious of the mysteries.
There is a great deal of historical evidence that this miracle happened.
It was the very core of Paul's teaching during the next twenty five years
after it happened and nobody would have believed him if all the
eyewitnesses were not in agreement with him and his teaching.
Glory is that which manifests the unmanifest even in its unmanifestness.
The *agape* which Jesus taught becomes manifest in Luke's Gospel.
As we see how Jesus lived and died and arose from the dead.
Luke's Jesus is especially warm and forgiving of all with a love
that is a mix of agapeic affection, friendship or *eros* for each.
Already in Luke Jesus' agapeic synthesis goes out with affection
to everyone and friendship to some and with *eros* to some
in a special sublimation that lets his love have a special power.
The charismatic Jesus as a celibate has the freedom and time to love
all with affection and the beloved John and the beloved Magdalen.

Part Three: Glorious Finishings

IV. The Four Loves

IV,7 Luther protests the four natural loves

IV,7.1 With an agape that hates the self

In 1515 when Luther was 32 years old in his "First Lectures on the Psalms" as Bernard Lohse writes in his book *Martin Luther An Introduction to his Life and Work:*

> The themes of judgment, self accusation,
> humbling oneself, and confessing oneself
> to be a sinner, as well as righteousness,
> justification, and grace were already
> the central focus on his theology.

Luther's theology of love is also strongly stated in 1515 in his *Lectures on Romans* for in part 9:3 he writes:

> For to love is to hate oneself,
> to condemn oneself, and to wish the worst,
> in accord with the statement of Christ:
> "He who hates his life in this world
> will keep it for eternal life." (John 12:25)

As Nygren has so well pointed out *agape* or true love is the sacrificial love of self for others and especially enemies and Luther thinks that in each of the natural loves there is a great self love. Luther protests everything that the Fathers, Doctors and mystics of the church thought about *agape* and the four loves for they each found a way to synthesize *agape* with *eros*, friendship, affection and even the natural *agape* which Plotinus used to explain his emanation. Luther ushered in Modernity with an absolutely new theology of love that nobody had ever worked out or even thought of before and it all began with the total depravity of humanity because of Adam's sin. Of course, there was always an interplay of incarnation love theology such as Abelard's and atonement justice theology such as Anselm's. So if there is self love in any affection, friendship or *eros* will Luther practise only *agape* toward his children, wife and associates and in some way even hate them because they are the other part of himself?

Agape and the Four Loves

IV,7.2 *Because the law shows that humanity is sinful*

Luther's reformation not only saw the four natural loves as sinful but he greatly downplayed the role of *agape* which had been central. *First Corinthians*, Chapter 13, is Paul's famous ode to love in which he shows how there are faith, hope and charity but the greatest of these is charity and for the Catholic tradition that was always the case. But for Luther it is faith alone and not love that can give us hope. The reformation is a transition from the God of love to the God of wrath. As a monk Luther had always been overly scrupulous going to confession often and feeling that he was a sinner and not justified. Jesus summarized the Law with the two great commandments: Love the Lord your God with your whole heart, mind and soul and your neighbor as yourself but this was not the Law for Luther. Faith and not love is the first and most important reality for Luther. Luther speculates about love very little and in his commentary on Galatians about 15 pages in, in the section called *Even We, I say, have believed in Christ Jesus, that we might be Justified* he does discuss I Cor. 13 and writes concerning the Catholics or the Papists as he calls them:

> Wherefore we must avoid this gloss
> as a most deadly and devilish poison,
> and conclude with Paul, that we are justified,
> not by faith furnished with charity,
> but by faith only and alone ...
> This faith justifieth without and before charity.

So as we are trying to understand what happened to *agape* and the four loves with Luther we can see that he stresses not the law of love but the law in its "evangelical use" which is to humble, terrify, and spiritually "kill" the sinner; this is "evangelical" because it is the true preparation for the Gospel, a preparation performed by God, not us, for we can do nothing of worth. As children of Adam and Eve we cannot begin to follow the law.

IV,7.3 But we can be justified by faith alone

Luther's theology is consistent for once he believes in the total
degradation of all things human because of Adam's sin then
there follows the belief that none of our works can have any merit.
Thus faith alone without any works can let us be justified
before the just and wrathful God who sent his Son to die for us.
Faith in God's promise that he will save us through the incarnation,
crucifixion and resurrection of his Son can save us from the Law
which reveals how impossible it is to be righteous without God's help.
We are made righteous by faith alone, apart from works, because
we receive what is promised not by doing anything about it but
simply by believing that it is true that Christ won it for us by dying.
The object of our faith is God's promise and thus Luther's motto
"Believe it and you have it." shows the new direction of his spirituality.
Whereas Augustine would teach that we flee to grace by prayer
Luther teaches that we flee to grace by taking hold of God's promise.
He says, "The promise of God gives what the commandment requires."
Luther gave a sermon probably in 1519 called *Two Kinds of Righteousness*.
Here he makes a very helpful distinction concerning faith and love.
He begins by saying:

> There are two kinds of Christian righteousness,
> just as man's sin is of two kinds.
> The first is an alien righteousness, that is,
> the righteousness of another, instilled from without . . .
> This righteousness, then, is given in baptism.

Then he says that there is

> The second kind of righteousness,
> not because we alone work it,
> but because we work with
> that first and alien righteousness.
> This is that manner of life
> spent profitably in good works.

Agape and the Four Loves

IV,7.4 *In the gospel's loving grace alone*

So, the central thought of Luther has to do with Law and Gospel. Augustine and all the Catholics of Holy Mother Church believed that God did not make junk and that the human is capable of very much good, of course, always with God's grace and help. Thus, Augustine was thankful for and used the wonderful insights of the Platonists, just as Thomas did of Aristotle and as the Franciscans also built upon the great tradition of the Stoics as also did St. Paul. When Luther thought of all this from his viewpoint about man as a condemned sinner he didn't think Plato or any Pagan could do anything worthwhile or think anything that had to do with truth. Luther saw how the Papists thought of grace as being infused in the first place in baptism, and renewed after each mortal sin in the sacrament of penance and that any prayer or good thought, word or deed would increase that grace and bring holiness to self and others. This grace ultimately cast man back upon himself in Luther's mind, towards his own striving for sanctification and thus uncertainty. This brought Luther to his new doctrine that we are justified by grace alone and if we have faith we can be certain that we are saved. However, Luther does distinguish two kinds of righteousness in his Sermon of that title and he goes on to say of the second:

> This righteousness goes on to complete the first
> for it ever strives to do away with the old Adam
> and destroy the body of sin.
> Therefore, it hates itself and loves its neighbor;
> it does not seek its own good, but that of another,
> and in this way its whole way of living consists.

The Catholics saw us as belonging to the mystical body of Christ and so what I do for the other I also do for myself because we are interpersonal persons and I should love myself as my neighbor. But, Luther denies or disregards more scripture than he believes and thus thinks of *agape* as being totally self-sacrificial and self-hating

Part Three: Glorious Finishings

IV,7.5 Which is revealed in scripture alone

Luther has faith in God's promise to save us by his loving
grace alone and Luther knows of all this through scripture alone.
This network of faith alone, grace alone, scripture alone all
fits together for Luther because fallen man can do nothing
of worth by himself so only faith in the promise he finds
only in scripture can give him the grace that alone can save.
Luther's sensitive conscience sought certainty and he found that
he could stand alone before God's judgment with certainty in his
own justification because he could prove God's promise of grace
by a literal reading of scripture centered on Christ's atonement.
Luther insists on the clarity of scripture and that it interprets itself.
Because we are sinners we will be blind to the message of scripture
but if we submit to the guidance of the Holy Spirit we will get its truth.
If we start with law and gospel all scripture will clarify that relation.
Already Augustine had read Paul as treating the Law as a way
in which the just God punishes us for the sins of Adam and from
Augustine Luther got his ideas about the Law as that which terrifies us.
But as Professor Phillip Cary puts it in his course Guide Book
  on *Luther: Gospel, Law and Reformation:*

> "The Law" in Paul means the Jewish Law,
> not God's method of terrifying consciences.
> Paul's doctrine of justification by faith
> is not about how we stand before God
> on judgment day but about the relation
> of Jews and Gentiles in the Church of Christ.
> Luther has, in effect, transformed a question
> about the Christian community into a question
> about the individual Christian conscience.

This notion of the individual Christian conscience is all important
in getting modernity launched and in emphasizing hatred so much.
Letting scripture interpret itself from this starting point changes love.

Agape and the Four Loves

IV,7.6 *Urging us to approach our neighbor with works of love*

We have faith in God's promise and become justified or righteous. Then we should spend our life profitably in good works that are not for ourselves but are works of love for all of our neighbors. To let our *agape* be pure we should hate ourselves for we should not perform the works of love to merit further grace for ourselves. Rather we should hate ourselves in order to become totally altruistic. This emphasis upon hatred seems to be new with Luther for none of the Greek philosophers or other religions would see it as good. Augustine said that if you go after someone with the sword of hatred it must pass through your own body first before it can touch him. But while Luther has faith in God and does not stress loving God and while he hates himself he does preach loving our neighbor. In his Preface to the New Testament he writes as we read in *Martin Luther: Selections from his writings* by John Dillenberger on page 18:

> Christ never gave any other commandment
> than that of love, because He intended
> that commandment to be the test
> of His disciples and of true believers.
> For if good works and love do not blossom forth,
> it is not genuine faith, the gospel has not yet
> gained a foothold, and Christ is not yet rightly known.

As we try to understand Luther's new theology of love we must pay attention to his network of key concepts: sin, grace, righteousness faith and good works and see how this network develops in his thought. Grace and good works are the two main points for grace is God's love for us and good works are our works of love for others. When we think of God's love there is always an interplay between love and wrath for as Bernard Lohse writes on page 158

> Even the cross of Christ is not just the fixed symbol
> of divine love but is God's sharpest judgment
> on human sin.

Part Three: Glorious Finishings

IV,7.7 But opponents, peasants and Jew are excluded

Toward the end of his Course Guidebook Cary has a chapter on
Luther and His Enemies and then one on Luther and the Jews and
on page 96 he writes:

> The level of verbal abuse Luther directs
> at his opponents is shocking
> and needs to be explained.
> Especially in his later writings, his use
> of metaphors of filth (usually excremental
> rather than sexual) must be heard to be believed . . .
> How is Luther's harsh attitude toward his enemies
> related to his view of the Gospel?

Luther believes in a tough love as he sees it in his God of wrath.
As Carey puts it:

> For Luther, defending the Gospel against its enemies
> is always, fundamentally, a battle with the spirit
> that speaks through them, which is the devil.

Carey asks if Luther's frequent battles with the devil sound crazy.

> Is there any justification or value
> in Luther's tendency to see the devil
> speaking in the words of his theological opponents.

He sees the devil in Augustine, Benedict, Aquinas, Bernard and Francis.
He sees the devil in the peasants when they rise up against the wealthy.
As Lohse writes on page 56

> Luther's very severe treatise
> *Against the Robbing and Murdering*
> Hordes of Peasants, challenges the Princes
> to suppress the revolt.

In 1543 he wrote *On the Jews and Their Lies* and recommended
burning their synagogues, confiscating their property and
expelling them so that later Hitler would look like a Lutheran.
Of course, Luther loved his enemies but this is a new kind of *agape*.

Agape and the Four Loves

IV,7.8 And Luther spends his life speculating with reason

Lohse has a chapter on *Reason and Faith* in which he discusses the uniqueness of Luther's understanding of Reason and shows how

> Luther clearly stood out as
> an especially sharp critic of reason.

Luther wrote about "blind faith" and saw reason as "the devil's whore." On page 159 Lohse writes concerning Luther's view of reason that

> We are at this point dealing with a dynamics
> similar to those in Luther's doctrine of law and gospel.

He writes that Luther's answer to the question about the natural knowledge of God was ambivalent for there is a knowledge written in the hearts of all that God exists and it can see that

> God is a terrible, wrathful judge,
> who leaves us no place to hide
> neither in this world nor in hell.

So reason can let us understand the law and then faith in scripture can let us see the good news of the promise of our justification for as Lohse puts it on page 163

> Luther simultaneously described faith and reason
> as in opposition to each other and as beginning
> to coexist in service to each other.
> The dialectic underlying this paradox
> has to do with our being sinners and justified
> at the same time and with the tensions
> and the unity between law and gospel.

Once Luther begins with the premise that everything human is totally sinful and degraded then, of course, all natural reason, philosophy and religion is corrupt and can only degrade us. Luther is totally opposed to the love of wisdom and the wisdom of love and all that goes with it for the sake of loving his neighbor. The best way to love our neighbors is to make clear to them what terrible sinners they are and to frighten then into getting faith.

Part Three: Glorious Finishings

IV,7.9 About a love that condemns all but true Lutherans

When it came to loving Luther was a very consistent man
and Lohse tells on page 33 that Luther's marriage

> was not a marriage of love
> in the modern sense of the term

Luther wrote

> I feel neither passionate love nor burning
> for my spouse, but I cherish her.

And yet on page 91 Lohse writes:

> Just as we are not able to remain silent
> about Luther's coarse polemic, so we must
> emphasize that Luther could also express
> tender feelings and empathy . . .
> As a husband and as a father to his children,
> and also as a friend and a colleague
> in relation to his prince, Luther could
> demonstrate empathy and consideration
> that would be hard to equal.

As Lohse puts it on page 171:

> We need to flee from this wrath to the love
> of God that has appeared in Christ.

Luther's whole talk as a scripture scholar and in practise was to do
just this and he was positive and empathetic toward those who found
the love of God and he showed wrath to those who had not.
On page 221 Lohse tells us that Harnack gave an excellent
interpretation of Luther for

> Harnack clearly showed that we cannot understand
> Luther's thinking simply on the basis of God's love.
> Alongside this love stands the reality of God's wrath.

Luther brought this new dimension of the wrath of God to the world
of *Agape* in a way that not even the Bible emphasized.

Agape and the Four Loves

IV,8 Calvin in systematizing Luther says little about agape

IV,8.1 *For Once the Natural Loves Go* Agape *Is Diminished*

In the two volume set of *The Institutes* translated by Henry
Beveridge in 1952 there are two mentions of love in the index.
Love ought to be extended even to enemies on page 360, and
it is enjoined by the second table of the Law on page 324.
In the 700 pages of Calvin's most important theological text love
is discussed in only two short treatises so what has happened?
Why is it that Luther greatly diminishes the role of *agape*
in his theology and practise and why is it nearly gone with Calvin?
Luther is right about there being a self love in the natural loves.
If you see any self love as sinful and if you must hate yourself
in order to love others properly then you have to get rid of all
the emotion and passion and desire that belong to the natural loves.
And if *agape* can have none of that then it is greatly diminished
in comparison with what it was for Augustine, Thomas, Francis and
all the Catholics who in their *agape* had affection, friendship and *eros*.
With Luther and Calvin the secularization of Modern Europe begins.
The second commandment said: "Love your neighbor as yourself."
For the Catholics this means that we should love ourselves in the
right way and a neighbor in the right way for we can love
ourselves and ours to the exclusion of others or we can love all persons
as being of equal worth and then love each in their own uniqueness.
But Luther got rid of the second commandment and any love of self.
Luther and Calvin loved their neighbor without emotion or desire
and performed the works of love for them by working very hard
in explaining to them faith in God and the works of love.
So religion was no longer a matter of fervent loving prayer
for all around me but a matter of secular work for others.
Lutherans and Calvinists think it is sinful to try to become
holy by loving God, the self, the neighbor and all of creation.
Theirs is an *agape* without any self loving natural love.

Part Three: Glorious Finishings

IV,8.2 And double predestination urges me to seek a sign

Augustine had already developed a theology of predestination for
before his conversion he was not free to practise chastity.
But, once he read Paul and was given a special grace he was able
to become celibate and to love God and neighbor with an ordered love.
Of course, Augustine did believe in good works and in their merit.
But, Luther who stressed grace alone and denied any good works
thought that it is God alone who saved anyone who is saved
and condemns to hell anyone who does not receive grace
for even the decision to receive grace is a gift of God's grace.
Ambrose told Monica that she need not worry because
a child of so many prayers and tears would never perish.
Monica's prayers and tears could merit grace for Augustine
and someday she would no longer shed tears and she would be
so happy because of her son's conversion and his new celibacy.
But for Luther and Calvin predestination is totally different
than it was for Augustine because they believed that we are saved
by God's grace alone and our work can merit nothing for us.
Lutherans and Calvinists when they take Luther and Calvin seriously
can become very anxious about whether God has chosen them or not.
They both pretty well see hell as populated by all non-Lutherans
and non-Calvinists and in getting rid of purgatory with their logic
of the exclusive opposites of either heaven or hell they have far more
anxiety than Catholics who see themselves eventually going to heaven.
Origen by 250 A.D. claimed there was no hell and all Catholics
pray for their blessed dead and ask their blessed dead to pray for them.
So the hellfire and brimstone of the double predestinationists
made them search for a sign that could let them be certain
as to whether they belonged to the elect or the condemned.
Max Weber's wonderful book on *The Protestant Work Ethic and
the Rise of Capitalism* can help us see what denying the value
of the natural loves and downplaying *agape* meant for the West.

Agape and the Four Loves

IV,8.3 *Of my Lutheran vocation and my Calvinist election*

On page 82 Max Weber writes:

> The salvation of the soul and that alone
> was the centre of their life and work.
> Their ethical ideals and the practical results
> of their doctrines were all based on that alone,
> and were the consequences of purely religious motives.

The Lutheran and the Calvinist could be very anxious about whether they would be saved or damned and the Lutheran idea of the Beruf or vocation or profession could give them tranquility. As Weber puts it on page 80

> The only way of living acceptably to God was
> not to surpass worldly morality in Monastic
> Asceticism, but solely through the fulfillment
> of the obligations imposed upon the individual
> by his position in the world. That was his calling.

So Luther and Calvin in seeing the four natural loves as evil and in reducing the four dimensional *agape* to two dimensions saw us as being predestined so that our works count for nothing. God loves us with his merciful *agape* and we should love our neighbor with the works of agapeic love and those are *agape's* two dimensions for we are no longer to love God or to love ourselves. Performing the works of love for the neighbor is the Lutheran's vocation. In Catholicism everyone had a vocation whether it be to the religious, the married or the single life but as Weber mentions certain persons did have special vocations to love God, self, neighbor and enemies by living the ascetic life of poverty, celibacy and obedience to a superior. Once Luther saw all that as monstrous because it had self love asceticism shifted to the life of the layman who with precociousness and hard work would live out his profession within the division of labor by performing his job as the works of love for his society. If one did this he could be certain he was chosen by God for heaven.

IV,8.4 For as Max Weber shows modernity begins

Max Weber gets right to the heart of the Lutheran faith on page 81:

> The monastic life is not only quite devoid of value
> as a means of justification before God, but Luther
> also looks upon its renunciation of the duties
> of this world as the product of selfishness,
> withdrawing from temporal obligations.
> In contrast, labour as a calling appears to him
> as the outward expression of brotherly love.

Luther hated the self love that is involved in loving your neighbor
as you love yourself and he saw this in all the monastic sublimation
of *eros*, friendship and affection and he hated his enemies, the monks.
To move now from Lutheran predestination and the vocation
to Calvin's predestination and the work ethic we might think
with Weber on page 102

> With Calvin the *decretum horribile* is derived not,
> as with Luther, from religious experience, but
> from the logical necessity of his thought.

This horrible decree can make Calvinists terribly anxious as
they see that their good works have no role to play in saving them.
Their faith alone brings them to believe that only a part of humanity
is saved, the rest damned and as Weber puts it on page 103:

> For the damned to complain of their lot
> would be much the same as for animals
> to bemoan the fact they were not born as men.

Weber begins to explain the connection between predestination and
the work ethic on page 108

> God requires social achievement of the Christian
> because He wills that social life shall be organized
> according to His commandments.

The commandments all have the purpose of an orderly Christian society
and the work ethic when lived out lets one know that he is chosen.

Agape and the Four Loves

IV,8.5 With the Protestant asceticism that replaces the Catholic

On page 110 Weber writes:

> The elect differ externally in this life
> in no way from the damned . . .
> For them the *certitudo salutis* in the sense
> of the recognizability of the state of grace
> necessarily became of absolutely dominant importance.

So what we have to understand is how becoming a good capitalist is the best sign of the certitude of salvation for as Weber writes on page 112:

> In order to attain that self-confidence
> intense worldly activity is recommended
> as the most suitable means. It and it alone
> disperses religious doubts and gives the certainty of grace.

God helps those who help themselves and building up a strong habit of work in society for the glory of God is the best sign of one's salvation. The Catholic sees the gradual accumulation of his good works as the way to holiness and happiness for himself and all others. The Lutherans accused the Reformed Churches and sects that came from them as reverting back to the doctrines of salvation by works. But the Calvinist did not have the repeated sacrifice of the Mass and the opportunity to go to confession and have his sins forgiven. As Weber puts it on page 117:

> The God of Calvinism demanded of his believers
> not single good works, but a life of good works
> combined into a unified system. There was no place
> for the very human Catholic cycle of sin,
> repentance, atonement, release, followed by renewed sin.

So as Weber argues the Calvinists worked out the religious foundation of worldly asceticism for they were as strict and thoughtful as Catholic monks but all of this for them was for the purpose of being certain that they were predestined to eternal salvation.

IV,8.6 And lets capitalism replace Catholic sublimated love

Catholic asceticism was all about love and aimed at continuing
the ongoing process of transforming the natural loves with *agape*.
Luther got rid of the four natural loves and Calvin got rid
of *agape* altogether and even justice for a God of Calvinistic
predestination does put forth the horrible decree that is truly horrible
because the Calvinist God created many only to suffer forever.
To understand secular asceticism we need to understand Calvin's
conception of God and the concept of the psychological test that
can let a person know whether or not they really have a saving faith.
For the Calvinist you know you have true faith by the evidence
of a changed life and a worldly ascetic life is the sign of certainty.
On page 126 Max Weber writes:

> The combination of faith in absolutely valid norms
> with absolute determinism and the complete
> transcendentality of God was in its way a product
> of great genius.

So for Calvin God is transcendent for there are no mediators
except Christ the God-man so that the angels and saints and Mary
and the church and the blessed dead cannot intercede for us at all.
God is not with us in his love in the sacraments and our prayer life.
Augustine said:

> You have made us for yourself, oh God,
> and our hearts are restless until they rest in Thee.

Augustine's heart could find rest in the blessed life even here but
the Calvinists with the loving imminent God never finds that rest.
As Weber says again on page 126:

> We shall see again and again how fundamental
> is the idea of proof for our problem.

Given the doctrine of double predestination there develops
a psychological basis for a rational morality which is the
ascetic worldly life and is the sign of salvation for the Calvinist.

Agape and the Four Loves

IV,8.7 With work rather than prayer that makes life sweet

The Germans have a proverb that "work makes life sweet" and that goes back to the Benedictines who stressed the ascetic life of work and prayer for all the people of the church which was made possible by their ascetic vows of poverty, celibacy and obedience. For the Calvinists waste of time is the deadliest of all of our sins. St. Paul said: "He who will not work shall not eat." and Calvinists as Weber puts it on page 158:

> continually repeated the most passionate preaching
> of hard, continuous bodily or mental labour.

Hark work is even an antidote to the other seven deadly sins for the idle mind is the devil's workshop and as Weber puts it on page 163

> The parable of the servant who was rejected
> because he did not increase the talent
> which was entrusted to him seemed to
> say so directly. To wish to be poor was,
> it was often argued to wish to be unhealthy.

So the Calvinist is exactly the opposite of the Franciscans who wish to be poor as did *Il Poverello* in order to serve the poor. Prayer also gets the Catholic in touch with the imminent God who is with us through Jesus and his Mother and all the angels and saints. The Calvinist believes in none of this and trusts completely in the life of hard work and becoming wealthy because that is the sign that our life has changed as a result of our conversion to Christ. Weber clearly relates asceticism and capitalism on page 172

> When the limitation of consumption is combined
> with this release of acquisitive activity,
> the inevitable practical result is obvious:
> accumulation of Capital through ascetic
> compulsion to save.

One's being a serious ascetic capitalist proved he was saved.

IV,8.8 Loving prayer for enemies predestined to hell

In the index to Max Weber's book love is not mentioned and as we said it is only mentioned twice in the index of *The Institutes*. However, in the 100 aphorisms summarizing *The Institutes* the 56th Aphorism says:

> The fruit of prayer is fivefold, 1. When we are accustomed to flee to God, our heart is inflamed with a stronger desire to seek, love and adore him . . . 3. We receive benefits with thanksgiving.

Whereas Luther stresses having faith in God but not loving him Calvin does seem to recover an agapeic love for God and a love of neighbor insofar as that neighbor is a fellow predestined one. Also in aphorism 70 when Calvin is discussing the government of the church when he writes of them who are to rule he says:

> We have a most excellent training to humility and obedience, and it is singularly fitted to bind us to mutual charity.

So Calvin has his version of the two great commandments:

> Love the Lord your God with your whole heard, mind and soul and your neighbor as yourself.

Calvin and Weber do occasionally mention love even though it does not receive a sustained treatment even as it did for Martin Luther. But what is beginning with Luther and going much further with Calvin and the Calvinists is the move toward secular humanism. Of course, there are two steps involved in this, the first toward secularism and then the move toward humanism and away from theism. The Calvinists great interest in a worldly asceticism can hardly be called a new spirituality for it is rather a new materiality. Whereas the monks would spend half their working life working and half of it praying there is no longer daily Mass for our secularists, or a daily rosary but much effort making money.

Agape and the Four Loves

IV,8.9 *Makes no more sense than loving hell-bent neighbors*

Just as Luther will have no loving prayer for Catholic opponents or peasants or Jews so there is no sense in Calvinists praying for those who are predestined to hell because prayer cannot help them. If they are predestined that is it and our prayer for them is worthless. So we can be united in charity with those predestined for heaven but there is no sense in loving and praying for those on their way to hell. Purgatory can make no more sense for Calvinists than for Lutherans. Either we have been good capitalists or not and that is the story. What the Calvinists and the sects that followed them did was to start building up a strong middle class of thrifty and responsible workers. If we think of late modernity as divided into the 20% at the bottom of the economic ladder and the 60% in the middle and the 20% at the top, then still the middle is made up of those who have the work ethic. What brought tranquility to the anxious Calvinist who was worried about whether he was predestined for heaven or hell was to pass the test and live the work ethic with great seriousness and building his Capital. So as the West moved with Calvinists and Lutherans toward secularity they promoted the way not only toward modern western economics but also toward a new politics and law that work with that economics. Luther was quite consistent and while he thought about the three persons of the Trinity he did not like the Tradition's application of the equal worth and uniqueness and interpersonal personhood of the Divine persons to human persons for we stand alone before God. And for Calvin all persons are definitely not of equal dignity for the majority were created as no good and destined for hell. But the notion of *agape* and personhood as well as *agape* and the four loves is basic to the Christian West and a special thanks can be given to the Protestants and especially Calvinists for their work ethic and the new economy and the middle class. The fruits of this ethic are being sought by the family of man today.

Part Three: Glorious Finishings

IV,9 The agapeic roots of modern economics, politics and law

IV,9.1 Are like the roots, trunk, branches and fruit of Descartes' tree

Modernity began with a great flourish of new wealth for Europe.
In 1492 Columbus sailed the ocean blue and soon Spain and then
Portugal and then Holland and then England were bringing home all
kinds of new goods and the new economy of the Renaissance began.
The Swiss and the Germans and those who first became protestants
were going nowhere economically in the hinterland and they could
hardly do their share in supporting the Renaissance building of
St. Peters and the Sistine Chapel and the other works of Renaissance art.
At the heart of Luther's protest was the economy of indulgences for
he and the Germans did not want to see good German money
going out of their relatively poor country to support the Church.
So he got on the slippery slop and in denying the Pope and Bishops
he go rid of the Priesthood and thus took away the basis for what
he wanted to keep such as the real presence of Christ in the Eucharist.
There was the new Lutheran idea of the calling to one's profession and
Calvin and the Calvinists as we have seen got the new economy
of the middle class going with the idea that "Time is money" and
"a penny saved is a penny gained" and before long Puritans,
Methodists, Mennonites and Quakers were all becoming capitalists.
Up until now *agape* had been the basis for a communism in which
you would sell your belongings, give to the poor and follow the Lord.
One's vocation could be to the religious life where all was shared,
but that asceticism now became worldly and as time went on
a new politics and a new system of law was developed in Europe and
North America which protected human rights and personal relations.
Just as Descartes got modern philosophy going with the three
metaphysical roots and the trunk of physics and the branches
of medicine, mechanics and morals so *agape* and personhood
supported the new economy and then the new politics and
finally the new system of jurisprudence protecting all persons.

Agape and the Four Loves

IV,9.2 *For the seeds of modern health, education and welfare*

After Weber treats Calvinism and the rise of Capitalism he goes on to treat Pietism, Methodism and the Baptist sects which include the Mennonites and the Quakers all of which promote capitalism. Concerning the Baptist Sects he writes on page 144,

> The feature of all these communities, which is
> both historically and in principle most important . . .
> is something with which we are already familiar,
> the believer's Church . . . as a community
> of personal believers of the reborn, and only these.

These communities wanted to be like early church communes and take care of each other by producing capital. In a footnote on this on page 254 Weber writes:

> The preaching of the mendicant friars, especially
> the Franciscans, probably did much to prepare the way
> for the ascetic lay morality of Calvinist Baptist Protestants.

The Franciscans and the Dominicans brought forth a new spirituality to help take care of the poor in the new cities and when the Jesuits first went to India in the time of the Counter Reformation they wanted to especially help the untouchables with health, education and welfare. They found that they were not welcomed by the Brahmins of the upper class caste system so when they went to China they were careful to be friendly to the wealthy too that they might be able to help the poor. Modernity aimed at a proper distribution of wealth and to accomplish that as time went on the New Spiritual Orders of Modernity: Franciscans, Dominicans, Jesuits and Carmelites all stressed more education. The Public and the Catholic school systems stressed education for all. The coming to be of the working class, that 60% in the middle, between the wealthy and the poor is the essence of Western Modernity. The idea that we should give glory to God by the asceticism of work and thrifty living came out of Calvin's theology of God's Sovereignty.

IV,9.3 Were planted by Calvin to give glory to God

The very essence of Calvinism had to do with the doctrine of double predestinationism and the test by which we could know whether or not we have been elected to be saved or to be damned. Because of God's absolute transcendence and no immanence through the church, or the sacraments or mystical union Calvin thought of God as demanding

> of his believers not single good works,
> but a life of good works
> combined into a unified system.   Max Weber (p. 126)

Only if we pass this test can we have any certainty that we are predestined to be saved and any sinning and repentance as with Catholics, or being justified and a sinner at the same time as with Lutherans, only proved they are predestined for damnation. If I am called to serve the mundane life of the community for the greater glory of God and I do it then I am saved. Once Calvin and the Calvinists came up with this idea capitalism, the spirit of Modernity, was born for these were the agapeic roots that stressed the value of the health, education and welfare of the mundane community and building God's kingdom on earth. To give glory to God is to let the unmanifest become manifest even in its unmanifestness and if God makes one into an animal rather than a man the animal should not complain but give glory to God just as should the non-elect in not questioning God. This view did motivate the West to a great work ethic, but many would agree with Milton as Weber says on page 101,

> Though I may be sent to Hell for it,
> such a God will never command my respect.

There is still in its great seriousness a certain productive value. Calvin planted this seed of being motivated by our eternal salvation to give our all to a mundane capitalist work ethic and that belief is the seed that differentiates the West from any other culture.

Agape and the Four Loves

IV,9.4 And the pietist roots of sublimated affection sprouted

The Pietists which was the religion of Nietzsche and which provided
the background for Wesley and the Evangelicals slowly moved
away from the notion of predestination toward religious feeling.
As Weber tells us on page 135:

> Zinzendorf's peculiar principle that
> the childlikeness of religious feeling
> was a sign of its genuineness and
> strongly counteracted the influence
> of rationality in conduct

strongly suggests the spirit of Nietzsche and a new agapeic affection.
Whereas modernity began with the pure agape of Luther that was
suspicious of the self love in affection and proceeded further
with the double predestination of the Calvinists who thought that
being a successful capitalist was a sign of our salvation we
now begin to recover the pious affection of the childlike Jesus.
Zinzendorf followed the Puritans in expressing the John Wesley of 1740

> that even though a man himself could not,
> others could know his state of grace
> by his conduct. Weber p. 135.

Even though the Pietists felt that the non-emotional were
second-rate Christians they still believed in the asceticism of hard work.
So one root coming out of the Calvinistic seed of ascetic modernity
was that of the Pietists who however returned to a sublimated
agapeic affection which was not self-centered in its childlikeness.
Given this kind of emotional love for God the Evangelicals have
become a popular and widespread Church of Modern Christianity.
Whereas in our day the Lutherans and Calvinists have a hard time
appealing to people given their rugged individualism and their
lack of a community spirit the Evangelical Pietists do have
an affectionate childlike agape that appealed to Nietzsche and also
to our postmodern world which emphasizes love more than justice.

Part Three: Glorious Finishings

IV,9.5 As did the Quaker roots of sublimated friendship

As Max Weber tells us on pages 144–145:

> While Pietism on the continent and the Methodism
> of the Anglo-Saxon peoples are secondary movements
> coming out of Calvinism
> the Baptist Movement and sects are
> an independent source of Protestant Asceticism . . .
> Baptists, Mennonites and above all Quakers
> did not have a church but were each
> a sect or community of personal believers
> of the reborn, and only these.

These peoples who did not believe in infant baptism strongly stressed
the working of the Divine Spirit in the individual and their holy
communities were made up of those who were reborn through
the Spirit upon whom the Quakers would wait in their meetings.
Since predestination was rejected especially by the Quakers
there was a silent watching for the Spirit to descend and this
Holy Spirit who came to some but not all let them be special friends.
George Fox the founder of the Quaker community demanded
an absolutely blameless conduct for good works are necessary for
salvation and those without the inner light and the good moral life
that flow from it were condemned more harshly than by the Calvinists.
As Luther pointed out friendship loved self in loving the friends
and this is true of the Quakers for they did love their own group
to the exclusion of other groups so there was no love of enemy here.
The friends as the Quakers called themselves had a new kind
of agapeic friendship for their agape or love of God gave them
a new kind of friendship or love of each other and their community.
This was a very responsible love that contributed greatly to
our modern health, education and welfare especially for each other.
For their friendship did give them a new version of agape that let
them with a capitalist spirit build up God's kingdom on earth.

Agape and the Four Loves

IV,9.6 And the Catholic roots of sublimated eros.

The Sermon on the Mount brought forth a new kind of personal
responsibility for the repeated assertion, "But I say unto you"
not only brought the debate out of the context of Jewish legalism
to a new level of universal significance but the very notion
of the institutional church got a new meaning for belonging
had to do with loving and not only a mutual, reciprocal love.
The Pietists with their affection for each other and the Quakers
with their friendship are almost more Jewish in working with
the notion of a chosen people than Catholics with their universalism.
In the early church Paul called for a reconciliation with the enemy
and all were seen as persons: male and female, Jew and Greek,
Master and slave and the new institutional church under Peter
was called upon to practise almsgiving, prayer and sacrifice
primarily for the poor but even for one's enemy and persecutor.
At the coming of the Holy Roman Empire with Constantine
and a new level of the institutional church the notion of
personhood began to be worked out at Nicea and again the emphasis
was on a love for all persons as equal, as unique and as
interpersonally connected not only institutionally but in love.
With Augustine's *Confessions* and *City of God* the Church
was explicated as the bipolar relation between institution
and individual responsibility to God, neighbor and self.
Of course, for Augustine as with all Catholics the love of *eros*
is central in letting the institution work because the priests
and religious practise a sublimated *eros* that their agape
might go out with great energy in loving all persons personally
as did Jesus in his self sacrificial agape for all flesh.
The word became flesh that all flesh might see the salvation
of the Lord and Catholic religious imitate Jesus by letting
the institutional church be made up of all lovers like Paul
and Augustine and Benedict and Scholastica and Francis and Clara.

Part Three: Glorious Finishings

IV,9.7 And with Adam Smith the trunk of the wealth of nations grew

So Luther and Calvin planted the seeds of our modern western world with the idea of a vocation or call to work and of our becoming wealthy so that we might pass the test and prove that we are saved. That work ethic had little to do with being motivated by love and Luther wanted to keep religious love free of any natural self love. But those seeds sprouted and the roots of Pietistic affection, Quaker friendship and Catholic *eros* were all connected with agape and were passionately felt as the motivational source of our work. The new economy of the Industrial age was very successful because persons were willing to work on the assembly line because as Zinzendorf put it:

> One does not only work in order to live
> but one lives for the sake of one's work,
> and if there is no more work to do
> one suffers or goes to sleep.   Weber, p. 264.

The Mormons also put it very clearly:

> But a lazy or indolent man
> cannot be a Christian and be saved.
> He is destined to be struck down
> and cast from the hive.   Weber p. 264

So we are like bees working together for the community of the hive and from this religiously motivated work the wealth of the western nations came and Adam Smith as he analyzed this saw that a natural self love is at the bottom of what motivates our work. Hobbes, Locke and Rousseau with their three developing versions of the social contract theory did not believe in a natural community. They thought it had to be artificially set up, but Adam Smith like Hume disputed the contract theory of society, government and law. Adam Smith and Hume set out to examine the passions of the soul and to show how they let us see values and motivate us to prepare some values more than others because of their greater value.

Agape and the Four Loves

IV,9.8 And the Branches Were Seen as Growing out of Self Love

So the Scottish philosophers Hume, Hutcheson and Adam Smith
began to return to the premodern concept of man and get
beyond the notions of individualism and the need for a social contract.
They analyzed our human passions in the way the Stoics and
St. Paul and the Franciscans had analyzed them and Adam Smith
saw that the two chief passions are the desire for self-preservation
and the desire to reproduce and these were motivated by self-love.
However, even though Smith saw that self-love motivates our
work he still did not totally get beyond Luther and modernity
in working out a proper self-love in relation to love of the other.
In the *Wealth of Nations*, ed. E Cannan, London, 6th ed., 1950,
page 181, Smith wrote:

> It is not from the benevolence of the butcher,
> the brewer or the baker, that we expect our dinner
> but from their regard to their own interest.
> We address ourselves, not to their humanity,
> but to their self love, and never talk to them
> of our necessities but of their advantages.
> Nobody but a beggar chooses to depend
> chiefly upon the benevolence of his fellow citizens.

So Smith is getting close to the both-and logic of Catholic
theology and of the postmodernity of Kierkegaard and Nietzsche.
But he does not argue that there can be benevolence or agape
and self love together so that the owner of a butcher shop
and the butcher could serve the customer with both self-interest
and a genuine, benevolent love for his neighbor and for God.
Smith does speak of the benevolence that can care for the beggar
and this is an important part of modernity with its politics
of health, education and welfare that can be rooted in agape
and its belief that all persons even beggars have a worth
that is equal to other persons and so they should be cared for.

Part Three: Glorious Finishings

IV,9.9 And the fruit of a well ordered self love becomes postmodern

There were the Lutheran and Calvinist seeds of modernity
which brought forth the roots of Pietistic affection, Quaker
friendship and Catholic *eros* and these became the trunk of
the tree of modernity with the assembly lines of the industrial age.
Marx brought forth the communist branch from out of this
trunk, and the Catholics of *Rerum Novarum* in arguing
for labor unions brought forth the Catholic branch and many
liberal protestants such as Tommy Douglas brought forth the
Protestant branch with the Political Party of the NDP leading the way.
From these branches have come forth the fruit of western
systems of health, education and welfare which are today
beginning to take root in the cultures of China, India and Islam.
These cultures which do not have agape in the very soil and
seeds of their culture and do not value all persons as of equal
worth do like the economic fruits of the agapeic cultural tree.
Kierkegaard, Nietzsche, Max Scheler and Sartre have gone beyond
even Adam Smith and have given full accounts of persons
as interpersonal and how all persons belong to the human family.
As we look at the history of Western Modernity we can see
the unfolding existential dialectic that set up the thesis of agape
and excluded the antithesis of the natural loves with their
built in self love but then went through stages of synthesis.
Now the thesis of Western agape is being appreciated by the
antithetical cultures of Bhakti, Karuna, Jen, Tao and Rahim,
and a new synthesis is beginning especially in terms of economics.
But this does imply a new politics and a new law that can
make sense of the new economy by understanding it in terms
of Agape and personhood and Agape and the natural loves that
will let other religious loves bring something to Agape even
as Agape is offering them its own economy, politics and law.
This now brings us to Postmodernity and its new global logic.

Bibliography

Buber, Martin. *I and Thou*. Translated by Ronald Gregor Smith. New York: Charles Scribner's Sons, 1958.

Dillenberger, John. *Martin Luther: Selections from His Writings*. New York: Doubleday, 1951.

Glueck, Nelson. *Hesed in the Bible*. Translated by Alfred Gottschalk. Cincinnati: Hebrew Union College Press, 1967.

Kaufmann, Walter. *The Portable Nietzsche*. New York: Vintage, 1962.

Lohse, Bernard. *Martin Luther: An Introduction to His Life and Work*. Translated by Robert C. Schultz. Philadelphia: Fortress, 1986.

Mack, Burton. *The Last Gospel. The Book of Q and Christian Origins*. San Francisco: HarperSanFrancisco, 1994.

Nietzsche, Friedrich. *Beyond Good and Evil*. Translated by Walter Kaufmann. New York: Vintage, 1966.

———. *The Birth of Tragedy and the Case of Wagner*. Translated by Walter Kaufmann. New York: Vintage, 1967.

———. *On the Genealogy of Morals/ Ecce Homo*. Translated by Walter Kaufmann. New York: Vintage, 1969.

———. *Thus Spoke Zarathustra*. Translated by R. J. Hollingdale. New York: Penguin, 1969.

———. *Twilight of the Idols/ The Anti-Christ*. Translated by R. J. Hollingdale. New York: Penguin, 1990.

Nygren, Anders. *Agape and Eros*. Translated by Phillip S. Watson. Philadelphia: Westminster, 1953.

Sakenfeld, Katharine Doob. *The Meaning of Hesed in the Hebrew Bible: A New Inquiry*. Missoula, MT: Scholars Press, 1978.

www.ingramcontent.com/pod-product-compliance
Lightning Source LLC
Chambersburg PA
CBHW071145300426
44113CB00009B/1092